Alternatives t
in the 21st

CW00685441

Series Editors: **Lara Monticelli**, Copenhagen Business School, and **Torsten Geelan**, University of Copenhagen

---

Debates about the future of capitalism demonstrate the urgent need to envision and enact alternatives that can help tackle the multiple intertwined crises that societies are currently facing. This ground-breaking new series advances the international, comparative and interdisciplinary study of capitalism and its alternatives in the 21st century.

Forthcoming in the series:

Politics of the Gift:
Towards a Convivial Society
Frank Adloff

Capital to Commons
Hannes Gerhardt

Money Commons:
Remaking Money for an Inclusive and Sustainable Future
Ester Barinaga

Find out more at

bristoluniversitypress.co.uk/alternatives-to-capitalism-in-the-21st-century

Alternatives to Capitalism in the 21st Century

Series Editors: **Lara Monticelli**, Copenhagen Business School, and **Torsten Geelan**, University of Copenhagen

International Advisory Board:

Find out more at

bristoluniversitypress.co.uk/alternatives-to-capitalism-in-the-21st-century

THE FUTURE IS NOW
An Introduction to Prefigurative Politics

Edited by
Lara Monticelli

With a foreword by
Arturo Escobar

BRISTOL
UNIVERSITY
PRESS

First published in Great Britain in 2024 by

Bristol University Press
University of Bristol
1–9 Old Park Hill
Bristol
BS2 8BB
UK
t: +44 (0)117 374 6645
e: bup-info@bristol.ac.uk

Details of international sales and distribution partners are available at bristoluniversitypress.co.uk

British Library Cataloguing in Publication Data
A catalogue record for this book is available from the British Library

ISBN 978-1-5292-1565-6 hardcover
ISBN 978-1-5292-1566-3 paperback
ISBN 978-1-5292-1567-0 ePub
ISBN 978-1-5292-1568-7 ePdf

Cover design: Liam Roberts
Front cover image: The Nest by Zualidro, https://www.behance.net/zualidro

Bristol University Press uses environmentally responsible print partners.

Printed in Great Britain by CPI Group (UK) Ltd, Croydon, CR0 4YY

FSC
www.fsc.org
MIX
Paper | Supporting
responsible forestry
FSC® C013604

To Torsten,
and to all the 'holy fools' who dare to
prefigure alternative futures.

Are there still other possibilities? Of course, there are. …
Whichever option is chosen, it will not be the end of history,
but in a real sense its beginning. The human social world is
still very young in cosmological time.

In 2050 or 2100, when we look back at capitalist civilization,
what will we see?

Immanuel Wallerstein, *Historical Capitalism with Capitalist
Civilization* (2011), p 163. Reproduced with permission of
Verso through PLSclear.

Contents

List of Figures and Tables

Figures

Tables

List of Abbreviations

DIY	do-it-yourself
ESF	European Social Forum
G8	Group of Eight
PKK	Partiya Karkerên Kurdistanê (Kurdistan Workers' Party)
SASE	Society for the Advancement of Socio-Economics
STAP	Stadin Aikapankki (Helsinki Timebank)
UK	United Kingdom
US	United States
WSF	World Social Forum
WTO	World Trade Organization

Notes on Contributors

Viviana Asara is Assistant Professor in Sociology at the Department of Humanities at the University of Ferrara (Italy) and a research affiliate with the Institute for Multi-Level Governance and Development at the Vienna University of Economics and Business (Austria). Her work has focused on political ecology and environmental politics and governance; more particularly she has undertaken research on social movements, democracy, degrowth, commons, social innovations and political parties. Her most recent book is the *Handbook of Critical Environmental Politics* (Edward Elgar), edited with Luigi Pellizzoni and Emanuele Leonardi, forthcoming in autumn 2022.

Chiara Bottici is a philosopher and a writer, known for her philosophy of political imagination and her feminist writings. She is Director of Gender and Sexuality Studies and Associate Professor of Philosophy at The New School in New York (USA), and she is the author of, among others, *Imaginal Politics: Images beyond Imagination and The Imaginary* (Columbia University Press, 2014), *A Philosophy of Political Myth* (Cambridge University Press, 2007) and *Anarchafeminism* and *A Feminist Mythology* (both Bloomsbury, 2021). She also co-authored, with sociologist Benoît Challand, *Imagining Europe: Myth, Memory, and Identity* (Cambridge University Press, 2013) and *The Myth of the Clash of Civilizations* (Routledge, 2010).

Laura Centemeri is Senior Researcher in Environmental Sociology at the French National Centre for Scientific Research (CNRS) and a member of the Center for the Study of Social Movements (CEMS) at L'Ecole des Hautes Études en Sciences Sociales (EHESS, France). Her areas of research interest and projects include: sociology of (e)valuation and environmental conflicts, environmental movements, sociology of repair, and environmental disasters. She is currently doing research on agroecology and preparedness to climate change in agriculture in Italy, with a focus on the permaculture movement. Her most recent books are *La permaculture ou l'art de réhabiter* (Éditions Quae, 2019) and the edited volume *Rethinking Post-Disaster Recovery: Socio-Anthropological Perspectives on Repairing Environments* (Routledge, 2022, with Sezin Topçu and J. Peter Burgess).

Suryamayi Aswini Clarence-Smith is a researcher, educator and activist focused on prefigurative and utopian practice, based in the intentional community of Auroville. She has a PhD in international development (University of Sussex, UK) and is a founding member of The Auroville Research Platform, affiliated with the Sri Aurobindo International Institute of Educational Research (India). Her work primarily explores alternative practices in economy, governance and education. Recent and forthcoming publications are to be found in the Ralahine Utopian Studies series (forthcoming, Peter Lang), the *Palgrave Handbook of Learning for Transformation* (Palgrave Macmillan, 2022, with Bem Le Hunte, Katie Ross and Aditi Rosegger) and the journal *Sustainability Science* (2022, with Lara Monticelli).

Davina Cooper is Research Professor in Law and Political Theory at King's College London (UK). She is the author of six books, including *Everyday Utopias: The Conceptual Life of Promising Spaces* (Duke University Press, 2013) and *Feeling like a State: Desire, Denial, and the Recasting of Authority* (Duke University Press, 2019). Her research combines two strands of prefigurative work: analyses of radical and transgressive governance practices – state and non-state; and prefigurative conceptualizing, where conceptual meanings that speak to hoped-for futures are advanced. During 2018–2022, she directed an ESRC-funded project on the Future of Legal Gender, which researched the implications of abolishing legal sex status.

Joost de Moor is Assistant Professor at the Centre for European Studies and Comparative Politics at SciencesPo (France). His work focuses on the various ways in which citizens concerned about the environment become politically active – individually or collectively – to address their concerns. He is particularly interested in the ways environmental activists navigate a political context marked by the apparent inability of states and international organizations to address crises like climate change. He has published on these topics in journals including *Environmental Politics*, *Theory and Society* and the *International Journal of Urban and Regional Research*.

Antonia De Vita is Associate Professor in General and Social Pedagogy and co-founder of the Territori in Libera Transizione research group in the Department of Human Sciences at the University of Verona (Italy). Her research interests span gender studies, critical education and social pedagogy; she also researches ecological citizenship with a focus on informal and transformative learning. Her most recent publication is the edited volume *Fragilità contemporanee. Fenomenologie della violenza e della vulnerabilità* (Mimesis Edizioni, 2021).

Ana Cecilia Dinerstein (MA, PhD) is Reader in Sociology at the University of Bath (UK). She teaches political sociology and Marxist, critical, decolonial and feminist theory, and has opened up a new research field: the global politics of hope. She is a member of the core group of the Global Tapestry of Alternatives. Her publications include *The Politics of Autonomy in Latin America: The Art of Organising Hope* (Palgrave Macmillan, 2015), *Social Sciences for An Other Politics: Women Theorising without Parachutes* (Palgrave Macmillan, 2016, editor), *Open Marxism 4: Against a Closing World* (Pluto Press, 2019, co-edited With Alfonso García Vela, Edith González and John Holloway) and *A World Beyond Work? Labour, Money and the Capitalist State between Crisis and Utopia* (Emerald, 2021, with Frederick Harry Pitts).

Arturo Escobar is an activist researcher from Colombia, working on territorial struggles against extractivism, post-developmentalist and post-capitalist transitions, and ontological design. He was Professor of Anthropology at the University of North Carolina at Chapel Hill (USA) until 2018 and is affiliated with the PhD Program in Design and Creation, Universidad de Caldas, Manizales, Colombia. His most recent books are: *Designs for the Pluriverse: Radical Interdependence, Autonomy, and the Making of Worlds* (Duke University Press, 2018) and *Pluriversal Politics: The Real and the Possible* (Duke University Press, 2020). He is currently working on a book on relationality (*Designing Relationally: Making and Restor(y)ing Life*) with Michal Osterweil and Kriti Sharma.

Francesca Forno is Associate Professor in Sociology at the University of Trento (Italy). Her interests include political consumerism and sustainable community movement organizations. She has a special focus on the consequences of the spread of market-based forms of action for citizens' participation and mobilization. She has published on civic participation and social movements, and has conducted research on political consumerism, collaborative consumption, grassroots initiatives, social eco-innovation and alternative food networks.

Emil Husted is Associate Professor in the Department of Organization at Copenhagen Business School (Denmark). His research is centred on the internal orchestration of political parties and social movements, often with a focus on the mediating role of digital technology. Emil's research has been published in international journals such as *Organization Studies*, *Organization* and *The Information Society*. He is co-author of *Digital Organizing: Revisiting Themes in Organization Studies* (Bloomsbury, 2019, with Ursula Plesner). Furthermore, Emil is a member of the editorial collective at the independent journal *ephemera*.

Aris Komporozos-Athanasiou is the author of *Speculative Communities: Living with Uncertainty in a Financialized World* (University of Chicago Press, 2022). He is Associate Professor of Sociology at the Social Research Institute, UCL (UK), where he leads the Sociology & Social Theory Research Group. His current book project, tentatively titled *Real Fake*, is an intellectual history of distortion technologies and myth-making in finance capitalism.

Mikko Laamanen is Associate Professor in Marketing in the Lifestyle Research Centre at EMLyon Business School (France). His research focuses on everyday politics of inclusion and social change with empirical work on consumer lifestyle movements, alternative organizing, the sharing economy, multi-stakeholder value and arts-based community engagement. This research has been published in, among others, *Current Sociology*, *International Journal of Consumer Studies*, *Journal of Cleaner Production*, *Journal of Marketing Management*, and *Marketing Theory*, as well as in the *Handbook of Social Movements Across Disciplines* (Springer, 2010) and the *Handbook of the Sharing Economy* (Edward Elgar, 2019).

Marianne Maeckelbergh is Professor of Political Anthropology at Ghent University (Belgium) and Professor of Global Sociology at Leiden University (Netherlands). Her research explores how people's everyday political practices inform and transform the way we understand democracy. She is the author of *The Will of the Many: How the Alterglobalisation Movement Is Changing the Face of Democracy* (Pluto Press, 2009) and co-producer of the Global Uprisings film series. She is the principal investigator on the Property and Democratic Citizenship project funded by the European Research Council, which explores how property regimes structure experiences of citizenship.

Lara Monticelli is Assistant Professor and Marie Skłodowska-Curie fellow at Copenhagen Business School (Denmark). Her ongoing research project, Ecovillages as Laboratories of Sustainability and Social Change, focuses on the (re-)emergence of prefigurative social movements as laboratories experimenting with practices of resilience and resistance to environmental, economic and societal challenges. Lara is especially interested in how these movements re-politicize everyday life, representing radical attempts to embody a critique to capitalism and prefigure alternative futures. She is the co-founder of the Alternatives to Capitalism research network at the Society for the Advancement of Socio-Economics and co-editor of the book series Alternatives to Capitalism in the 21st Century, published by Bristol University Press.

Erik Mygind du Plessis is Associate Professor in the Department of Business and Management at the University of Southern Denmark. His research interests revolve around the ways organizational subjects are constituted through dynamics of power and resistance, and to this end he has studied phenomena such as mindfulness, self-help books, whistle-blowing, prepping and informal resistance. From a theory perspective, he is interested in post-structuralism, critical theory and new materialism, and from an empirical perspective, he looks for interstices in which alternatives to dominant forms of organizing might emerge.

Eleonora Gea Piccardi is a PhD candidate in the Centre for Social Studies at the University of Coimbra (Portugal). Her present work focuses on the Kurdish women's movement in Rojava and, at the transnational level, the revolutionary praxis it is producing around feminism, ecology and radical democracy. Her fields of interest are decolonial feminisms, feminist political ecology, social movements and praxis/pedagogies of socioecological organization. She carries out militant research and is a member of the Ecology and Society working group at the Centre for Social Studies. Her latest publication is 'The Challenges of a Kurdish Ecofeminist Perspective: Maria Mies, Abdullah Öcalan, and the Praxis of Jineolojî' (2021).

Frederick Harry Pitts is Lecturer in Work, Employment, Organization and Public Policy in the School of Management at the University of Bristol (UK), where he leads the Perspectives on Work research group in the Faculty of Social Sciences and Law. He also co-edits the Bristol University Press online magazine *Futures of Work*. He is a research fellow of the Institute for the Future of Work. He is co-author of *A World Beyond Work? Labour, Money and the Capital State Between Crisis and Utopia* (Emerald, 2021, with Ana Cecilia Dinerstein) and author of *Value* (Polity, 2021).

Paul Raekstad is Assistant Professor in Political Theory at the University of Amsterdam, working theories of freedom, critiques of capitalism and debates about alternative economic institutions and how to attain them, with a particular focus on prefigurative politics, direct action and proposals for a Green New Deal. They recently co-authored *Prefigurative Politics: Building Tomorrow Today* (Polity) and are currently completing a book on *Karl Marx's Realist Critique of Capitalism* (Palgrave).

Jilly Traganou is Professor of Architecture and Urbanism at Parsons School of Design. Her publications include *The Tōkaidō Road: Travelling and Representation in Edo and Meiji Japan* (RoutledgeCurzon, 2004), *Travel, Space, Architecture* (Ashgate, 2009, co-edited with Miodrag Mitrašinović), *Designing the Olympics: Representation, Participation, Contestation* (Routledge,

2016) and *Design and Political Dissent: Spaces, Visuals, Materialities* (Routledge, 2021, editor). She is currently working on an edited volume, tentatively titled *Design, Migration, Displacement*, with Sarah Lichtman, to be published by Routledge. She is co-editor-in-chief of the journal *Design and Culture*.

Francesco Vittori is Research Fellow in General and Social Pedagogy and a member of the Territori in Libera Transizione research group in the Department of Human Sciences at the University of Verona (Italy). His research interests cover critical and social pedagogy, gender studies and ecological citizenship, with a specific focus on agroecology. His most recent contributions appear in the journals *Sociologia Urbana e Rurale* and *Sustainability*, and the edited collection *Fragilità contemporanee: Fenomenologie della violenza e della vulnerabilità* (Mimesis Edizioni, 2021, edited by Antonia De Vita).

Stefan Wahlen is Professor of Food Sociology at the University of Giessen (Germany). His research and teaching focuses on everyday practices and their political, organizational and institutional parameters. He previously worked as Assistant Professor of the Sociology of Consumption at Wageningen University (Netherlands). He earned his PhD in consumer economics from the University of Helsinki (Finland) with a thesis entitled *Governing Everyday Consumption*. He is a member of the steering committee of the Sustainable Consumption Research and Action Initiative in Europe and editor of the journal *Consumption and Society*, published by Bristol University Press.

Luke Yates is Lecturer in Sociology and Researcher at the Sustainable Consumption Institute, University of Manchester (UK). His work explores collective action, everyday consumption practices and the new digital economy. His interest in prefigurative politics emerges from trying to better understand debates around social movement strategy. His current work explores the societal shifts associated with platform capitalism through looking at social movements and platform businesses' legitimation tactics.

Acknowledgements

It is well known that academic books require a long gestation before being ready to be published. Indeed, many years have passed since 2018, when I first started toying with the idea of publishing an edited collection on the multifaceted and often contentious concept of prefigurative politics. This elongated process gave the contributors and especially me, the editor, the rare – at least in contemporary academia – opportunity to carefully ponder, chisel and cross-reference the various chapters of the book to form what, hopefully, stands as a strong, cohesive and illuminating volume. However, this requires patience. For this reason, I'd like to begin by thanking each and every contributor for bearing with my demanding editorial requests and the many delays. A special thanks also goes to Arturo Escobar and Davina Cooper who very generously agreed to frame the volume with two powerful and brilliant pieces.

I'm also very grateful to my commissioning editors at Bristol University Press, Shannon Kneis and Paul Stevens, who shared my excitement for the project and remained encouraging despite the challenges encountered along the way. Thanks also to Hannah Austin for her extremely professional editorial support in the creation of the first full manuscript, and to artist and illustrator Giacomo Trivellini for creating a unique and provocative piece of art for the cover.

Like many other book projects, this one reflects my personal intellectual journey. Landing a postdoc in the Faculty of Political and Social Sciences at Scuola Normale Superiore in Florence gave me the push and the determination to shift my research focus from the sociology of work and labour market policy to political participation and social movement studies – for which the department is world-renowned and towards which my 'academic heart' has always been drawn. These years have been punctuated by very fruitful encounters and collaborations; most notably, with Francesca Forno and Paolo Graziano around sustainable community movement organizations, which led to the organization of two extremely successful mini-conferences in Berkeley (2016) and Lyon (2017) for the annual gatherings of the Society for the Advancement of Socio-Economics (SASE).

This engagement with SASE was formalized the following year when, together with Torsten Geelan, Katherine Chen and Joyce Rothschild, we launched the Alternatives to Capitalism research network, which now constitutes a vibrant and ever-growing community. These conferences attracted a great number of scholars from around the world interested in the study of non-conventional forms of activism and political engagement able to challenge contemporary capitalism. Many of them are contributing authors in this edited volume. Others passionately shared their ideas and perspectives during paper presentations, panels and themed round tables.

In particular, during the 2019 gathering held at The New School for Social Research in New York, I had the opportunity to engage in some fascinating and extremely useful conversations on prefigurative politics with Luigi Pellizzoni, Alice Dal Gobbo, Audrey Laurin-Lamothe, Maura Benegiamo, Salvo Torre, Dario Minervini, Onofrio Romano, Laura Basu, Philipp Degens, Jonathan Preminger, Dario Azzellini, Marion Maignan, Susanne Giesecke, Jason Spicer, Marcelo Vieta, Michele Bianchi, Lampros Lamprinakis, Sophie Dubuisson-Quellier, David Bailey, Elizabeth Bennet, Malu Villela, Bernd Bonfert, Jan Blažek, Dirk Holemans and many others. So a heartfelt thanks goes to SASE and to the entire Alternatives to Capitalism community, which played a crucial role in inspiring me to pursue this book project and sparked broader interest in prefigurative politics.

I would also like to thank Christian Fuchs and the organizing committee of the European Sociological Conference held in Athens in 2017 for kindly inviting me to the semi-plenary session titled '(Un)Making Capitalism'. This was a wonderful opportunity to try out loud, in front of a large and specialized audience, some of my reflections on the disruptive potential of prefiguration, with my speech titled 'Embodying the critique to capitalism'. These ideas have subsequently been published in a special issue I co-edited with Christian in the journal *Triple C: Communication, Capitalism & Critique*.

There are other academic and activist communities that I am deeply grateful to. Flor Avelino and Julia Witthmayer at the Dutch Research Institute for Transitions in Rotterdam, where I spent some months in 2017. The inhabitants of the intentional communities of Granara (Italy) and Auroville (India), which I have visited on multiple occasions. The Global Ecovillage Network and Anna Kovasna. The Territori in Libera Transizione research group and the faculty involved in the Saperi in Transizione master's programme, co-hosted by the universities of Trento, Verona and Parma (Italy). The Copenhagen contingent of wonderful friends and colleagues: Catia Gregoratti, Laura Horn, Nicole Doerr and Vasna Ramasar. The Women on the Verge collective, coordinated by Ana Cecilia Dinerstein. The Politics, Ontologies and Ecologies research group, spearheaded by Luigi Pellizzoni. The Heilbroner Center for Capitalism Studies at The New School, co-directed by William Milberg and Julia Ott.

The Global Tapestry of Alternatives and Ashish Kothari. The Real Utopias project in memory of Erik Olin Wright, coordinated by Tom Malleson.

Last but not least, colleagues in the Department of Management, Politics and Philosophy at Copenhagen Business School, in particular the Civil Society research group: Liv Egholm, Lars Bo Kaspersen, Andreas Møller Mulvad, Mathias Hein Jessen, Maj Grasten, Dimitra Makri Andersen, Anders Sevelsted, Christiane Mossin and Cristine Dyhrberg Højghaard. Liv Egholm, in particular, supported me during the preparation of my Marie-Skłodowska Curie fellowship application. She persistently believed in my project and sensibly suggested that I centre its theoretical focus on prefigurative politics. This edited volume, in fact, is among the publications stemming from the theoretical work I conducted for my Marie-Skłodowska Curie project titled 'EcoLabSS – Ecovillages as Laboratories of Sustainability and Social Change' (2018–2024), financed by the European Commission (grant number 798866).

I would also like to thank all the students, co-lecturers and guests involved in the 'Reimagining Capitalism: Towards Just and Sustainable Futures' course that I am thoroughly enjoying coordinating and teaching at Copenhagen Business School and which has worked as a sounding board for some ideas expressed in this book.

I would like to close these acknowledgments by thanking those who have given me constant unconditional emotional support during what have turned out to be difficult years. My close and extended family, spread across the four corners of the world. My childhood and university friends: Elena Aldi and Marina Maffezzoli, Serida Catalano, Matteo Bassoli, Alessio Bertolini, Laura De Boni, Anna Panarello, Serena Galligani and Maria Giovanna Scarale. And, above all, my mother, Elzbieta Jamroz, my late father, Riccardo Monticelli, and my husband and comrade in life, Torsten Geelan, to whom this book is dedicated.

Foreword

Arturo Escobar

David Graeber in memoriam.

In the early 1990s, situationist Raul Vaneigem wrote these prescient and angry words:

> The economy is everywhere that life is not: but however intertwined the two may become, they simply do not meld, and one can never be confused with the other. ... There is only one terror, from which all others derive. For most people it is the fear of losing the last illusion separating them from themselves, the panic of having to create their own lives. (1994, pp 17, 21)

He was also concerned with the relation between nature and the economy. 'Nature,' he said, 'cannot be liberated from the economy until the economy has been driven out of human life', offering the following prefiguration: 'As the economy's hold weakens, life is more able to clear a path for itself' (Vaneigem, 1994, pp 33, 36).[1]

I started my presentation at a small conference in Mainz, Germany, in 2004[2] by quoting these sentences. They caught the attention of one of my fellow panellists, David Graeber, whose short but influential *Fragments of an Anarchist Anthropology* – from which one of the most noteworthy characterizations of prefigurative politics is quoted in the first chapter of this volume – had just been published. As the session concluded, David was keen to express his happiness at the fact I quoted Vaneigem. "It's very rarely the case," I remember him saying, "that an anarchist is quoted in an academic conference." He was thrilled about that, and although that situation has not changed significantly, this collection is certainly a step in the right direction. I want to start this foreword by recalling David and his influence on the concept–practice this wonderful volume discusses and celebrates. Clearly, for David, there was an important – perhaps inextricable – link between anarchism and prefigurative politics.

Prefigurative politics: an idea whose time has come

Think deeply about any important area of social life at present and you will inevitably conclude that a radical reimagining of how it might be construed and made otherwise is greatly needed. From here follows the need for 'progressive social change' (Monticelli, this volume) – one able to envision, and help bring into existence, alternative forms of life. Such is the main thesis to which this timely volume is dedicated, focusing on prefigurative politics as a path towards reimagining and remaking social life. While largely anchored in theory and research from the Global North, the book harbours key inspirations from the Global South, particularly in featuring what most would agree are the two most prominent examples of prefigurative politics in the world today: the Zapatista autonomous communities in Chiapas, Mexico, and the Democratic Confederalism envisioned and practised in the Rojava feminist revolution.

The notion of prefigurative politics is understood in various ways – for instance, as 'practised by social movements that embody, in the here and now, the future society they desire' (Piccardi, this volume); as 'the alignment of means and ends' (Laamanen, this volume); in terms of 'the tendencies of the future (the Not Yet)' (Dinerstein and Pitts, quoting Santos, this volume); or as 'a repertoire of political action that presents a different form of resistance: dissenting through making' (Traganou, this volume). Throughout this volume's chapters – whether theoretical or empirical – prefigurative politics is amply and eloquently shown to involve not only a struggle against both capitalism and the state, and the multiple forms of power and material–semiotic arrangements of everyday life they deploy, but also a diverse set of political experiments to bring about new social orders. Succinctly, prefigurative politics is an idea whose time has come, as reflected by activists' increased interest in it and the number of academic publications on it (Yates and de Moor, this volume; du Plessis and Husted, this volume). This book lends coherence to these activist and academic trends, lucidly projecting them in new and exciting directions.

A main reason for the prominence of the notion of prefigurative politics, I believe, lies in the fact that its stakes – as Monticelli (this volume) cogently spells out – are the highest of all: the construction of a vision–practice for how our being in the world, and our human becoming, are in need of a radical transformation. The reason is deceptively simple: 'we' (humans – some more than others) have forgotten how to act properly, as living beings, on the planet, from which it follows that humanity's greatest task is relearning how to be non-destructive, non-exploitative, relational beings. This means prefiguration has an ontological dimension: it is about creating 'alternative worlds' – other ways of being, knowing and doing. This book is part of a planetary movement of mobilizing for a new way of dwelling on the Earth.

Prefigurative politics is led by the realization that everything needs to change significantly if 'humanity' is to confront the civilizational crisis it has wrought upon itself and the Earth. As such, prefigurative politics has a holistic orientation, which inspires the various chapters of this book. Taken as a whole, the book is devoted to exploring the proposition that prefigurative politics constitutes a novel approach to transformative social change – precisely because it addresses, simultaneously, the ontological and epistemological character of the multiple systems of domination embodied in contemporary forms of globalized capitalism (Monticelli, this volume). It seeks to denaturalize global/modern capitalist culture as our default setting of being, knowing and doing, so as to liberate the discursive, imaginative and material space for other worlds and worlds *otherwise*.

Throughout these pages, the reader will be treated to a wonderful spectrum of topics and cases in which prefigurative politics is being experimented with and conceptualized. Some of these include utopianism (Clarence-Smith, this volume), post-patriarchalism (Piccardi, this volume), ecology (Centemeri and Asara, this volume), anarchism (Raekstad, this volume), hope (Dinerstein, this volume), radical imagination (Komporosoz-Athanasiou and Bottici, this volume), social movements (Yates and de Moor, this volume), postwork (Dinerstein and Pitts, this volume), intentional communities and ecovillages (Clarence-Smith, this volume; Piccardi, this volume), commons, innovative forms of municipalism (Monticelli, this volume; Piccardi, this volume; Traganou, this volume) and critical pedagogies (De Vita and Vittori, this volume). Successive chapters provide engaging discussion on particularly salient issues of concern for prefigurative politics, such as everyday life as a key locus of change (Forno and Wahlen, this volume); the governance of prefigurative communities and their relation to the state and economy (Cooper, this volume); and the genealogies of prefiguration in Marxist, anarchist and spiritual frameworks and experiences (Raekstad, this volume; Clarence-Smith, this volume). There are constructive notes of caution, from what are seen as the concept's blind spots, as to whether it does 'too much' or 'too little' (Yates and de Moor, this volume). How people respond against capital in everyday life by enacting what, at times, seem to be utopian practices is a main site of exploration. This leads some contributors to focus on alternatives to capitalist production and the process of 'disalienation', in which seeds of alternative practices might be found – for instance, in food and the reconnection with nature, as in ecotopian initiatives (such as permaculture and bioregionalism) (Centemeri and Asara, this volume), or in horizontal forms of governance (such as intentional communities, discussed by Clarence-Smith and Piccardi in their chapters).

The volume's goal can be seen as joining the ongoing intellectual–activist task of exercising the radical imagination, at the service of the Earth and fellow humans, in a grounded manner. From here follows the emphasis on concrete utopias – embodying post-capitalism, post-development and post-patriarchalism at various levels of existence – and the analysis of a landscape of practices that defies capitalism's hold on work and its separation from the production and reproduction of life. The rising paradigms of care and commoning, together with matristic, re-communalizing and re-localizing experiments, appear as real forces transforming existing societies.

Finally, a rich set of open questions remains for further exploration and practical construction. Can prefigurative politics – by definition, a process that is genuinely emergent and pluriversal – be organized (Laamanen, this volume)? Can 'practical structures' be created to foster it? Should organization structures aim to balance horizontality and verticality? How to articulate the daily practices, strategies and chores of organizing ('process-time') with concrete moments of action and mobilization ('event-time') (Maeckelbergh, this volume)? Short- and long-term time frames? Another thorny issue – and an unresolved question in both social theory and activism – is that of the meaning of movements' 'successes' or 'failures'. In what ways can movement effectiveness be rethought without slipping back into objectifying assessments that reproduce the ontological order to be replaced? Can prefigurative politics work – let alone thrive – without a certain normativity (such as the postulation of ideal values for the new society) and without imposing subcultural lifestyles on all (du Plessis and Husted, this volume)? Can prefigurative politics overcome the always-present risk of preaching only to the converted (du Plessis and Husted, this volume)? What are the processes through which prefigurative politics becomes necessarily embodied and embedded in place-making spatial forms and practices, and even concrete designs (Cooper, this volume; Traganou, this volume)? Is it possible to balance presentism with a generative, recursive temporality that truly enables a multiplicity of open-ended futures? What lessons might we learn from the prefigurative utopianism of intentional communities – such as the well-known Auroville in India or Christiania in Copenhagen – for groups in other parts of the world attempting to create a new path amid much messier contexts? Can spatial enclosures be strategically designed to defend commons-orientated experiences from encroachment by antagonistic forces (see Traganou, this volume, on 'the paradox of enclosed commons')? And so forth.

In what remains of this short foreword, I would like to comment on three interrelated aspects: the onto-epistemic character of prefiguration; the relation between prefigurative politics and transformative alternatives; and the tensions – and potential synergy – between modernist and prefigurative pluriversal politics.

Progressive modernist politics and pluriversal politics

Let me start with the last issue. Can prefigurative and conventional Left politics work in tandem, reinforcing rather than undermining each other? I attempted to give the best answer I could to this question in a recent work, drawing a contrast between pluriversal politics and modernist Left politics (Escobar, 2020). I understand pluriversal politics as based on the perspective of radical interdependence and focused on fostering diverse movements for civilizational transitions to a world in which many worlds fit – whether in the Global North, the Global South or both. Do modern intellectuals and activists espousing progressive social change agendas have a role in this type of ontological politics towards the pluriversal? I believe multiple ways exist to build effective bridges between progressive modernist politics and pluriversal politics – for instance, around struggles for economic democratization, de-patriarchalization, environmental justice and an end to racism and homophobia. That said, it is also important to recognize that many progressive modernist forms of politics are counterproductive in relation to pluriversal politics; they reproduce and strengthen the modernist dualist ontology from which they stem. There are no readily available models for the articulation of both types of politics, although this is currently the subject of many social struggles' active experimentation (including in the case of radical municipalism, mentioned by Monticelli, this volume). How these kinds of politics might initiate rhizomatic expansions from below – effectively relativizing modernity's universal ontology and the imaginary of a single globalized world, which it actively produces – remains an open question.

Those committed to one or another form of Left politics and alternative modernity can usefully consider this question, among others: what habitual forms of knowing, being and doing does a given strategy contribute to challenging, destabilizing or transforming? For instance, does the strategy or practice in question help us in the journey of de-individualization and towards re-communalization? Does it contribute to bringing about more local forms of economy that might, in turn, provide elements for designing infrastructures for an ethics of interexistence and the deep acceptance of radical difference? Does it make us more responsive to the notions of multiple reals and a world in which many worlds fit? Does this shift encourage us to entertain non-realist notions of the possible? To what extent do efforts to de-patriarchalize and decolonize society transcend anthropocentrism, contributing to weaving the pluriverse effectively with others – human and not?

For conventional political strategies to move along pluriversal politics, in other words, they must take on an explicit political ontological character, pushing their anti-capitalist stance beyond the dominant ontologies. From this perspective, it seems to me, pluriversal principles of struggle – when genuinely conceived from the perspective of radical interdependence, such as autonomy, territoriality, communality and care – cannot easily be accommodated within existing Left discourses. While much can be done to advance these causes through modernist counter-hegemonic strategies, they also require an explicit ontological framing that advances the principles of relationality.

The relationship between modernist and pluriversal politics is relevant to a second question: what constitutes a genuinely transformative alternative from the perspective of a prefigurative pluriversal politics? The Global Tapestry of Alternatives – a collective endeavour devoted to fostering convergence among networks of alternatives – characterizes such alternatives in the following way:

> We focus primarily on what we call 'radical or transformative alternatives', which we define as initiatives that are attempting to break with the dominant system and take paths towards direct and radical forms of political and economic democracy, localised self-reliance, social justice and equity, cultural and knowledge diversity, and ecological resilience. Their locus is neither the State nor the capitalist economy. They are advancing in the process of dismantling most forms of hierarchies, assuming the principles of sufficiency, autonomy, non-violence, justice and equality, solidarity, and the caring of life and the Earth. They do this in an integral way, not limited to a single aspect of life. Although such initiatives may have some kind of link with capitalist markets and the State, they prioritise their autonomy to avoid significant dependency on them and tend to reduce, as much as possible, any relationship with them. (Global Tapestry of Alternatives, nd)

This statement resonates strongly with the contents of this volume. One may add that we need to push all strategies and forms of politics ontologically and decolonially. What I mean by this is, first, that we all need to actively unlearn the ontologies of separation that shape our bodies and worlds. For instance, can we unlearn the liberal individual – that anti-relational Trojan Horse that inhabits each of us in modern worlds – similar to how we endeavour to unlearn patriarchy, racism and heterosexism? Can we unlearn anthropocentrism and really, deeply relearn how to live well as a living being, and what would this entail in practical terms? Second, we all need to be mindful of the multiple ways in which our actions depend on – and often reinforce – the metaphysical infrastructure of the current dominant system, including its universal constructs and objectifying relations; its anthropocentrism, secularism and Eurocentrism; and its colonialist, hierarchical classifications in terms of race, gender and sexuality.

This brings me to my final observation. If prefigurative politics addresses the onto-epistemic dimension of social life, what does the exercise of prefiguration imply under conditions of ontological occupation? For our lives and thoughts are thoroughly occupied by the discourses, structures and practices performed by governments, corporations, organized religions and the academy as the main purveyors of the dominant onto-epistemic structure. Let us consider prefigurative politics as a form of ontological politics that foregrounds a vast array of ways of conceiving what exists, so as to make tangible the claim of multiple ontologies or worlds.

It seems to me, in the end, that prefigurative politics' most formidable rival today is the seductive technological imagination put forth by the technopatriarchs of cutting-edge technologies – be that nanotechnology, synthetic biology, genomics, robotics, geoengineering, cognitive enhancement or interstellar travel. In promising 'life beyond biology' – and, conceivably, beyond Earth – this imagination is becoming the most powerful ontological colonizing force of all. What becomes of prefigurative politics in the age of the artificial-as-totality – that is, as the artificial becomes the new horizon for being (for example, Dilnot, 2021)? It would be a mistake to reduce the full arrival of the artificial to just another manifestation of capitalism's latest phase. Today, the technopatriarchs are performing one of the most important forms of cultural work: imagining the future. This needs to be dealt with on its own.

Let us hope that prefigurative pluriversal politics gradually becomes a space for effectively telling other compelling stories of worldmaking, opening spaces for the enactment of the pluriverse, against ongoing terricide. Such politics might contribute to a sort of 'ontological detox' through practices of making that not only pluriversally engage with but also problematize and undermine object-centred worldmaking and designing. Prefigurative politics calls on us to consider anew the fundamental insight that the world does not exist 'out there', separate from us, but that we construct it with every one of our actions – that the world is always co-emergent with our actions, even if that is within a complex dynamic of causality, contingency and drift.

Healing the web of life

From 7–10 February 2020, the first Climate Camp, 'Peoples Against Terricide', met in a recovered territory in Wallmapu (Mapuche territory, in what is otherwise known as the province of Chubut in the Argentinean Patagonia), with the goal of launching a broad movement against terricide. Called for and organized by the Movimiento de Mujeres Indígenas por el Buen Vivir [Movement of Indigenous Women for Buen Vivir], the group issued a final declaration, which read, in part, as follows:

> We define terricide as the killing of tangible ecosystems, the spiritual ecosystem, and that of the *pueblos* [peoples] and of all forms of life. Confronted with the terricide, we declare ourselves to be in permanent struggle, resistance, and re-existence against this system. … We summon all peoples to build a new civilizational matrix that embraces Buen Vivir [good living, or collective wellbeing] as a right. Buen Vivir implies the retrieval of harmony and reciprocity among peoples and with the Earth. Summoned by the memory of our ancestors and the lands and landscapes that inhabit us, we have agreed on the creation of the Movement of Pueblos against Terricide.[3]

For this movement, the social emergent is Earth itself. Terricide is a new concept that does not easily fit into the thinking and cultural experience of the modern West. The closest notion would be that of the Anthropocene, which – even if important and useful – lends itself to managerial and technoscientific solutions to problems that clearly overflow technoscience's ability to solve them. The Anthropocene shelters the idea of a new global reality that all humans, without distinction, should rally around; this will easily yield to proposals for overarching biopolitical projects for a 'universal humanity', in the terms of 'Enlightened Man', again missing the point that what is at stake is the creation of new conditions for being human.

I end this foreword with an invitation to us all to heed the call for a broad movement – originating in Wallmapu – against terracide. This means engaging in the collective and patient but steady ontological and political task of constructing a different civilizational matrix – one that we can place at the heart of prefigurative pluriversal politics. Thus understood, prefigurative pluriversal politics becomes an active praxis for healing the web of life, which constitutes the bodies, places and communities we are and inhabit.

Notes

[1] And he added, among other things: 'Economics is the most durable lie of the approximately ten millennia mistakenly accepted as history. … The end of the reign of the economy is not the end of the world – merely the end of the economy's totalitarian hold over the world. … From the moment the market system minimizes the fruits of the earth by seeing them only in terms of the fruits of labor, the market system treats nature as its slave. … The commodity is the original form of pollution' (Vaneigem, 1994, pp 18, 30, 31). Here, we find a statement of prefigurative politics avant la lettre.

²   The session in question was 'Persuasion in Economic Life', organized by Stephen Gudeman and Ivo Strecker at the Fourth International Rhetoric Culture Conference, Johannes Gutenberg University, Mainz, 16–20 July 2005.

³   See the Movimiento de Mujeres Indígenas por el Buen Vivir, https://www.faceb ook.com/movimientodemujeresindigenasporelbuenvivir/. Readers can easily find Spanish-language, and a few English-language, sources online by searching for the Movimiento or for Moira Millán, a brilliant and courageous Mapuche activist and one of the movement's founders. On the definition and final declaration, see Plan B Noticias (2020) and Revista Resistencias (2020).

References

Dilnot, C. (2021) 'Designing in the world of the naturalised artificial', in T. Fry and A. Nocek (eds) *Design in Crisis*, London: Routledge, pp 93–112.

Escobar, A. (2020) *Pluriversal Politics: The Real and the Possible*, Durham, NC: Duke University Press.

Global Tapestry of Alternatives (nd) 'Alternatives', *GTA's Definitions* [online], available from: https://globaltapestryofalternatives.org/:definitions#term-Alternatives

Graeber, D. (2004) *Fragments of an Anarchist Anthropology*, Chicago, IL: Prickly Paradigm Press.

Plan B Noticias (2020) 'Participó vutá trawn: conformaron movimiento contra el "terricidio"' [online], 15 February, available from: www.planbn oticias.com.ar/index.php/2020/02/15/participo-wuta-trawn-conforma ron-movimiento-contra-el-terricidio/

Revista Resistencias (2020) 'Deliberó en el Lof Mapuche Pillán Mahuiza el Campamento Climático Pueblos contra el Terricidio' [online], 18 February, available from: https://revistaresistencias.wixsite.com/resistencias/post/deliber%C3%B3-en-el-lof-mapuche-pill%C3%A1n-mahuiza-el-campamento-clim%C3%A1tico-pueblos-contra-el-terricidio

Vaneigem, R. (1994) *The Movement of the Free Spirit*, New York, NY: Zone Books.

Introduction

Lara Monticelli

The future belongs to those who prepare for it in the present.

Malcolm X

Why prefigurative politics?

If you are reading this book, you've probably heard about the concept of 'prefigurative politics' before and are looking forward to knowing more about it; or maybe this is the first time that you're reading about it. Either way, you are in the right place. This edited volume aims to be an accessible, intriguing, non-exhaustive introduction to what one of the reviewers called the 'nomadic concept' of prefigurative politics. Indeed, the idea for this collaborative project came from the realization that despite the increasing popularity and extensive use of the term across the social sciences, it is hard to find articles or books that – rather than taking its meaning for granted – aim explicitly at introducing, defining and discussing it.[1] As will become clear throughout the next chapters, though, this is not an easy task.

The meaning of 'prefigurative politics' and the repertoire of actions referred to as 'prefigurative' have been in evolution since the 1970s, when the term was used in political manifestos calling for workers' self-management and democratic councils in the United States. The world we live in today, decades later, is profoundly different. However, social movements and civil society haven't run out of things to grieve, to protest against and to mobilize for. They also have *a lot* to prefigure. The gloomy prospect of human-driven ecosystems' collapse and the consequences for human and non-human life on this planet calls for an urgent and radical rethinking of the ways in which humans are working, producing, reproducing, consuming, travelling, eating and spending; in other words, the entire human way of life.[2] Prefigurative politics in the form of alternative production, consumption and food networks, cooperatives, transition towns, intentional and ecological communities, and worker-owned firms are proof that such a transformation, at least on a small scale, is imaginable and realizable.

The COVID-19 pandemic has only made the unsustainability of the status quo more evident. In fact, it is now almost impossible to ignore the importance of care work and emotional and reproductive labour for our collective wellbeing. The pandemic has brought into stark relief the inequalities and fragilities at the heart of our health systems and, more generally, our modern societies; think, for instance, of the burnt out, underpaid, racialized care workers at the frontline of intensive care units in US hospitals during the first wave of the pandemic. In this contemporary context, prefigurative politics in the form of grassroots, solidarity and mutual help groups can provide crucial spaces in which gender and body norms, stereotypes and discriminations, together with capitalist patterns of social reproduction, can be openly debated, deconstructed and sabotaged. Feminist activists and thinkers remind us, though, that democratizing care and strengthening our solidarity ties and mutual aid networks should be a daily practice, not just a lifebuoy we hold onto in cases of emergency (Sitrin and Colectiva Sembrar, 2020).

The pandemic has also revealed how crucial schools and universities are for the socialization and wellbeing of children and young people. And despite the dramatic disruption to their education, they remain at the forefront of unprecedented mobilizations calling for 'system change, not climate change' (for an overview, see Wahlström et al, 2019). These demands for change reflect an openness to think the world anew. This begs the question of whether we can transform educational institutions into spaces where centuries of colonial, racist, patriarchal and capitalist norms, values and beliefs can be questioned and unlearned. For the moment, activists' assemblies, local/neighbour solidarity groups and radical independent schools constitute safe environments where critical pedagogy, experimentation, learning by trial and error and doing *otherwise* is encouraged.

But it is not only our economies, our consumption patterns, our lifestyles and our educational institutions that need to be rethought. The way we live together, articulate our emotions and manage conflict also need to be addressed. The pandemic's toll on mental health, with a rise in anxiety, depression and addiction rates, has been particularly pronounced among certain groups: those who are unemployed and precarious workers, the elderly, sexual and gender minorities, women and single parents (see, for example, Cullen et al, 2020; Moreno et al, 2020). Some of these fragile parts of society are finding support in prefigurative initiatives. For instance, many intentional communities are helping their members to find constructive ways of supporting each other collectively when individual feelings of rage, distress and anxiety emerge. This effort is connected to the ongoing experimentation with non-violent communication methods and inclusive horizontal decision-making mechanisms within these communities.

At this point, it is important to stress that the main message of this book is not that prefigurative politics and prefigurative movements are the panacea to all of the problems in this world. The world is characterized by a great deal of violence, oppression, inequality, injustice and abuse of power that must be tackled through other means. However, prefiguration still has an essential role to play. In his last book, the late Erik Olin Wright (2019) concludes that in order to transcend capitalism and move towards a more just and sustainable socio-economic system, capitalism needs to be not only openly contested and opposed but also eroded *from within*. And prefigurative politics can be thought of as the ensemble of temporary or long-lasting movements, initiatives, collectives and networks that foster this erosion. The main takeaway of this book, then, is that prefigurative politics can be *one* way, among many (and very necessary) other ways, of bringing about progressive social change.

Throughout the chapters, the reader will encounter many definitions and attempts to characterize prefigurative politics, drawing from a range of social science disciplines such as philosophy, sociology, political economy, social movement studies, organization studies, and political ecology, thus reflecting the interdisciplinarity and transdisciplinarity of the concept. Indeed, the contributors to this volume have embraced a broad, encompassing understanding, rather than a narrow one, of what constitutes prefigurative politics. One particular feature, though, makes prefigurative politics unique with respect to other forms of political engagement: its ontological and epistemological nature. Unlike conventional or contentious politics, prefigurative politics focuses on the creation of alternative ontologies: alternative ways of being in the world and, one might even dare to say, 'alternative worlds'. Change is sought on multiple and interconnected levels: the private and the public, the individual and the collective, the socio-economic and the subjective–emotional. This 'holism' (in the literal meaning of the term, which comes from the Greek ολοσ, *holos*, meaning 'entire' or 'whole') captures not only the ontology, but also the epistemology of change in prefigurative politics (on this, see Monticelli, this volume).

Because of this 'holistic' ambition, prefigurative politics has attracted many criticisms; for instance, that it is an ineffective, purely performative exercise (see, for example, Blühdorn, 2017, criticizing the politics of hope). Such criticism must be taken into account and dealt with seriously when assessing the impact, effectiveness and usefulness of prefigurative politics. Indeed, the contributors to this volume – as demonstrated in the chapters by Monticelli, Yates and de Moor, and du Plessis and Husted – are well aware of the limitations of prefigurative politics; hence, they provide cautions that one should bear in mind while studying prefigurative movements. At the same time, though, critics sometimes fail to acknowledge that, as some scholars of prefiguration have previously pointed out (Brissette, 2016; Monticelli,

2021), we can't deploy the same epistemological lenses used to assess the effects of conventional and contentious politics to study prefigurative politics. To put it bluntly, it would be like using the instruction manual of a fridge to learn how to drive a car. More work is nevertheless needed to complement the existing body of empirical research with reflexive theoretical and methodological contributions. The chapters gathered in the third and last part of this book, together with the thoughtful afterword by Davina Cooper, are excellent steps in this direction.

In sum, this volume will not provide the reader with a crystallized definition of prefigurative politics, one to be used as a litmus paper to assess whether certain social phenomena are prefigurative or not. Rather, the point is to offer a critical overview of some of the most salient debates that a reader interested in prefigurative politics should be aware of. The chapters are written by scholars who are, and have been, working on prefigurative politics for a long time, some of them for more than a decade, producing scholarship that now constitutes the 'go-to' for anyone interested in the topic. At the beginning of this book project, each of these scholars was given the task of condensing her/his/their specialized knowledge into one short and punchy text, no longer than 6,000 words. As editor of this volume, I found curating the contents to have been a phenomenal learning experience. While trying to identify the best order in which to present the chapters, it was possible to recognize some recurring themes forming an invisible red thread. In the next section, I introduce those I believe to be the most significant.

Unpacking prefigurative politics

The first observation is that prefigurative initiatives are often described as being willing to oppose state power or state authority. However, looking closely at some of the examples in the chapters, such as the intentional community of Auroville in India (Clarence-Smith, this volume), Christiania in Copenhagen (Traganou, this volume) and the Jineolojî communes in Rojava (Piccardi, this volume), it is apparent that many prefigurative initiatives, more than opposing state power, are trying to *reimagine* these constituencies so that they follow radically different values and belief systems. As Davina Cooper poignantly reminds us in her work on prefiguring the state, 'state bodies can also be reimagined, including as democratic, horizontal, responsible, caring, permeable and stewardly' (Cooper, this volume). A key example of this is radical municipalism and the networks connecting several radical municipalities around the world, such as Fearless Cities or C40 Cities.

Inevitably, reimagining and enacting different state bodies through prefigurative initiatives requires (re)negotiating their relationship with existing institutions, laws and regulations (at the supranational, national, regional and local levels). Emblematic of this is the case of Auroville, which, after decades marked by independence and peaceful coexistence with the federal Indian government, has recently been put under pressure by the nationalist government of Narendra Modi to develop and expand its infrastructure (Kothari, 2022). This has caused tensions within the community, with factions either supporting or opposing the development plan, and it has ultimately pushed the inhabitants to gather in assembly to discuss their positioning with respect to the Indian government[3] (see Clarence-Smith, this volume). Another notable example is the urban intentional community of Christiania. As a response to pressure coming from the Danish government, Christiania has passed from an area of illegal squatting to the community setting up a bank loan to legally purchase the land that it has inhabited since 1971 (for an overview of Christiania's history, see Traganou, this volume). For both of these communities, the process of renegotiating is forever in flux.

Another distinctive element common to many chapters in the book is the relationship between prefigurative politics and capitalism. Many prefigurative communities and initiatives form 'diverse economies' with many coexisting types of labour, enterprise, transactions, property and finance. This term, coined by feminist economists Julie Graham and Katherine Gibson, refers to the existence of a plurality of different economies within the dominant context of capitalist economy characterized by waged labour producing for the market (Gibson-Graham et al, 2013). In this sense, prefigurative communities and initiatives do not exist *outside* capitalism. They exist within and despite capitalism, inextricably intertwined with it (on this, see also Chatterton and Pickerill, 2010). As a result, some prefigurative communities and initiatives end up being repressed or co-opted by the state and the market.

Whatever relationship exists between prefiguration and capitalism, this entanglement generates a set of theoretical and empirical questions that a researcher studying prefiguration must be aware of. How should one assess the transformative potential of prefigurative initiatives when these are following the frameworks, metrics and organizational forms of capitalism? In other words, should scholars interested in prefiguration solely analyse initiatives that envision *alternatives to* capitalism or should they also examine alternative capitalism*s*? Another question concerns whether prefigurative initiatives are always destined to be insular niches or whether they have the potential to eventually 'become sufficiently prominent in the lives of individuals and communities that capitalism could eventually be displaced from its dominant role in the system' (Wright 2019, p 60). Finally, to keep citing Wright, is there a 'viable, achievable and desirable' way of making them 'sufficiently prominent' (2019, p 60)? This last question is linked to the long-standing critique of prefiguration as lacking 'scalability' and societal impact, which is addressed in several chapters of the book (for example, those by Yates and de Moor, and du Plessis and Husted).

Suffice it to say that any radical transformation[4] is, by definition, 'multi-dimensional', 'intersectional' and 'multi-scalar' (Temper et al, 2018). Such a transformation entails a 'shift in society's value-normative system and shifting relations across the personal (beliefs, values, worldviews), political (systems and structures), and practical (behaviours and technical responses) levels simultaneously' (O'Brien and Sygna, 2013, p 19). Rather than being 'scaled up' from the grassroots to the mainstream institutional level, many prefigurative initiatives follow non-linear, rhizomatic, network-like and place-based patterns of change diffusion (on this, see Forno and Weiner, 2020). Finally, prefigurative politics – and the embodiment of alternatives it implies – integrates, rather than supplants, conflict and resistance-based social movements and collective actions (Temper et al, 2018, p 754; Monticelli, 2021).

Another reflection is that research on prefigurative politics hasn't paid enough attention to how the intersectionality between class, gender, race and ethnicity affects individual access to, and participation in, prefigurative initiatives and movements. In fact, some critics have pointed out that prefigurative politics is inherently exclusionary, attracting mostly Western, white, middle-class, highly educated individuals (see, for instance, Smucker, 2014, on the Occupy Wall Street movement). Indeed, looking at both the contributors' list and the examples discussed throughout the chapters, this book reflects such a bias. This is unfortunate because there are plenty of thriving prefigurative movements around the world and in the so-called Global South – some of which are discussed in Arturo Escobar's foreword. But as Ana Cecilia Dinerstein rightly points out in her chapter, titled 'Decolonizing prefiguration', it is not only that the *focus* of research ought to be expanded, but also that the *epistemological framework* through which the empirical cases are analyzed needs to be decolonized.

A final observation relates to the (yet unexplored) potential of cross-pollinating scholarship on prefigurative politics with other emerging areas of research within and outside of the social sciences. A promising example is represented by the 'New Materialism(s)' turn within the humanities (for an overview of the concept, see Dolphijn and van der Tuin, 2012). The thrust towards a 'flat', immanent ontology – one where dichotomies such as human/non-human, agency/structure, mind/matter, anthropocentrism/ecocentrism are overhauled – is aligned with the holistic character of prefigurative politics. The chapter by Laura Centemeri and Viviana Asara, where new socioecological ontologies are expounded as being prefigurative, epitomizes this affinity. Although not explicitly discussed in this volume, a dialogue between scholars working on these themes is set to produce compelling and cutting-edge scholarship in the near future.

An invitation to read: overview of the book and its chapters

The book is structured in three thematic parts and is meant to be read following the order in which the chapters are presented. In fact, the various chapters 'speak' to each other, and the reader will find the thorough cross-chapter referencing quite useful. That said, the reader is of course also welcome to browse through the table of contents and jump to the chapters that are particularly appealing. The volume begins with Arturo Escobar's foreword, which allows the reader to get a curated overview and to spot unforeseen interconnections. In it, he describes prefigurative politics as 'an idea whose time has come', drawing fruitful parallels with his famous notion of the pluriverse. Through paragraphs punctuated by concerned yet hopeful words, he contrasts decolonial, anti-racist and anti-capitalist prefigurations of the future with 'technopatriarchal' ones, characterized by ambitions of interstellar colonization and promises of 'life beyond biology'.

The first part of the book, titled 'Contextualizing prefigurative politics', offers a comprehensive discussion of the broader historical, philosophical and sociological debates revolving around the concept. My opening chapter considers the extent to which prefigurative politics can develop alternatives to capitalism *within* capitalism, and it defines prefigurative politics as possessing an onto-epistemic character – that is, a type of politics conceiving social change in an ontologically and epistemologically different way than conventional and contentious politics. Paul Raekstad then delves into the use of prefigurative politics in anarchist, Marxist and syndicalist theory and strategy, ranging from the First International in 1864 to Bernie Sander's recent calls for democratic socialism. He concludes with a strong case for prefigurative politics as a tool to overcome the 'paradox of self-emancipation': how can we achieve a free and equal society when dominant institutions prevent us from doing so?

In the chapter that follows, Ana Cecilia Dinerstein cross-pollinates Ernst Bloch's theory of hope with a reflection on the 'resilience of the colonial' in the epistemological understandings of prefiguration. Dinerstein argues that Bloch's concept of multiversum can usefully complement the concept of pluriverse (coined by Arturo Escobar and other post-development scholars) because it incorporates the workings of multiple, non-synchronous temporalities. Moving the discussion along, Aris Komporosoz-Athanasiou and Chiara Bottici's chapter scrutinizes the relation between prefigurative politics and radical imagination understood – deploying Castoriadis' work – as the capacity to produce ideas and visions of the future able to materially condition the present. Seen in this light, prefigurative politics is a (radical) 'imaginal practice' that collapses the future into the present, thus working as a 'homeopathic strategy' against the spectacle of contemporary capitalism.

In a similar vein, the first part is brought to a close by Antonia De Vita and Francesco Vittori's chapter. Drawing from Paulo Freire's scholarship on the pedagogy of the oppressed, prefiguration is thought of as a set of informal collective 'learning practices' that are based on 'affinity for affinity' (Day, 2005); these practices shape social relationships that the hegemonic system of power (capitalism) is not able to assimilate or suppress.

The second part of the book, titled 'Prefigurative politics in practice', fleshes out the concept of prefigurative politics through concrete examples and rich case studies. In the opening chapter, Ana Cecilia Dinerstein and Frederick Harry Pitts examine the prefigurative potential of (human) work. Distancing themselves from depictions of postwork and fully automated futures – currently quite popular among the Left – the authors criticize the view that transcending work equals transcending capitalism; work doesn't necesarily mean *capitalist work*. Indeed, instead of rejecting tout court the idea of work, one should focus on the relations of social reproduction characterizing work in contemporary capitalism. But what would such a prefigurative society look like? In the chapter that follows, Suryamayi Aswini Clarence-Smith takes the reader on a vivid journey through Auroville, one of the oldest and largest intentional communities in the world: 'the universal town where men and women of all countries are able to live in peace and harmony … to realize human unity' (The Mother, 1968). Thanks to her personal experience as a born and raised Aurovilian, Clarence-Smith's auto-ethnographic work provides a nuanced description of daily practices, social relations and value/belief systems in a 'utopian prefigurative' microsociety. In doing so, she also opens up a much-needed dialogue between utopian studies and prefigurative scholarship.

But prefigurative modes of living are not found exclusively in intentional communities. In fact, as Francesca Forno and Stefan Wahlen's thought-provoking chapter shows, the mundane can be prefigurative, political and *politicized*. By focusing on three key facets of everyday life – time, space and modality – the authors contend that the 'everyday' is a *locus* of resistance, change and prefiguration. Through the case of alternative food networks, they go on to illustrate how food production, provisioning and consumption can be reimagined and re-enacted in more sustainable, fair and democratic ways. The politicization of the mundane can, in turn, raise political awareness and willingness to engage in other forms of political participation outside the everyday sphere. If, according to Clarence-Smith, prefiguration is by definition utopian, in the following chapter Laura Centemeri and Viviana Asara convincingly add that prefiguration can also be 'ecotopian' – emphasizing social as well as ecological relations. Such ecological prefiguration can shape new ontologies, new forms of coexistence between humans and non-human nature. By way of illustration, the authors examine the permaculture movement and show that it is more than just a social movement; it's also a value practice and a design method useful to envision uncontaminated socioecological relations.

The next chapter turns to the question of how prefigurative politics affects the surrounding world, especially physical space. In Jilly Traganou's view, prefigurative politics is 'dissenting through making'. This making often involves the planning, creation and maintenance of autonomous spatialities, materialities and infrastructures. Because, as touched on earlier, prefigurative initiatives are never completely insulated from the outside world, these processes of spatial creation and maintenance are rarely predictable; indeed, they are often contentious and can sometimes lead to paradoxical outcomes. In her chapter, Traganou describes the results of her research stay in Christiania Freetown, an urban intentional community in the heart of Copenhagen, Denmark. Through a close examination of this case, the above-mentioned processes are dissected and problematized against the backdrop of rising tensions between Christiania's insiders and outsiders. The book's second part closes with Eleonora Gea Piccardi's chapter on the Kurdish Rojava revolution, geared towards the subversion of patriarchal and colonial relations and the establishment of a liberated socioecologically just society. Central to this contribution is the description and analysis of Jineolojî, a matristic epistemology that condenses the philosophical beliefs and world view of the Kurdish women's struggle within the Kurdistan Workers' Party. Thanks to her immersive period of militant ethnographic research in Rojava, Piccardi avoids essentialist or romanticized accolades, succeeding instead in delivering an incredibly informative piece of research on one of the most significant contemporary examples of prefigurative politics.

The third and final part of the book, titled 'Doing research on prefigurative politics', presents valuable reflections, including limitations, cautions and caveats that scholars should keep in mind. Luke Yates and Joost de Moor begin with an overview of the (implicit and explicit) use of prefigurative politics in modern social movements from 1968 to 2019. Systematically examining literature from social movement studies, the authors demonstrate how the term 'prefigurative politics' has been used to refer to distinct yet overlapping logics of activism: the *imagination* of alternatives, the practical *implementation* of alternatives, or the political/*decisional processes* through which these alternatives are implemented. The chapter ends with a useful appraisal of potential areas for future research on prefigurative politics. In this respect, a promising strand of research is emerging from critical management studies and organization studies. Mikko Laamanen's chapter draws from and, at the same time, contributes to the research conducted within these fields by reflecting on the (apparent) paradox of what it means to 'organize prefiguratively'. The chapter is based on the author's first-hand action research in the Finnish time bank organization Stadin Aikapankki, which has approximately 4,000 members. Reading Laamanen's chapter, we are reminded that translating prefigurative ideals into inclusive and horizontal day-to-day practices, while also guaranteeing the organization's survival and functioning, is a challenging endeavour that entails a constant process of (re)structuring and (re)negotiation. In sum, and not so paradoxically, it a constant process of organization.

Prefigurative organizing is also central to Marianne Maeckelbergh's chapter. She deploys her own previous work on the alter-globalization movement in the 2000s, as well as the wave of assembly-based movements in the early 2010s, to explore how horizontal decisional practices and structures are implemented. By defining two types of temporalities – event-time and process-time – Maeckelbergh stresses how blurred the lines are between success and failure within prefigurative social movements, and how significantly the outcome of this assessment can change when choosing different time frames. Part three of the book draws to close with a chapter that is, as stated in the title itself, 'a sympathetic polemic'. Following on from the meta-analytic exercise of Luke Yates and Joost de Moor, du Plessis and Husted present five challenges for future research on prefigurative politics: the assumption of effectiveness; the (excessive) puritanism of ideals; the exclusive focus on progressive movements (rather than conservative or regressive ones); the conceptual confusion and conflation between prefiguration as a premise and as a point of arrival; and, finally, the uber-performativity often implied by the term. These challenges are not meant to deter anyone from conducting research on prefigurative politics. On the contrary, they are intended as an encouraging invitation to chart new lines of enquiry and push the boundaries of existing knowledge.

The book ends with a masterly afterword by Davina Cooper, who provides a compelling reading of this edited volume through the prism of three central questions: What is being prefigured? What does prefiguration do and need? And what academic methods support and advance prefigurative work? In answering these questions, she crucially reminds us that prefigurative politics implies the prefiguration of *new meanings* along with the common understanding that prefigurative politics entails remaking organizational and decisional processes, and developing new everyday practices and subjectivities. Finally, by describing how new meanings of 'state' and 'gender' – which Cooper has worked on extensively – can be reimagined and enacted, she emphasizes the importance of incorporating reflections on power, capacity and meaning in the study of prefigurative politics.

As the reader will by now have understood, scholarship on prefigurative politics represents a vibrant, thriving and interdisciplinary area of research. And this trend is set to continue as the demand grows for sociological research that can help envision alternative futures and elucidate ways to transition to more just, democratic and sustainable societies. This volume hopefully constitutes a valuable companion for current and future cohorts of scholars willing to explore why, drawing on the words of Malcolm X, the future belongs to those who prepare for it today.

Notes

[1] A recently published book titled *Prefigurative Politics: Building Tomorrow Today* by Paul Raekstad and Sofa Saio Gradin (2020) is an excellent exception.

[2] That said, as Jason Moore, Raj Patel, Stefania Barca and other political ecologists remind us, we are not all equally responsible for what is happening. The 'imperial mode of living' of the few is undermining the possibility to live for the many (Brand and Wissen, 2021).

[3] An overview of what is currently happening in the intentional community around the federal government's development plan is available via the Twitter account @SaveAuroville.

[4] Some scholars working on socioecological transitions and sustainability innovations distinguish between radical transformations and reformist transitions. Temper et al describe a radical transformation as 'confronting the basic structural reasons for unsustainability, inequity and injustice, such as capitalism, patriarchy, state-centrism, or other inequities in power resulting from caste, ethnic, racial, and other social characteristics' (2018, p 752). These involve 'diverse, emergent, and unruly political alignments' (Stirling, 2015, cited in Temper et al, 2018, p 748) that challenge the status quo, such as citizen-led initiatives, grassroots innovations and place-based social movements.

References

Blühdorn, I. (2017) 'Post-capitalism, post-growth, post-consumerism? Eco-political hopes beyond sustainability', *Global Discourse*, 7(1): 42–61.

Brand, U. and Wissen, M. (2021) *The Imperial Mode of Living: Everyday Life and the Ecological Crisis of Capitalism*, London: Verso Books.

Brissette, E. (2016) 'The prefigurative is political: on politics beyond "the state"', in A.C. Dinerstein (ed) *Social Sciences for an Other Politics*, Basingstoke: Palgrave Macmillan, pp 109–19.

Chatterton, P. and Pickerill, J. (2010) 'Everyday activism and transitions towards post-capitalist worlds', *Transactions of the Institute of British Geographers* 35(4): 475–90.

Cullen, W., Gulati, G. and Kelly, B.D. (2020) 'Mental health in the COVID-19 Pandemic', *QJM: An International Journal of Medicine*, 113(5): 311–12.

Dolphijn, E. and van der Tuin, I. (2012) *New Materialism: Interviews and Cartographies*, Ann Arbor, MI: MPublishing, Open Humanities Press.

Forno, F. and Weiner, R.R. (2020) *Sustainable Community Movement Organizations: Solidarity Economies and Rhizomatic Practices*, London: Routledge.

Gibson-Graham, J.K., Cameron, J. and Healy, S. (2013) *Take Back the Economy: An Ethical Guide for Transforming Our Communities*, Minneapolis: University of Minnesota Press.

Kothari, A. (2022) 'Bulldozing a dream? Auroville's importance as an experiment in alternative living', *Wall Street International Journal* [online], 9 January, available from: https://wsimag.com/economy-and-politics/68234-bulldozing-a-dream

Monticelli, L. (2021) 'On the necessity of prefigurative politics', *Thesis Eleven*, 167(1): 99–118.

Moreno, C., Wykes, T., Galderisi, S., Nordentoft, M., Crossley, N., Jones, N., et al (2020) 'How mental health care should change as a consequence of the COVID-19 pandemic', *The Lancet Psychiatry*, 7(9): 813–24.

O'Brien, K. and Sygna, L. (2013) 'Responding to climate change: the three spheres of transformation', in *Proceedings: Transformation in a Changing Climate: International Conference in Oslo 19–21 June 2013*, Oslo: University of Oslo, pp 16–23.

Raekstad, P. and Saio Gradin, S. (2020) *Prefigurative Politics: Building Tomorrow Today*, Cambridge: Polity Press.

Sitrin, M. and Colectiva Sembrar (eds) (2020) *Pandemic Solidarity: Mutual Aid during the Covid-19 Crisis*, London: Pluto Press.

Smucker, J.M. (2014) 'Can prefigurative politics replace political strategy?', *Berkeley Journal of Sociology* [online], 58, available from: https://berkeleyjournal.org/2014/10/07/can-prefigurative-politics-replace-political-strategy/

Temper, L., Walter, M., Rodriguez, I., Kothari, A. and Turhan, E. (2018) 'A perspective on radical transformations to sustainability: resistances, movements and alternatives', *Sustainability Science* 13: 747–68.

The Mother (1968) *The Auroville Charter*, Puducherry: Sri Aurobindo Ashram.

Wahlström, M., Kocyba, P., De Vydt, M. and de Moor, J. (eds) (2019) 'Protest for a future: composition, mobilization and motives of the participants in Fridays for Future climate protests on 15 March, 2019 in 13 European Cities' [online], available from: https://protestinstitut.eu/wp-content/uploads/2019/07/20190709_Protest-for-a-future_GCS-Descriptive-Report.pdf

Wright, E.O. (2019) *How to Be an Anticapitalist in the 21st Century*, London: Verso Books.

PART I

Contextualizing Prefigurative Politics

1

Prefigurative Politics Within, Despite and Beyond Contemporary Capitalism

Lara Monticelli

Introduction

As Rahel Jaeggi (2013) notes, the critical approaches to capitalism that emerged after the financial crisis of 2007–08 have, at times, had an inflationary character, as evidenced by hyperbolic newspaper articles on the forthcoming 'end of capitalism' (see, for instance, Mason, 2015b). Nevertheless, this has provided a clearance of sorts for a vibrant discussion to emerge around alternatives to capitalism – a debate that has spread well beyond the walls of academic political philosophy, critical theory and sociology departments. Indeed, the recent and simultaneous crises at the ecological, economic, social and sanitary levels seem to have brought about the realization that capitalism is an unsustainable socio-economic system and that, if we are to safeguard the continuation of life on this planet, it needs to be either reformed or completely transcended towards a post-capitalist future. Interestingly, this position – traditionally the slogan of the most progressive political and environmental activists – is starting to be shared by not only international institutions (such as the European Union and the United Nations) but also multinational corporations' top managers, investment banks, think tanks and consultancy companies (Cacciari, 2020). The *Financial Times* recently launched a new column titled 'Time for reset', and the World Economic Forum at Davos in 2021 produced a new agenda that, in the words of business guru Klaus Schwab, envisions 'a global economy that works for progress, people and planet' (Schwab, 2021). Ironic as it may seem, critiquing contemporary capitalism as unsustainable is the new mainstream mantra.

As a consequence of this shared realization, many governments are starting to call for the implementation of a Green New Deal – one able to foster the transition to a more ecological and sustainable economy. Following a similar trend, the energy sector's multinational corporations are claiming they will 'turn the switch' towards more sustainable ways of producing energy, investment banks are proposing new green assets and sustainability-linked loans, and consultancy companies are beginning to rate companies according to their impact on the environment, society and governance. Even the allocation of the European Union's recovery fund, whose purpose is to relaunch the European economy during and after the COVID-19 pandemic, is linked to new taxonomies and climatic benchmarks. In reaction, then, it is legitimate to wonder whether we are witnessing a true 'awakening' or just another way to allow 'business as usual' to continue – what Immanuel Wallerstein has labelled (recalling the closing sentence of the novel *Il Gattopardo* by Italian novelist Giuseppe Tomasi di Lampedusa), the 'changing everything so that nothing changes' strategy (in Wallerstein et al, 2013, p 34). Many social theorists and historians of capitalism claim that capitalism's survival strategy is to evolve and adapt over time in the face of the crises it produces. Moreover, many critics claim that what is needed is not to reform or reimagine a more responsible, conscious or greener capitalism, but rather to shift towards a totally new socio-economic paradigm, one capable of overcoming the basic functioning assumptions of capitalism – growth, acceleration, profit and the exploitation of nature and humans. The term 'post-capitalism' has become increasingly popular in recent years in both academic circles and the media, perhaps the most popular example being Paul Mason's (2015a) book, *Postcapitalism: A Guide to Our Future*.

Several proponents of post-capitalist alternatives, such as Mark Fisher (2009) and Paul Mason (2015a), consider neoliberalism a specific 'mode' of capitalism; they therefore focus their critique and analyses on capitalism rather than neoliberalism. This necessitates broadening the Marxist definition, which reduces capitalism to economic production based on private property with the goal of accumulating capital and seeking profits. To achieve this, Nancy Fraser defines capitalism as an 'institutionalized social order' thriving along multiple boundary lines or separations: economic vs social reproduction, supranational economy vs national polity and human vs non-human nature (see Fraser and Jaeggi, 2018). Rahel Jaeggi goes a step further, overcoming the 'economy vs society' dualism typical of Polanyi (2001) and arguing for a monistic social theory in which the economy is not a separate sphere from society but rather a set of practices that constitute – together with cultural, social and personal practices – a form of life (Fraser and Jaeggi, 2018, p 51).

Accepting Fraser and Jaeggi's invitation to 'de-orthodoxify' the understanding of capitalism implies first recognizing that capitalism exists and that it manages to reproduce itself over time so successfully precisely because of its 'background conditions of possibility' (Fraser and Jaeggi, 2018, p 28) – that is, the undervalued economy of care and social reproduction, the accumulation of resources through the exploitation of nature and the primacy of business over politics. Second, it means redefining capitalism as a form of life: a set of practices that 'are configurations of human coexistence, and thus (are) continually reproduced' (Cole and Ferrarese, 2018, p 106). It is precisely the reproduction of capitalist practices over time, and the process of their sedimentation into shared habits, beliefs, organizations and institutions, that ends up creating what Fraser calls an 'institutionalized social order'. From this perspective, capitalism is an ossified configuration of human life, and its existence is made possible by expropriative and exploitative mechanisms. Thus, to transcend capitalism, it is necessary to envision and embody alternative forms of life capable of 'breaking with the comfort of the familiar' (Cole and Ferrarese, 2018, p 106).

Given this context, this brief chapter aims to outline the role of prefigurative politics in transcending contemporary capitalism and the characteristics that render prefigurative politics – in my view – a necessary (but not sufficient) element of that endeavour. In the next section, I develop this argument by emphasizing that prefiguration entails an understanding of social change that is 'holistic' and, as such, different from any other form of political participation. This allows me to engage with strands of the debate that depict prefigurative politics as concerning mere apolitical (or post-political) lifestyle changes – and, therefore, as incompatible with any sort of emancipatory strategy. To conclude, I argue that prefigurative politics constitutes a fundamental component of any political strategy that aims to transcend contemporary capitalism, because it approaches progressive social change in a way that is both ontologically and epistemologically unique.

Understanding prefiguration: a holistic approach to progressive social change

The word 'prefiguration' comes from the Latin *praefigurare*, a verb composed by the prefix *prae-* (before) and *figurare* (to represent, to depict). It means, literally, anticipating or representing something that will happen in the future. In its contemporary political meaning, the term was first used by the American thinker Carl Boggs in a 1977 essay on workers' control strategies in the United States. In the essay, the author underlines the need for democratic, local and collective structures able to 'anticipate the future liberated society' (Boggs, 1977). The idea that the means of change should not only be consistent with their ends but also strive to embody, in the present, the type of society envisioned for the future – without necessarily waiting for a revolutionary, disruptive event – has traditionally been a point of contention between anarchist and Marxist thinkers (see van de Sande, 2015, 2018; Raekstad, this volume). But it was not until the antiglobalization protests in Seattle in 1999 and the subsequent wave of mobilizations, which began with Occupy Wall Street and were followed by the Arab Spring, that the term 'prefigurative politics' really returned to the fore, popularized by the late anthropologist David Graeber:

> When protesters in Seattle chanted 'this is what democracy looks like,' they meant to be taken literally. In the best tradition of direct action, they not only confronted a certain form of power, exposing its mechanisms and attempting literally to stop it in its tracks: they did it in a way which demonstrated why the kind of social relations on which it is based were unnecessary. ... The diversity was a function of the decentralized form of organization, and this organization *was* the movement's ideology. (Graeber, 2004, p 84)

This emphasis on decentralized self-organization and the daily (re)production of activists' collective subjectivities is guided by a 'moral and political mandate to match means and ends' (Hardt and Negri, 2017, p 275). In the case of Occupy Wall Street, this resulted in the creation of various encampments in Zuccotti Park – including public kitchens, libraries and facilities – that were meant to embody and actualize the movement's ideology and to materially sustain the mobilization over time. Seen from a global perspective, however, it is evident that these 'assembly movements' represent only a small number of the movements deploying prefigurative practices. As Paul Raekstad (2018, this volume) argues, many contemporary social movements around the world are 'potentially prefigurative in nature' (Raekstad, 2018, p 363) – for example, the Zapatista communities in Chiapas, the network of recuperated factories in Argentina and the ecological villages and intentional communities scattered across the world. Many of these movements – albeit differing in their political histories, goals and strategies – blend, to various degrees, contentious action with prefigurative practices.

At this point, it is useful to reflect further on the difference between means and ends – ideals and visions for the future and the strategies through which we pursue them. When it comes to means (that is, repertoires of action), prefigurative politics can be found either alone or in combination with other types of action, whether in the realm of representative democracy (for example, voting, parliamentary and legal opposition, referendums) or extra-parliamentary politics (for example, blockades, riots, strikes, demonstrations). Turning to political ends, prefiguration largely aims to challenge and transcend the culture and structures of contemporary capitalism, the capitalist state and representative democracy by embodying a different type of society within the old one. Among the most notable prefigurative movements in recent memory is the Kurdish project of Democratic Confederalism, to be 'implemented through communes, academies, councils, and cooperatives', which intends to go beyond 'the conventional idea of democracy as representative politics' to form a 'stateless democracy' (Dirik, 2018, pp 222–3; Piccardi, this volume). Another notable movement comprises ecological villages and intentional communities focused on self-sufficiency and unwilling to engage in any type of confrontational activity with the state. Prefigurative politics, in sum, can be deployed to *defend* subjects and spaces from capitalist expropriation and exploitation, to *restore* spaces of former capitalist (re)production or to *create*, from scratch, new collective subjects and spaces through experimentation (Monticelli, 2018, p 510).

Discussions on the usefulness of prefigurative politics are usually held within well-defined disciplinary fields, notably social movement studies and, more recently, organizational studies (for example, see Yates and de Moor, this volume; Laamanen, this volume). In these fields, prefiguration has mostly been described as an important part of social movements' and alternative organizations' reproduction, coordination and mobilization strategies (Yates, 2020), or as playing an important developmental and pedagogical role in social movements' experimentations and internal learning processes (Swain, 2019; De Vita and Vittori, this volume). More rarely, social theorists have deployed the concept of prefiguration in relation to the study of contemporary capitalism and its future. One important exception is the formation of a new collective, Women on the Verge,[1] comprised of scholar–activists from the United States, Italy, Mexico, Australia and the Netherlands and coordinated by Ana Cecilia Dinerstein. Dinerstein belongs to the intellectual tradition of Open Marxism, a current of thought encouraging a greater focus on praxis and a departure from the strictly deterministic, positivist views of history typical of Marxism's more orthodox strands.[2] Alongside developing new ways of conceiving and doing research, the collective sets out to engage in another kind of critique – one that considers unexplored territories with respect to the mainstream social sciences. As Dinerstein puts it: 'The realm of possibility refers to things that are not-yet, things whose becoming lurk in the darkness of the present, ready to be activated, enacted, anticipated, made real' (Dinerstein, nd). In the edited volume *Social Sciences for an Other Politics*, Dinerstein (2016) articulates these 'things that are not-yet' as concrete utopias and shows that, by exploring these utopias as a method (Levitas, 2013), 'capitalist-colonial' society becomes 'denaturalised' – from being the only possible society to being one of many possible societies (Dinerstein, 2016, pp 50, 54). In this sense, Dinerstein thinks of prefiguration as entailing both a *negation* of the status quo and an *affirmation* of what is possible. Concrete utopias, however, are never detached from the dominance of capitalism and the capitalist state; on the contrary, they develop 'within, against and beyond' capitalism (Dinerstein, 2016, p 52; see also Chatterton and Pickerill,

2010). As a result, concrete utopias are always under the threat of being 'translated' – that is, circumscribed, co-opted, appropriated and subsumed (Dinerstein, 2016, p 53; see also Dinerstein, this volume).

The idea of transcending capitalism by developing prefigurative alternatives within its cracks is also evident in the work of the late sociologist Erik Olin Wright and his seminal book *Envisioning Real Utopias* (2010). In the book, Wright outlines three mechanisms of change: the *ruptural* system change (revolution), the *symbiotic* system change (carried out through the compromise between the spheres of exchange, production and politics – typical of social democracy) and the *interstitial* system change (occurring in the 'interstices' of capitalism through the social and solidarity economy, collectives and cooperatives – this is the mechanism most aligned with prefigurative politics). Wright dismisses the first mechanism as undesirable (in light of past attempts), the second as ending up reinforcing capitalism and the third as lacking the force to bring about radical change. In the last book he published before his death, Wright elaborates on his scepticism regarding the 'erosion' of capitalism from within and embraces a more open, encompassing view whereby 'a new strategic idea may be emerging that combines the bottom-up, civil-society-centered initiatives of resisting and escaping capitalism with the top-down, state centered strategy of taming and dismantling capitalism' (2019, p 58). He labels this new strategic configuration as 'eroding capitalism'. Nonetheless, he describes this strategy as simultaneously 'enticing and far-fetched': enticing because it gives hope that change can happen, and far-fetched because it underestimates the power of capitalism to incorporate or crush any alternative economic system capable of becoming big enough to threaten it (Wright, 2019, p 58). Following his reasoning, the only realistic option would be the formation of a 'sufficiently homogeneous subject of history' – necessarily unified around the values of democracy, equality and solidarity, not just class – to strive for a 'democratisation of democracy' (Santos, 2007, p 64).

At first glance, Dinerstein's concrete utopias and Wright's real utopias seem to be similar concepts. Looking more closely, though, it becomes clear that their visions are slightly different. The first discernible distinction concerns the role of the state. For Dinerstein, the state 'translates' concrete utopias realized at the grassroots level by either co-opting or appropriating them, while for Wright, the state is functional in enabling alternatives (which focus on the economic sector) to emerge and thrive within the dominant capitalist system. But the differences between Dinerstein's concrete utopias and Wright's real utopias are also noticeable at a deeper epistemological level. In Dinerstein's view, striving to create more spaces in the economy to implement alternatives is not enough to transcend capitalism; it is equally (if not more) important to focus on the patterns of social reproduction underlying capitalism – in other words, to 'denaturalize' capitalist society through prefiguration. Such a denaturalizing entails reconfiguring needs, shifting values and, in the words of the late founding father of ecosocialism, Joel Kovel, 'offsetting the belief-system' to generate a collective, shared intention 'that can withstand the power of capital's force' (2007, p 211). Indeed, this is why many prefigurative communities around the world call themselves 'intentional' communities: they are organized and structured around shared intentions, which are often markedly different from dominant sets of values and beliefs (Kovel, 2007). In his book *The Enemy of Nature* (2007), Kovel proposes leaving behind a system in which the economy is driven by the exchange value of things to focus, instead, on use value and the post-economic 'intrinsic' value of things, in a 'transformative and receptive relation to nature' (2007, p 213). This demands a 'struggle for the qualitative side of things' that simultaneously incorporates control over work and its product and 'subjectivity, beauty, pleasure, and the spiritual' (Kovel, 2007, p 213).

Looking at many prefigurative social movements and practices, such as the confederalist women's movement in Rojava and intentional communities across the world, it is clear that the struggle for change goes well beyond the political and economic spheres. While these movements share some characteristics with the past generation of so-called 'new social movements', they are best understood when compared with the alter-globalization movement of the late 1990s and Occupy, which both targeted global social injustices at the macro level, acted at the micro/local level and were highly interconnected, transnationally, through organizational networks and digital platforms (Monticelli, 2018). Moreover, unlike single-issue movements (such as the environmental or gay rights movements), prefigurative social movements emphasize the need to tackle – simultaneously – economic, social and environmental issues, which are seen as deeply interrelated (for a recent depiction of capitalism as a 'world system', see Patel and Moore, 2020). When it comes to their action repertoire, it is possible to recognize the presence of a strong affirmative tendency, which outplays the contentious aspect; the focus is on embodying, creating and enacting alternatives, rather than on the act of protesting.

It is an integral, holistic (from the Greek *holos*, meaning whole) type of approach that seeks to oppose capitalism – understood as the dominant form of life, not as a mere economic form of production and consumption (Fraser and Jaeggi, 2018) – through experimental practices which simultaneously allow for autonomy, playfulness and interconnectedness between (and within) other human and non-human beings (see Table 1.1). Change is sought at both the individual/subjective/psychological and collective/objective/ performative levels, which are understood as inseparable, interconnected and mutually influential, albeit not without tensions or conflicts (Cornish et al, 2016). Similar to Alain Badiou's (2005) 'break', Kovel's (2007) 'value

Table 1.1: Prefigurative social movements: a holistic approach to change

Who	What	When	Where	Why
Subjects experiencing and enacting change	Fields in which change is sought	Time in which change is enacted	Interstitial spaces in which change is enacted	Motivation
Individual (subjective and psychological level) ↕ Collective (group and performative level)	Psychology Economy Politics Environment Culture Spirituality	Present	Existing spaces (squatted buildings, public spaces/squares) New spaces (newly formed/built intentional communities/ecovillages) Restored/recuperated spaces (transition towns, recuperated factories)	Creation, diffusion and reproduction of alternatives

Source: Author's elaboration, based on Monticelli (2018)

off-setting' and Dinerstein's (2016) 'denaturalisation of capitalism', Tom Moylan – a prominent scholar within the field of utopian studies – claims that change happens first at the 'socio-psychological level', thus allowing for a 'radical reconfiguration' of the person who breaks with her ideological formation and 'becomes a utopian subject' (2021, p 8).

Prefigurative politics: ontologically and epistemologically different

The growing interest in prefigurative politics and the widespread use of the term 'prefiguration' among scholars and activists have been accompanied by critiques on the supposed futility of prefigurative politics in bringing about progressive social change. Among the most recent sceptical voices, Blühdorn and Deflorian (2021) discuss prefigurative politics and its transformative capacity in new forms of environmental activism. The authors emphasize that prefigurative initiatives can either be co-opted by the market or represent 'short-term articulations of otherness', during which the subject temporary suspends its conventional mode of living and simulates alternative, non-capitalist forms of life (Blühdorn and Deflorian, 2021, p 266). Deflorian continues, in a special issue of *Social Movement Studies* on prefiguration, by describing how 'collective everyday practices' – a broadly defined category that includes alternative modes of consumption mostly diffused in the Global North, such as recycling, clothes swapping and recycling cafés – are 'volatile modes of participation' (2021, p 348) – attempts by the late modern subject to (re)consolidate and refigure her identity. In the same special issue, Luigi Pellizzoni takes a strong position by highlighting the limits of affirmative thinking and emphasizing instead the 'subtractive element' in prefiguration (2021, p 374). Such a stance is reminiscent of both Paolo Virno's (2002) exodus strategy and Erik Olin Wright's 'escaping capitalism' strategy, in which individualistic micro-alternatives are often built and dependent on accumulated capitalist wealth (2019, p 52). Wright's example of the banker who decides to 'give up the rat race' (2019, p 52), move to Vermont and live off his trust fund illustrates this. Sherilyn MacGregor takes a more nuanced position, stressing the importance of differentiating between 'lifestyle' and 'everyday activism' and not underestimating the transformative potential of what she calls – again, following Wright – 'interstitial environmental politics' (2021, p 334).

But scepticism of prefigurative politics dates back to the aftermath of the financial crisis of 2007–08 – and, in particular, of the Occupy Wall Street movement. Some critics, including Occupy activist Jonathan M. Smucker (2014), describe the prefigurative tendency within the movement as an expression of its middle-class status. According to Smucker, it is exactly the socio-economic background and privileged material circumstances of many activists in advanced capitalist nations that pushes them towards less contentious types of action, focusing more on what he calls 'a project of private liberation' than on 'the larger common realm of power and politics' (Smucker, 2014). In other words, prefigurative practices within Occupy have been criticized not only for being an obstacle to the movement achieving its external political goals but also for their inherently exclusionary character. Imaginative self-organizing and radical everyday practices are accused of being a luxury that only people with enough time, health, energy and wealth can afford.

Along similar critical lines, Fraser and Jaeggi (2018) discuss the extent to which social movements that deploy prefigurative practices can foster progressive social change and be 'truly' emancipatory. To do so, they apply three normative evaluative criteria: nondomination (of one group over the other), functional sustainability (over time) and democracy (of decisional processes). Fraser and Jaeggi (2018) specify that it is when these practices constitute the core of a political programme, rather than a mere organizational mode, that they fail to comply with these three criteria. As early as 2013, Fraser expressed some critical positions regarding anarchism and anarchist practices, which, she argued, ignore the necessity of a 'two-track' political system – that is, a political system in which, on the one hand, civil society raises grievances and requests and, on the other, public institutions or governing bodies address these grievances (and, ideally, are held accountable by the public). To Fraser (2013), anarchist and prefigurative practices instead aim to reduce politics to a 'single-track' system in which these two layers overlap. To her, this is problematic because it inevitably ends up replicating the very system these practices aim to overcome. As she so eloquently puts it, a one-track system 'presupposes that everyone can always act collectively on everything that concerns them. ... In what way and to what extent are a council's actions accountable to non-participants who are affected by or subjected to its decisions? These 'others' are, in effect, the council's public(s)' (Fraser, 2013).

This interpretation of prefigurative practices and the other 'assembly movements' derives, in part, from the inability of dominant academic frameworks to understand and provide fitting interpretive lenses for the concept (Brisette, 2016). Indeed, these frameworks usually describe social movements as 'demanding' and 'grieving' with respect to the separate and reified entity of the state, and as engaging in confrontational, contentious politics whenever these grievances are not taken into account or met. This, in Emily Brisette's (2016, p 114) view, creates a dangerous conceptual bifurcation between the state and civil society, which resembles Fraser's two-track political system. I would add that in the case of Blühdorn and Deflorian (2021), the understanding of prefigurative politics is confined to the realm of economic production and consumption, underestimating the holistic approach to change, typical of prefiguration. Focusing on recycling, repair cafés and clothes swapping, moreover, does not include what feminist scholar Sara C. Motta calls 'multiple knowledges, multiple subjects of knowing and multiple practices of creating knowledge' (2016, pp 44–5). Many scholars and critics of prefiguration almost unconsciously focus on knowledges, subjects and practices that stem from the Global North. A greater awareness of this situation must lead, on the one hand, to the examination of different 'knowledges' (as Motta calls them) and, on the other, to a better acknowledgement of the different prefigurative practices from a decolonial perspective (see Dinerstein, this volume).

Prefigurative politics aims to imagine, produce and reproduce – materially – new collective subjects and subjectivities, new democratic modes of participation and new decision-making processes – in other words, new forms of life. In this way, 'the discussion is raised up to the question of being' (Hardt and Negri, 2017, p 245). The creation of these new subjectivities is intrinsically a reaction to not only the ideology backed by dominant institutions but also their functioning and organizing principles. It is the result of a critique addressing both their form and their substantive nature, as exemplified by the case of Kurdish confederalism (Piccardi, this volume). In this sense, our understanding of what is 'political' must be broadened beyond those activities that *directly* aim to overthrow and overtake a position of hegemony. Prefigurative movements, instead, envisage change in an *ontologically* and *epistemologically* different way from political parties and traditional protest movements. Nonetheless, the type of change they envisage remains fundamentally and intrinsically 'political'. To understand the ontological and epistemological nature of progressive social change as it is conceived in prefigurative politics, one must reflect on three interrelated features: the mechanism of change; the relationship to (state) power; and the temporality of change.

Prefigurative politics strives to embody alternative forms of social relations, decision-making, culture, belief systems and direct experience. Looking at prefigurative politics through the lens of feminist political philosopher Rosi Braidotti's (2019) 'radical materialism' (or 'neomaterialism') is fruitful in that it allows us to grasp the core of its episteme: the 'political' is affirmative and immanent, and develops within and despite capitalism. Progressive social change is thus achieved through a karst-like mechanism of erosion (à la Wright) and, simultaneously, affirmation from within. Prefigurative politics grounds change in material reality and experimentalism (Martell, 2018, p 442) – indeed, experimentalism is a central feature of prefigurative politics. Long after Marxist critiques of utopian socialism dismissed the importance of experimentalism, scholars such as Axel Honneth (2018, p 53) resuscitated it in critical theory. Similar to Wright's argument, however, its use is too often limited to the realm of economic production and exchange. In contrast, the ontological and epistemological nature of prefiguration digs its roots into radical feminist and ecological thought in that its focus extends beyond production to centre on alternative modes of social reproduction and the preservation of life. Prefiguration shares this perspective with the feminist and autonomist theories on the commons, for which everyday life, the personal sphere and the body are arenas of political struggle, and commoning is a means of reclaiming and 're-enchanting the world' (Federici, 2019).

Turning to the relationship with power, political parties and protest movements mostly focus on taking state power, whereas in prefiguration, power is understood as a possibility, one that takes place through 'micro-instances that are embodied and interrelated' (Braidotti, 2019, p 87). Following Foucault and Deleuze, power is defined as empowering and creative *potentia* – Latin for 'ability' or 'capacity to do something' – rather than coercive *potestas* – which, in Roman law, referred to the power of promulgating edicts or initiating military actions (Braidotti, 2019, pp 110–11). Prefigurative politics is embodied by a multiplicity of communities within different social and political contexts worldwide, each of which is organized and networked differently and holds a distinct belief regarding whether, and how, to relate to the state and capitalism. For example, indigenous populations, refugees and migrants, LGBTQI+ activists and dismissed workers have created some of the most enduring prefigurative movements and communities. Through prefiguration, these communities do not demand recognition or redistribution (as Nancy Fraser would put it); rather, they affirm their identities and strive to create the material conditions for a more equitable, democratic and cooperative way of living – essentially, they endeavour to achieve self-determination, emancipation and empowerment.

Understanding how prefigurative politics interacts with (and reacts to) power brings me to the third feature of prefiguration: temporality. The focus of prefigurative politics is undeniably the *immanence* of the present moment. This does not imply, however, that the change happens abruptly (Maeckelbergh, 2017); on the contrary, the material creation of infrastructures that enable alternative modes of production and forms of social reproduction requires time, energy and resources. For this reason, prefigurative politics entails a change that happens in the present but develops processually, immanently and slowly; again, because of its karst-like nature, it may require time to produce visible changes on a large scale. If we compare this with the change envisaged by the accelerationists, for instance, it is clear that prefiguration involves a different kind of temporality: accelerationism aims to develop after capitalism has exhausted its energies, and to utilize and reconvert capitalism's infrastructures. This is why accelerationists refer to their envisioned society as 'post-capitalist' (Snircek and Williams, 2015).

Having sketched these constitutive features – the mechanism of karst-like erosion from within; focus on self-determination, emancipation and empowerment; and processual temporality – it is evident that prefigurative politics' understanding of progressive social change is ontologically and epistemologically different from how change is conceived in both representative and contentious politics. As such, any comparison of representative politics, contentious politics and prefigurative politics does not hold (see Table 1.2). This does not mean, though, that prefigurative politics and other forms of political participation are incompatible; on the contrary, they can mutually reinforce each other. There are ways of taking the best of both worlds. The key is to accept that prefigurative politics *cannot* bring the type of change sought by political parties or protest movements, but it *can* complement their actions with its holistic perspective and focus on experimentation and materiality. Even the relationship with the state can – under some circumstances – be constructive, and prefiguration can – in some cases – positively feed into representative politics.

As discussed, the translation of prefigurative politics often coincides with co-option, simulation or repression. But translation could also entail a positive diffusion and democratization of transformative niche practices, with the support of political forces that are willing to offer it. One illustrative example is the resurgence of radical municipalism. Despite the presence of similar initiatives in many European countries during the first half of the 20th century, radical municipalism has undergone a renaissance in reaction to the implementation of austerity policies in the aftermath of the financial crisis of

Table 1.2: Ontology and epistemology in representative, contentious and prefigurative politics

	Mechanism of change	Relationship to state power	Temporality
Representative politics	Delegation	Legitimizing	Future
Contentious politics	Rupture	Conflictual	Present
Prefigurative politics	Interstitial erosion and embodiment	Avoiding	Processual

Source: Author's elaboration, drawing from Wright (2010) and Maeckelbergh (2017; this volume)

2007–08. Radical municipalism promotes the deployment of participatory democracy in decision-making processes at the municipal level. The ideology of the movement is strongly influenced by the concepts of 'libertarian municipalism' and 'eco-communalism', coined by American social theorist Murray Bookchin (Biehl, 2015). Programmes vary from city to city, but the overall aim is to defend human rights and the common good, to feminise politics and to fight the rise of the far right.[3] Radical municipalism gained prominence after Ada Colau was elected mayor of Barcelona in 2015, and it is now constituted by a global network of cities and towns across the world. The movement is growing internationally, as demonstrated by the almost 700 municipalities that participated in the 2017 Fearless Cities summit in Barcelona. These ongoing experimentations, driven by prefigurative imaginaries of what alternative 'political governance formations' could look like (Cooper, 2016), show that prefigurative politics has the potential to ignite progressive social change in an inclusive, democratic and scalable manner (Russell, 2019).

Conclusion

The financial crisis of 2007–08 reinvigorated critical analyses of capitalism and interest in alternatives. Some groups on the Left have emphasized the need to oppose capitalism by striving to enact more localized, ecological and decelerated alternatives in the present – within, and despite, capitalism. For the latter and the concrete utopias they have inspired across the world – such as the Zapatistas in Chiapas, the indigenous communities in Latin America and the global network of ecovillages and intentional communities – prefiguration is a foundational principle because it conceives progressive social change *holistically*, in a way that is *ontologically* and *epistemologically* different from representative and contentious politics. If contemporary capitalism is conceived as an encompassing form of life, rather than a mere system of economic production, then the only way to transcend it is by embodying alternative forms of life. Thus, change has to be sought on multiple, interconnected levels – economic, political, cultural, personal and even spiritual. And this is exactly what prefigurative politics does: experiment with alternative practices of production and social reproduction, and with alternative values and beliefs, in a constant process of trial and error. As such, prefiguration cannot be dismissed as a mere project of private liberation or a withdrawal from society.

The multiple crises we are facing on the economic, social and ecological levels require the combination of what I have argued are two *mutually reinforcing* types of politics: prefigurative politics (to imagine and experiment with embodied alternatives) and representative politics (to counteract hegemonic and regressive forces, such as Right-wing populism). This synergetic interplay, which is not just possible but necessary, can lead to the diffusion of transformative niche practices, such as radical municipalism. Indeed, some of the most recent social movements – such as Black Lives Matter, Extinction Rebellion and the Sunrise Movement – recognize the interconnectedness of socio-economic, racial, reproductive and ecological struggles, and are blending prefigurative practices with more conventional counter-hegemonic tactics. Exploring the interactions and potential alliances between prefigurative, representative and contentious politics constitutes one of the most promising pathways for achieving progressive social change in the years to come.

Acknowledgements

This chapter is an adapted and revised version of the article 'On the necessity of prefigurative politics' written by Lara Monticelli and published in the journal *Thesis Eleven* Vol 167, No 1 (2021). The article is available in Open Access here: https://journals.sagepub.com/doi/full/10.1177/0725513621 1056992, and is reporoduced with permission from SAGE Publishing.

Notes

1 See https://www.anaceciliadinerstein.com/women-on-the-verge-1
2 Other distinguished thinkers belonging to the current of Open Marxism are John Holloway and Henry Lefebvre.
3 See Fearless Cities: http://fearlesscities.com/

References

Badiou, A. (2005) *Being and Event*, trans O. Feltham, London: Continuum.

Biehl, J. (2015) *The Politics of Social Ecology: Libertarian Communalism*, Montreal: Black Rose Books.

Blühdorn, I. and Deflorian, M. (2021) 'Politicisation beyond post-politics: new social activism and the reconfiguration of political discourse', *Social Movement Studies*, 20(3): 259–75.

Boggs, C. (1977) 'Marxism, prefigurative communism, and the problem of workers' control', *Radical America*, 11(6): 99–122.

Braidotti, R. (2019) *Materialismo Radicale: Itinerari Etici Per Cyborg e Cattive Ragazze*, Parma: Meltemi Editore.

Brisette, E. (2016) 'The prefigurative is political: on politics beyond "the state"', in A.C. Dinerstein (ed) *Social Sciences for an Other Politics*, Basingstoke: Palgrave Macmillan, pp 109–19.

Cacciari, P. (2020) *Ombre Verdi: L'imbroglio del capitalismo green*, Milan: Altraeconomia.

Chatterton, P. and Pickerill, J. (2010) 'Everyday activism and transitions towards post-capitalist worlds', *Transactions of the Institute of British Geographers*, 35(4): 475–90.

Cole, A. and Ferrarese, E. (2018) 'How capitalism forms our lives', *Journal of Cultural Research*, 22(2): 105–12.

Cooper, D. (2016) 'Transformative state publics', *New Political Science*, 38(3): 315–34.

Cornish, F., Haakeb, J., Moskovitz, L. and Jackson, S. (2016) 'Rethinking prefigurative politics: introduction to the special thematic section', *Journal of Social Psychology*, 4(1): 114–27.

Deflorian, M. (2021) 'Refigurative politics: understanding the volatile participation of critical creatives in community gardens, repair cafés and clothing swaps', *Social Movement Studies*, 20(3): 346–63.

Dinerstein, A.C. (nd) 'Women on the Verge and mainstream social science', *Ana Cecilia Dinerstein* [online], available from: https://www.anaceciliadinerstein.com/women-on-the-verge/

Dinerstein, A.C. (ed) (2016) *Social Sciences for an Other Politics*: *Women Theorizing Without Parachutes*, Basingstoke: Palgrave Macmillan.

Dirik, D. (2018) 'The revolution of smiling women: stateless democracy and power in Rojava', in R. Shilliam and O. Rutazibwa (eds) *Routledge Handbook of Postcolonial Politics*, London: Routledge, pp 222–38.

Federici, S. (2019) *Re-Enchanting the World: Feminism and the Politics of the Commons*, Oakland, CA: PM Press.

Fisher, M. (2009) *Capitalist Realism: Is there No Alternative?* London: Zero Books.

Fraser, N. (2013) 'Against anarchism', *Public Seminar Blog* [online], 9 October, available from: http://www.publicseminar.org/2013/10/against-anarchism/

Fraser, N. and Jaeggi, R. (2018) *Capitalism: A Conversation in Critical Theory*, Cambridge: Polity Press.

Graeber, D. (2004) *Fragments of an Anarchist Anthropology*, Chicago, IL: Prickly Paradigm Press.

Hardt, M. and Negri, A. (2017) *Assembly*, Oxford: Oxford University Press.

Honneth, A. (2018) *The Idea of Socialism*, Cambridge: Polity Press.

Jaeggi, R. (2013) 'What (if anything) is wrong with capitalism? Dysfunctionality, exploitation and alienation: three approaches to the critique of capitalism', *The Southern Journal of Philosophy*, 4(1): 44–65.

Kovel, J. (2007) *The Enemy of Nature*, London: Zed Books.

Levitas, R. (2013) *Utopia as Method: The Imaginary Reconstitution of Society*, Basingstoke: Palgrave Macmillan.

MacGregor, S. (2021) 'Finding transformative potential in the cracks? The ambiguities of urban environmental activism in a neoliberal city', *Social Movement Studies*, 20(3): 329–45.

Maeckelbergh, M.E. (2017) 'The prefigurative turn: the time and place of social movement practice', in A.C. Dinerstein (ed) *Social Science for an Other Politics*, Basingstoke: Palgrave Macmillan, pp 121–34.

Martell, L. (2018) 'Utopianism and social change: materialism, conflict and pluralism', *Capital & Class*, 42(3): 435–52.

Mason, P. (2015a) *Postcapitalism: A Guide to Our Future*, London: Penguin Books.

Mason, P. (2015b) 'The end of capitalism has begun', *The Guardian* [online], 17 July, available from: https://www.theguardian.com/books/2015/jul/17/postcapitalism-end-of-capitalism-begun

Monticelli, L. (2018) 'Embodying alternatives to capitalism in the 21st century', *tripleC: Communication, Capitalism & Critique*, 16(2): 501–17.

Motta, S.C. (2016) 'Decolonising critique: from prophetic negation to prefigurative affirmation', in A.C. Dinerstein (ed) *Social Sciences for an Other Politics*, Basingstoke: Palgrave Macmillan, pp 33–48.

Moylan, T. (2021) *Becoming Utopian: The Culture and Politics of Radical Transformation*, London and New York: Bloomsbury Academic.

Patel, R. and Moore, J.W. (2020) *A History of the World in Seven Cheap Things: A Guide to Capitalism, Nature, and the Future of the Planet*, London: Verso Books.

Pellizzoni, L. (2021) 'Prefiguration, subtraction and emancipation', *Social Movement Studies*, 20(3): 364–79.

Polanyi, K. (2001) *The Great Transformation: The Political and Economic Origins of Our Times*, Boston, MA: Beacon Press.

Raekstad, P. (2018) 'Revolutionary practice and prefigurative politics: a clarification and defense', *Constellations*, 25(3): 359–72.

Russell, B. (2019) 'Beyond the local trap: new municipalism and the rise of Fearless Cities', *Antipode*, 51(3): 989–1010.

Santos, B. (ed) (2007) *Democratizing Democracy: Beyond the Liberal Democratic Cannon*, London: Verso Books.

Schwab, K. (2021) *Stakeholder Capitalism: A Global Economy that Works for Progress, People and Planet*, Hoboken, NJ: Wiley.

Smucker, J.M. (2014) 'Can prefigurative politics replace political strategy?', *Berkeley Journal of Sociology* [online], 58, available from: http://berkeley journal.org/2014/10/can-prefigurative-politics-replace-political-strategy/

Snircek, N. and Williams, A. (2015) *Inventing the Future: Postcapitalism and a World Without Work*, London: Verso Books.

Swain, D. (2019) 'Not not but not yet: present and future in prefigurative politics', *Political Studies*, 67(1): 47–62.

van de Sande, M. (2015) 'Fighting with tools: prefiguration and radical politics in the twenty-first century', *Rethinking Marxism*, 27(2): 177–94.

van de Sande, M. (2018) 'Prefiguration', *Krisis: Journal for Contemporary Philosophy*, 2: 135–7.

Virno, P. (2002) *Esercizi di Esodo: Linguaggio e Azione Politica*, Milan: Ombre Corte.

Wallerstein, I., Collins, R., Mann, M., Derluguian, G. and Calhoun, C. (2013) *Does Capitalism Have a Future?* Oxford: Open University Press.

Wright, E.O. (2010) *Envisioning Real Utopias*, London: Verso Books.

Wright, E.O. (2019) *How to Be an Anti-Capitalist in the 21st Century*, London: Verso Books.

Yates, L. (2020) 'Prefigurative politics and social movement strategy: the roles of prefiguration in the reproduction, mobilisation and coordination of movements', *Political Studies* [online], available from: https://doi.org/10.1177%2F0032321720936046

2

Prefiguration: Between Anarchism and Marxism

Paul Raekstad

Introduction

Humanity is facing a planetary crisis. With the advent of the Anthropocene and capitalism driving us into disastrous global warming and a new mass extinction, we desperately need to reconfigure our societies in ways better able to sustain life on this planet. We have the technology we need (solar energy, mass transit and so on); what we lack are the kinds of free, equal and democratic socialist relations and institutions that can harness this technology in ways that secure an ecological way of life, enabling the development and flourishing of all. Achieving these will require radically transformative mass politics. Here, history has clear lessons for us. Just as capitalism developed from and built on relations already developed under feudalism, USSR-type central planning built on the forms of organization developed by capitalism, the nation state and the Bolshevik party (Lebowitz, 2012). These revolutions didn't conjure up new societies ex nihilo; rather, they further developed, generalized and systematized elements that already existed in the societies preceding them. We might say the figures of these new societies were prefigured in those that came before. In a sense, prefigurative politics is politics that takes a conscious, deliberate and experimental approach to prefiguring the future. If this is correct, then a successful revolution driven by our current needs to secure a more free, equal, democratic and ecologically sustainable society requires the kinds of prefigurative politics developed by the world's socialist movements.

   In this chapter, I explain how various socialist thinkers and movements have developed and used ideas of prefigurative politics. They typically talked about prefigurative politics in terms of means–ends coherence, or 'building a new society within the shell of the old'; indeed, this was the concept to which Carl Boggs (1977a, 1977b) and Wini Breines (1980, 1982) began applying the term 'prefigurative politics'.[1] More precisely, we can define prefigurative politics as '*the deliberate experimental implementation of desired future social relations and practices in the here-and-now*' (Raekstad and Gradin, 2020, p 10, emphasis in the original).[2]

So understood, prefigurative politics is a core commitment of a great deal of anarchist, Marxist and syndicalist thought. This chapter takes a brief look at some of the core ideas and arguments of these strands of thought. It examines the historical origins of debates over prefigurative politics within the International Workingmen's Association (aka the First International), the main arguments for and against prefigurative politics, and associated debates about relating to – and dealing with – state power.

To this end, the chapter is structured as follows. The next section very briefly discusses how ideas about prefigurative politics arose within the First International and how they filtered down into later anarchist, syndicalist and Marxist movements. I then reconstruct three of the main arguments for prefigurative politics that such movements have developed. Subsequently, I look at related arguments against taking existing state power and the challenges such arguments pose for anyone concerned about transitioning to a free, equal and democratic society. Finally, I discuss the relevance of these ideas to contemporary politics – particularly the recent rise of socialist candidates in the United Kingdom and United States – and the development of approaches that seek to combine prefigurative politics with taking existing state power – namely, 21st-century socialism and Democratic Confederalism.

Federalism, the First International and beyond

Although prefigurative politics, in various forms, is likely as old as politics itself, the issues that inform a lot of anarchist and Marxist debates about prefigurative politics rose to prominence within the First International in the late1860s. A diverse association of Leftist and workers' organizations founded in 1864, the First International developed the idea that, in the words of its Belgian section, the International 'carried within itself the institutions of the society of the future', where trade unions 'would be responsible for organizing production in the future society' and 'local sections, being geographically based, would establish consumer cooperatives for selling at a fair price the goods produced by the workers' cooperatives' (quoted in Graham, 2015, p 92). As such, the First International was seen not only as resisting capitalism, but also to be developing the social structures of the future.

Key to this idea is the concept of federalism, which played an important role in subsequent debates about how the First International should be structured. The most famous statement of this idea is the Sonvillier Circular of 1871, which argues:

> The society of the future should be nothing other than the universalization of the organization with which the International will have endowed itself. We must, therefore, have a care to ensure that that organization comes as close as we may to our ideal. How can we expect an egalitarian and free society to emerge from an authoritarian organization? Impossible. The International, as the embryo of the human society of the future, is required in the here and now to faithfully mirror our principles of freedom and federation and shun any principle leaning towards authority and dictatorship. (Quoted in Graham, 2005, pp 97–8)

The basic idea here is clear: if the First International aims to bring about a free society, it must itself constitute that sort of organization. If it instead organizes in unfree and authoritarian ways, it will make itself unable to achieve the free future it is aiming for. More concretely, the federalists argued that the First International's member sections and congresses (to which member sections sent delegates) should make all important decisions, while the standing General Council should mostly be limited to communicative and administrative functions. Here, federalism refers essentially to a participatory and non-hierarchical system of collective self-rule. It should not be confused with – indeed, is fundamentally incompatible with – today's so-called 'federal states' (such as the United States), which the First International's federalists would see as exemplifying the inherently unfree, centralist modes of organization they opposed.

The federalists included people like Mikhail Bakunin (who became one of the most influential anarchist theorists), and the federalist sections were generally among the largest in the First International, particularly those in Belgium, Italy, Spain and Switzerland. These went on to become important parts of the world's anarchist and syndicalist movements (Thorpe, 1989; van der Linden and Thorpe, 1990; Damier, 2009; Hirsch and van der Walt, 2010; Darlington, 2013; Solidarity Federation, 2014), which continued to be committed to both prefigurative politics and rejecting taking existing state power, the arguments for which I examine later on (see 'The case for prefigurative politics' and 'The question of existing state power'). Anarchism is notoriously hard to define, and I won't venture a definition here. However, we can loosely characterize the kind of anarchism embraced by the international movement that labelled itself 'anarchist' as follows:

> Fiercely opposed to all forms of social and economic inequality and oppression, anarchism rejected capitalism, the state and hierarchy in

general. A revolutionary and libertarian doctrine, anarchism sought the establishment of individual freedom through the creation of a cooperative, democratic, egalitarian and stateless socialist order. This would be established through the direct action of the working class and peasantry, waging an international and internationalist social revolution against capitalism, landlordism and the state. (Hirsch and van der Walt, 2010, pp xxxvi–xxxvii)

Syndicalism is a kind of revolutionary trade unionism that seeks to replace capitalism with a society based on union structures, either in whole or in part (Darlington, 2013, p 5). Anarcho-syndicalism, then, can be defined as a form of syndicalism that 'explicitly aims for an anarchist society by employing anarchist means' (Raekstad and Gradin, 2020, p 9). Anarchism and syndicalism were 'the main vehicle of global opposition to industrial capitalism, autocracy, latifundism, and imperialism' at the turn of the 20th century (Anderson, 2006, p 54) – so much so that the Marxist historian Eric Hobsbawm claimed that during 1905–14, 'the bulk of the revolutionary left was anarcho-syndicalist' (1993, pp 72–3). We find various ideas of prefigurative politics in all these strands of socialist theory and practice.

The centralist sections of the First International, by contrast, formed part of the basis for what became Second International Marxism, from which Lenin, Trotsky, Stalin and the other Third International Marxists eventually split. This went on to include a number of Marxist theorists who advocated prefigurative politics, including the council communist Anton Pannekoek, Rosa Luxemburg, Antonio Gramsci, Sylvia Pankhurst and Herman Gorter. A number of later Marxists also advocated such politics, including the various autonomists such as Antonio Negri and John Holloway. Collectively, these thinkers are often labelled Left Marxists, a term that refers to various strands of Marxism that emphasize the anti-authoritarian aspects of Marx's thought. Usually focused on establishing and securing participatory democratic workers' councils, they also often reject taking existing state power. Many recent writers draw on various strands of Marxism in their work on prefigurative politics (see, for example, Wright, 2010; Dinerstein, 2014, 2017a, 2017b; Monticelli, 2018; Raekstad, 2018; Swain, 2019; Raekstad and Gradin, 2020), as do approaches like 21st-century socialism (see 'Combined approaches to transition'), which combines prefiguration with taking existing state power.

One of the most productive stands of socialist practice in this tradition was anarcho-syndicalism. There is a host of erroneous myths about anarcho-syndicalist organizations, so it's worth noting the fact that they were more than able to organize at scale. For instance, the Federación Obrera Regional Argentina (Argentine Regional Workers' Federation) at one point had 100,000–120,000 members, the Spanish Confederación

Nacional del Trabajo (National Confederation of Labour) at one point had 1.58 million members, and both fought and won numerous victories while facing severe state repression. Anarchist influences have continued to be felt in recent years, including in the global justice movement (Maeckelbergh, 2011, 2012), the new democracy movement (including Occupy) (Bray, 2013; Graeber, 2013; Sitrin and Azzellini, 2014; Raekstad, 2020) and the currently resurging anarchist and syndicalist movements worldwide. Some of these – particularly the global justice movement and much of Occupy – employed a form of consensus decision-making that differed markedly from the voting and delegate systems used by most historical and contemporary anarchist and syndicalist organizations. Instead, the historical anarchist and syndicalist mass movements tended to favour directly voting on issues and sending mandated, instantly recallable and rotated delegates to make decisions on higher levels.[3] This contrasts markedly with the practices of almost all political parties and existing state structures, no matter how 'democratic' they claim to be.

The sheer number of, and strategic variation among, these movements indicates the errors in thinking that prefigurative politics constitutes a strategy of its own or ignores strategy altogether (Breines, 1982; Farber, 2014). Prefigurative politics is just one – varied, contested and important – component of a wide range of broader strategies that vary on a number of issues, including the centrality of trade unions and the strategic value of taking existing state power.

Traditionally, debates about prefigurative politics among anarchists, Marxists and syndicalists focused on formal decision-making structures. As the 20th century went on, however, this began to change. First, thinking about prefigurative politics tended to expand to include a much broader range of social phenomena, such as culture and daily life, and sometimes also to *shift focus* towards these phenomena and away from the structure of mass organizations. Virtually all the large anarchist, Marxist and syndicalist movements created their own counterculture, practiced forms of mutual aid, and reconstructed their daily lives in various ways, but they often didn't conceptualize these actions in terms of prefigurative politics.

Second, many anti-racist, decolonial and feminist thinkers and activists within socialist movements have rightly argued that overcoming (for example) racism and sexism requires understanding and actively addressing them within movements and organizations in ways that go beyond formal decision-making. This has involved challenging the neat separation of the personal from the political, and arguing for the importance of understanding and addressing various informal hierarchies and inequalities. Far from being new, these concerns have been raised and advocated in various anarchist and syndicalist movements for well over a century, but usually weren't implemented as consistently or as well as they're expected to be today.

A variety of informal norms, practices, values and so on can deeply affect whether, for example, a formally democratic organization functions in a substantially democratic way. If some members are routinely ignored or expected to do much more work outside of organizing – for example, all the childcare and cooking – then the most perfect rules and procedures won't be enough. This suggests a more general point: prefiguring a free, equal and democratic future society requires recognizing and addressing a broad range of informal hierarchies.

Leaving (for example) racist and sexist social structures unchallenged within organizing prevents them from effectively prefiguring free, equal and democratic formal decision-making structures – much less the broader social relations and practices they want to be part of it. Addressing these informal hierarchies can be (and is) done in many different ways, including constructing organizations, events, materials and so on that do not exclude members of marginalized groups; adding caucuses for those groups (for example, women's or people of colour's caucuses within unions); and utilizing workshops, skill shares and other events to help empower members of those groups to participate more effectively.[4] These measures would be unnecessary in a fully free, equal and democratic socialist society, but under present conditions they help to prefigure the kinds of social relations that radical groups want the future to have.

The case for prefigurative politics

The case for prefigurative politics starts from the premise that our basic institutions – capitalism, the state, the patriarchal family and so on – are inherently unfree and unequal. This is part of the reason why they need to be replaced. Replacing them with truly free, equal and democratic institutions requires agents with the powers, needs and consciousness to do so. Enough people have to be able to introduce such institutions, feel a need to do so and have the knowledge and understanding necessary for all of this. However, the basic institutions we have don't develop any of these things, because they are inherently unfree and unequal. Having never organized complex deliberation and decision-making in free, equal and democratic ways, most people haven't learned to do so well, haven't developed a real drive to do so and/or don't have much concrete consciousness about what it would be like. If current basic institutions don't help people to develop – and even prevent them from developing – these skills, how is self-emancipation possible? Put differently: how can we emancipate ourselves if current institutions prevent us from developing the powers, drives and consciousness we need to do so? Call this the 'paradox of self-emancipation' (similarly, Campbell, 2006, 105, refers to a 'chicken-and-egg dilemma for a transition to socialism') (see Ackelsberg,

2004; Campbell and Tutan, 2008; Raekstad, 2018; Raekstad and Gradin, 2020; for more on the pedagogical implications of some of these ideas, see Antonia De Vita and Francesco Vittori, this volume).

Prefigurative politics offers an answer to this paradox. Organizations of struggle and transition must begin to implement the social relations and practices they want for the future in the here and now. This is because doing so is important for developing the right kinds of revolutionary agency; for developing the powers, drives and consciousness necessary to bring about universal human emancipation.

First, prefigurative politics is needed to develop the powers – the abilities or capacities – to reorganize social life in truly free, equal and democratic ways. People must 'prepare themselves for revolution' and a new society 'by participating in activities and practices that are themselves egalitarian, empowering, and therefore transformative' (Ackelsberg, 2004, pp 53–4). Revolutionary movements need to create and embody an 'emancipatory climate' to enable the 'enhancing [of] the capabilities buried within the people' (Zibechi, 2012, pp 52–3). To do this, 'it is essential to build those institutions through which people are able to develop their capacities and make themselves fit to create a new world' (Lebowitz, 2012, p 88). The general idea here is that we learn how to do something well – whether that's playing football, dancing or flying aeroplanes – by practising. To be sure, instructions from coaches, books, videos and so on can be invaluable, but it's rarely possible for people to become proficient at complex and difficult tasks without ever actually practising them. How many skilled dancers, pilots or mechanics do you know who got good without ever practising dancing, flying or repairing things?

Second, prefigurative politics is needed to develop the drives to take us to a free, equal and democratic society. As Marina Sitrin rightly points out, to 'see oneself as an actor, when historically one has been a silent observer, is a fundamental break from the past' (2012, p 84). The experience of much more free, equal and democratic social relations is inherently empowering and enjoyable. The effects of such lived experiences, and the enjoyment that comes along with them, help people to develop a taste for these more free, equal and democratic ways of organizing and living together. This drives them to seek these things in other areas of their lives as well, such as their local communities and workplaces. These 'new drives, and the pleasure of satisfying them, also provide powerful motivation to continue to struggle and win' and, in so doing, 'push against the system and drive us towards transcending it' (Raekstad and Gradin, 2020, p 74).

Third, prefigurative politics is needed to develop the right kinds of revolutionary consciousness. David Graeber has discussed how the global justice movement and Occupy sought to use prefigurative politics for consciousness-raising:

We all knew it was practically impossible to convince the average American that a truly democratic society was possible through rhetoric. But it was possible to show them. The experience of a thousand, or two thousand, people making collective decisions without a leadership structure, motivated only by principle and solidarity, can change one's most fundamental assumptions about what politics, or for that matter, human life, could actually be like. (Graeber, 2013, p 89)

For Marxists, anarchists and syndicalists, consciousness isn't something that's 'elevated above the this-worldly realm of human practice' (Cox and Nielsen, 2014, p 32); rather, it is part of, and embedded within, a nexus of social and historical relations and practices. There are many ways of developing people's consciousness, such as convincing them through arguments in a book or an article. But these aren't the only things that affect our consciousness; our practices and experiences do so as well. One important way to develop revolutionary consciousness is through practices that can nurture and sustain such consciousness. For example, by embodying the kinds of free, equal and democratic social relations that we can come to better understand, appreciate, actively participate in and potentially spread to other aspects of our lives.

Reaching a free, equal and democratic socialist society requires a lot of people to realize that – and how – such a society can be made a reality; who are able to understand and make sense of the new institutions that such a transition requires; and who are able to apply, adapt and modify these institutions as needed. Here too the best way to develop such consciousness is through the lived practices and experiences of producing and reproducing them.

If these arguments are correct, universal human emancipation requires prefigurative politics because prefigurative politics is needed to develop the necessary powers, drives and consciousness for transitioning to such a society. This has often been viewed as being in tension with strategies that involve taking control of the existing state apparatus, to which I now turn.

The question of existing state power

Based on the perceived failures of the 18th- and 19th-century republicans, the authoritarian socialism of the Blanquists and the early experiences with participatory elections (like the Swiss cantonal elections of 1868), many in the First International rejected the idea of participating in the existing state. In their view, the republicanism of, for example, the French Revolution failed to provide real freedom and equality for all, and the radicals elected in the 1868 Swiss cantonal elections quickly betrayed their promises. As a result, the federalists of the First International argued against taking existing state power and in favour of constructing organs of popular power outside of, and opposed to, it.

The federalists, and later anarchists and syndicalists, developed four main arguments against taking existing state power. Note that, because anarchist and Marxists often define the state differently, I here use the term 'existing state' to refer to the kind of hierarchical and centralized state institutions we see in current capitalist societies and in centrally planned 'socialist' societies. The debate between anarchists and some Marxists, on the one hand, and other Marxists and socialists, on the other, is principally about the strategic usefulness and value of taking control over this kind of apparatus to facilitate a transition to socialism.

First, they argue that taking existing state power is insufficient for introducing socialism. Today, this is not a controversial point; the experiences of social democratic parties committed to a reformist road to socialism show that having a socialist party in power is far from sufficient to introduce socialism. Second, they argue that taking state power will change those who do so in ways that will cause them to undermine any project of transition to a fully emancipated society, because such a transition would threaten their new-found positions of power, wealth and privilege. Third, critics of taking over the existing state argue that it will result in neglecting to build the new institutions needed for the new society they want. Fourth, they argue that taking state power and trying to transition to socialism through nationalizing the economy paves the way for dictatorship (Goldman, 1911, 1998; Bakunin, 1973, 1990, 2016; Parsons, 2004; Reclus, 2013; Kropotkin, 2018).

Later anarchists further argue that these ideas enable them to explain why all attempts to reach socialism through taking state power result in, at best, a slightly better managed capitalism (welfare state capitalism or social democracy) or, at worst, a single-party dictatorship with central planning that just becomes an intermediate stage between capitalism and more capitalism. Either way, they fail to bring about the universal human emancipation aimed for. For instance, Emma Goldman argues that the Russian Revolution aimed for 'the negation of authority and centralization', while the Bolshevik party, in contrast, aimed to 'force the activities of the people into forms corresponding with the purposes of the Party', which they did by monopolizing 'all economical, political, and social activities' (1998, p 391). Whether one agrees with their conclusions or not, socialists who reject taking existing state power are neither ignoring the question of state power (contra Dean, 2016) nor rejecting doing so for merely 'ideological reasons' (contra Harvey, 2017, p 242). Rather, they do so for strategic reasons rooted in their commitment to prefigurative politics.

These arguments pose an important challenge to the revival of support for socialist candidates we've seen in recent years, even in the United States. In many ways, these candidates' proposals are spectacular compared with the last few decades of neoliberal authoritarianism – for example, commitments to strong wealth redistribution, ownership transfer and a Green New Deal – and they are committed to these things, in part, because their goal is not a 'better capitalism' but a free, equal and democratic socialism. So far, however, their ideas have done little to incorporate prefigurative politics or address concerns about the likely effects of taking existing state power.

Given social democracy's track record and the failures of recent socialists in power (for example, Syriza in Greece), can these candidates manage to ensure they will succeed where their predecessors have failed? Any answer to this question will require grappling with the necessity of prefigurative politics and its concerns about the existing state. One solution could be to reject seizing the existing state altogether, focusing instead on social movements and organizations winning changes through direct action and building popular counterpower, in prefigurative ways, outside of it. Another solution could be combining taking and using existing state power with developing and empowering various forms of prefigurative politics. Two models for doing so today are 21st-century socialism and Democratic Confederalism.

Combined approaches to transition

Twenty-first-century socialism is a strand of Marxism that aims to combine taking existing national-level state power with prefigurative politics (Mézsáros, 1995; Lebowitz, 2010, 2014; Harnecker, 2015). Particularly influential in Venezuela, it aims to create a socialist society based on social ownership of the means of production (where means of production are controlled by workers themselves, not corporations or existing states), production organized by workers themselves (rather than by capitalists or managers) and production for the satisfaction of social needs (as determined democratically by individuals and communities). These three elements make up the elementary triangle of socialism (Lebowitz, 2010, 2014).

This approach advocates taking existing state power to enable and support the development of this triangle by setting up, legalizing and financially supporting a network of local, bottom–up, participatory councils and a non-capitalist social economy. The aim is to gradually replace capitalism and the inherited state with a free federation of associated producers. Critics argue that, since the inherited existing state remains hierarchical and capitalist, it will have the same effect on those who wield it as it's had on all who came before, causing them, in time, to seek to undermine and prevent transition. Given how dependent the local councils and social economy are on the inherited state, what prospects do they really have to survive and transition beyond it?

Democratic Confederalism was initially developed by Murray Bookchin (1993, 2005, 2015; see Biehl, 1998) and further developed by Abdullah Öcalan (2017), playing an important role in the revolution in Rojava (Strangers in a Tangled Wilderness, 2015; Dirik, 2016; Dirik et al, 2016; Knapp et al, 2016; Piccardi, this volume). It aims to replace capitalism and the state with a network of bottom-up local and municipal councils where all policies are debated and decided in face-to-face assemblies, which send delegates to higher-level confederal councils that, in turn, administer and carry out the decisions the former have made. Its economic vision is unclear, but the economy is supposed to be governed democratically by territorially based councils in combination with some sort of worker self-management. As Öcalan writes:

> Democratic Confederalism is based on grassroots participation. Its decision-making processes lie with the communities. Higher levels only serve the coordination and implementation of the will of the communities that send their delegates to the general assemblies. For one year they are both mouthpiece and executive institution. However, the basic decision-making power rests with the local grassroots institutions. (Öcalan, 2017, p 46)

To achieve this society, democratic confederalists typically advocate combining setting up local, directly democratic assemblies with taking existing local or municipal (but not national) state power. They aim to use state power to empower the local assemblies by rooting local institutions in these assemblies and combining them into a confederation outside of state control. This was not qute what took place in Rojava, where, facing a situation of state collapse, both a network of bottom-up democratic councils and a layer of more top-down state-like institutions were set up. These were combined with, among other things, a gendered system of dual leadership, gender-based quotas and both mixed and women-only organizations to specifically secure women's emancipation (on this, see Piccardi, this volume).

Some commentators, like Graeber (2016), have expressed concerns that by largely sidelining questions of class and class struggle, not formalizing the precise relationship between bottom-up councils and institutions that are more state-like, and employing a time- and energy-consuming council structure, democratic confederalists may be unable to achieve the kind of free, equal and democratic socialist society they aim for. If an attempted transition to a free and democratic socialism doesn't address class power, won't the upper classes, in time, be able to reassert their power and prevent the transition from succeeding? If more centralized and top-down state structures are also retained, won't they in turn assert their power and suppress their less hierarchical competition?

Conclusion

In this chapter, I have explored how ideas about prefigurative politics developed in the First International and their importance to subsequent anarchist, Marxist and syndicalist movements and thinkers. I then looked at three important arguments for prefigurative politics and the distinct but connected critiques developed by anarchists, in particular, of taking existing state power. I also looked at the challenges these arguments continue to pose for contemporary socialist politicians pursuing a mainly electoral route to socialism. Finally, I discussed two approaches that seek to combine prefigurative politics with taking existing state power.

I'd like to finish by emphasizing that what our world needs now, more than ever, is a transition to a much more free, equal and democratic society – one that can enable us to live in harmony with the rest of nature. We need to think constructively about what the transition to such a society needs to be like. This demands, I think, that we are able to openly, honestly and critically discuss the ideas and arguments put forward by different strands of socialism to chart a suitable path forward for our current conditions. I hope this chapter manages to do some of the necessary ground-clearing to help make that possible.

Notes

[1] There were sporadic uses of 'prefigurative' and 'prefiguring' in earlier socialist texts, but discussion of the ideas we today label 'prefigurative politics' typically spoke in terms of coherence between means and ends. By contrast, the term 'prefiguration' has a long history that is largely disconnected from these ideas (see Raekstad, 2018, this volume; Gordon, 2019; Raekstad and Gradin, 2020). In general, this chapter draws heavily on Raekstad and Gradin (2020).

[2] Prefigurative politics may be as old as (human) politics itself, and we find variations of it in a variety of anti-racist, decolonial, feminist and socialist movements – including, of course, in various strands of anarchism, Marxism and syndicalism. For more on this, see Raekstad and Gradin (2020, chapters 1 and 2).

[3] Some historical anarchists did advocate a kind of consensus decision-making for separate anarchist federations, but these approaches were different from the set of deliberation and decision-making procedures that today's advocates of consensus decision-making typically employ.

[4] For much more on this, see Raekstad and Gradin (2020), Chapter 5.

References

Ackelsberg, M.A. (2004) *Free Women of Spain: Anarchism and the Struggle for the Emancipation of Women*, Oakland, CA: AK Press.

Anderson, B. (2006) *Under Three Flags: Anarchism and the Anti-Colonial Imagination*, London: Verso.

Bakunin, M. (1973) *Selected Writings*, London: Jonathan Cape.

Bakunin, M. (1990) *Statism and Anarchy*, Cambridge: Cambridge University Press.

Bakunin, M. (2016) *Bakunin: Selected Texts 1868–1975*, London: Merlin Press.

Biehl, J. (1998) *The Politics of Social Ecology: Libertarian Municipalism*, Montreal: Black Rose Books.

Boggs, C. (1977a) 'Marxism, prefigurative communism and the problem of workers' control', *Radical America*, 11(6): 99–122.

Boggs, C. (1977b) 'Revolutionary process, political strategy, and the dilemma of power', *Theory and Society*, 4(3): 359–93.

Bookchin, M. (1993) *Urbanization without Cities: Rise and Fall of Citizenship*, Montreal: Black Rose Books.

Bookchin, M. (2005) *The Ecology of Freedom: The Emergence and Dissolution of Hierarchy*, Oakland, CA: AK Press.

Bookchin, M. (2015) *The Next Revolution: Popular Assemblies and the Promise of Direct Democracy*, London: Verso.

Bray, M. (2013) *Translating Anarchy: The Anarchism of Occupy* Wall Street, Alresford: Zero Books.

Breines, W. (1980) 'Community and organization: the New Left and Michels' "iron law"', *Social Problems*, 27(4): 419–29.

Breines, W. (1982) *The Great Refusal: Community and Organization in the New Left: 1962–1968*, New York: Praeger.

Campbell, A. (2006) 'Competition, conscious collective cooperation, and capabilities: the political economy of socialism and transition', *Critique*, 34(2): 105–26.

Campbell, A. and Tutan, M. (2008) 'Human development and socialist institutional transformation: continual incremental changes and radical breaks', *Studies in Political Economy*, 82(1): 154–79.

Cox, L. and Nielsen, A. (2014) *We Make Our Own History: Marxism and Social Movements in the Twilight of Neoliberalism*, London: Pluto Press.

Damier, V. (2009) *Anarcho-Syndicalism in the 20th Century*, Edmonton: Black Cat Press.

Darlington, R. (2013) *Radical Unionism: The Rise and Fall of Revolutionary Syndicalism*, Chicago: Haymarket Books.

Dean, J. (2016) *Crowds and Party*, London: Verso.

Dinerstein, A.C. (2014) *The Politics of Autonomy in Latin America: The Art of Organising Hope*, London: Palgrave Macmillan.

Dinerstein, A.C. (2017a) 'Coconstruction or prefiguration? The problem of the "translation" of social and solidarity economy practices into policy', in P. North and M. Scott Cato (eds) *Towards Just and Sustainable Economies*, Bristol: Policy Press, pp 57–71.

Dinerstein, A.C. (ed) (2017b) *Social Sciences for an Other Politics: Women Theorizing without Parachutes*, London: Palgrave Macmillan.

Dirik, D. (2016) 'Building democracy without the state', *ROAR Magazine*, 1: 32–41.

Dirik, D., Strauss, D.L., Taussig, M. and Wilson, P.L. (2016) *To Dare Imagining: Rojava Revolution*, New York: Autonomedia.

Farber, S. (2014) 'Reflections on "prefigurative politics"', *International Socialist Review* [online], 92, available from: https://isreview.org/issue/92/reflecti ons-prefigurative-politics/index.html

Goldman, E. (1911) *Anarchism and Other Essays* (2nd edn), New York: Mother Earth Publishing Association.

Goldman, E. (1998) *Red Emma Speaks: An Emma Goldman Reader*, ed A.K. Shulman, New York: Humanity Press.

Gordon, U. (2019) 'Prefigurative politics between ethical practice and absent promise', *Political Studies*, 66(2): 521–37.

Graeber, D. (2013) *The Democracy Project: A History, a Crisis, a Movement*, London: Allen Lane.

Graeber, D. (2016) 'Foreword', in M. Knapp, A. Flach and E. Ayboga (eds) *Revolution in Rojava: Democratic Autonomy and Women's Liberation in the Syrian Kurdistan*, London: Pluto Press, pp xii–xxii.

Graham, R. (2005) *Anarchism: A Documentary History of Libertarian Ideas: Volume 1, From Anarchy to Anarchism (300 CE to 1939)*, Oakland, CA: AK Press.

Graham, R. (2015) *We Do Not Fear Anarchy? We Invoke It: The First International and the Origins of the Anarchist Movement*, Oakland, CA: AK Press.

Harnecker, M. (2015) *A World to Build: New Paths toward Twenty-First Century Socialism*, New York: Monthly Review Press.

Harvey, D. (2017) '"Listen, anarchist!" A personal response to Simon Springer's "Why a radical geography must be anarchist"', *Dialogues in Human Geography*, 7(3): 233–50.

Hirsch, S. and van der Walt, L. (2010) *Anarchism and Syndicalism in the Colonial and Postcolonial World, 1870–1940*, Leiden: Brill.

Hobsbawm, E. (1993) *Revolutionaries*, London: Abacus.

Knapp, M., Flach, A. and Ayboga, E. (2016) *Revolution in Rojava: Democratic Autonomy and Women's Liberation in Syrian Kurdistan*, London: Pluto Press.

Kropotkin, P. (2018) *Modern Science & Anarchy*, Oakland, CA: AK Press.

Lebowitz, M. (2010) *The Socialist Alternative: Real Human Development*, New York: Monthly Review Press.

Lebowitz, M. (2012) *The Contradictions of Real Socialism: The Conductor and the Conducted*, New York: Monthly Review Press.

Lebowitz, M. (2014) 'Proposing a path to socialism: two papers for Hugo Chávez', *Monthly Review* [online], 65(10), available from: https://monthl yreview.org/2014/03/01/proposing-path-socialism-two-papers-hugo-chavez/

Maeckelbergh, M. (2011) 'Doing is believing: prefiguration as strategic practice in the alterglobalization movement', *Social Movement Studies*,10(1): 1–20.

Maeckelbergh, M. (2012) 'Horizontal democracy now: from alterglobalization to occupation', *Interface: A Journal for and about Social Movements*, 4(1): 207–34.

Mézsáros, I. (1995) *Beyond Capital: Toward a Theory of Transition*, London: Merlin Press.

Monticelli, L. (2018) 'Embodying alternatives to capitalism in the 21st century', *tripleC: Communication, Capitalism & Critique*, 16(2): 501–17.

Öcalan, A. (2017) *The Political Thought of Abdullah Öcalan: Kurdistan, Woman's Revolution and Democratic Confederalism*, London: Pluto Press.

Parsons, L. (2004) *Lucy Parsons: Freedom, Equality & Solidarity – Writings & Speeches, 1878–1937*, Chicago: Charles Kerr.

Raekstad, P. (2018) 'Revolutionary practice and prefigurative politics: a clarification and defence', *Constellations*, 25(3): 359–72.

Raekstad, P. (2020) 'The new democracy: anarchist or populist?', *Critical Review of International Social and Political Philosophy*, 23(7): 931–42.

Raekstad, P. and Gradin, S.S. (2020) *Prefigurative Politics: Building Tomorrow Today*, Cambridge: Polity.

Reclus, E. (2013) *Anarchy, Geography, Modernity: Selected Writings of Elisée Reclus*, Oakland, CA: PM Press.

Sitrin, M. (2012) *Everyday Revolutions: Horizontalism and Autonomy in Argentina*, London: Zed Books.

Sitrin, M. and Azzellini, D. (2014) *They Can't Represent Us! Reinventing Democracy from Greece to Occupy*, London: Verso.

Solidarity Federation (2014) *Fighting for Ourselves: Anarcho-Syndicalism and the Class Struggle*, London: Freedom Press.

Strangers in a Tangled Wilderness (eds) (2015) *A Small Key can Open a Large Door: The Rojava Revolution*, Charleston, SC: Combustion Books.

Swain, D. (2019) 'Not not but not yet: present and future in prefigurative politics', *Political Studies*, 67(1), 47–62.

Thorpe, W. (1989) *'The Workers Themselves': Revolutionary Syndicalism and International Labour, 1913–1923*, London: Kluwer Academic Publishers.

van der Linden, M. and Thorpe, W. (eds) (1990) *Revolutionary Syndicalism: An International Perspective*, Aldershot: Scolar Press.

Wright, E.O. (2010) *Envisioning Real Utopias*, London: Verso.

Zibechi, R. (2012) *Territories in Resistance: A Cartography of Latin American Social Movements*, Oakland, CA: AK Press.

3

Decolonizing Prefiguration: Ernst Bloch's Philosophy of Hope and the Multiversum

Ana Cecilia Dinerstein

Introduction

> But the prospect-exploration of What-Is-In-Possibility goes towards the horizon, in the sense of *unobstructed, unmeasured expanse*, in the sense of the Possible which is still unexhausted and unrealized.
>
> Bloch, 1986, p 209

> We are not your past, but your contemporaries.
>
> Zapatista women to European feminists, cited in Vázquez, 2009

The debate about prefiguration is vast, and this book addresses many of the significant arguments therein. As a concept, prefiguration has a long trajectory. A Marxist take on prefiguration refers to the 19th century's anarchist, syndicalist and communist struggles. It relates to radical socialist politics (Boggs, 1977, p 100), which include the creation of 'counter-institutions' (Murray, 2014) in both the production and social reproduction domains of social life that aim to foster revolutionary change. In the 20th century, approaches to prefiguration moved away from this revolutionary edge (Murray, 2014) towards focusing on radical organizational processes among activists (Graeber, 2011). However, Raekstad (2018, p 364) correctly defends prefigurative politics as a revolutionary practice beyond the radical democratization of movements' organizing. The critical issue is not to separate the strategic (confronting and contesting power) and the prefigurative (reinventing the world) dimensions of movements' collective actions. This separation allows for a 'false dichotomy' (Maeckelbergh, 2016, p 121). Prefigurative politics involve a struggle in and against capitalism and an experiment to bring about a new society (Raekstad, 2018, p 364; see also Raekstad, this volume).

In the past four decades, together with workers' protests and strikes, subjectivities other than the organized working class – including indigenous peoples' movements – have become stronger and more visible in the global struggle against global capitalism and for social, cognitive and environmental justice. These resistances are not only rejecting the present critical condition of the planet by demanding that the state act with urgency; these grassroots collectives, movements and community networks are also experimenting with alternative practices and social relations around issues of social reproduction of life amid the global capitalist 'crisis of civilisation' (Figueroa Helland and Lindgren, 2021; see also Escobar, 2021). The new crisis signals the increasing impossibility of attaining a peaceful, sustainable and dignified human and non-human life on the planet. It combines crises of social reproduction, food and water, ecology, economy and finance, and energy and resources (Figueroa Helland and Lindgren, 2021).

The long-term transformation in the radical agency (Monzó, 2019) has awoken global solidarity, but the significant differences among these collective struggles still deserve attention. These differences point to the classic North–South divide but *also* to the historically differentiated geopolitical and temporal locations of different subjects of struggle with, against and beyond the myriad of political institutions, legislation and economic policy in the world political economy. Prefiguration scholars and activists still lack (self-)reflection on the persistence of views on prefiguration that neglect, ignore or subsume non-Western and indigenous struggles to the universality of the West, thus reproducing the 'coloniality of power' (Quijano, 2008) that movements are struggling against. Coloniality designates the resilience of the colonial in the present postcolonial world: coloniality of power and knowledge, and of gender persist and are constantly reproduced in society, and rather than being cultural, it is grounded on capitalism as a universalizing project (Nail, 2020). Today's struggles demand a recognition of difference: they are 'epistemic struggles' for cognitive justice by challenging universality and the 'dominant ways of thinking and ordering of the real' and how we understand them (Icaza and Vázquez, 2013, p 684). The question is whether our prefigurative practice is reproducing the coloniality of power, and what are the clues to challenge the universalizing power of capital and to decolonize prefiguration by finding adequate ways of understanding *difference*?

In this chapter, I aim to contribute to the this question and to the debate around prefiguration more generally by presenting and discussing Ernst Bloch's material praxis philosophy of hope and, in particular, his concept of multiversum. In the following, I explore three ways in which Bloch's philosophy of hope can enhance our prefigurative praxis: first, I expose Bloch's understanding of 'possibility' as a condition grounded in the (utopian) material world; second, I present Bloch's notion of 'concrete utopia' as praxis and reposition prefiguration within, and not outside, the accumulation of capital, mediated by the state; third, I propose that Bloch's notion of the multiversum offers a decolonising – non-linear – reading of history that enables us to decolonize prefiguration – that is, to comprehend prefigurative struggles as non-synchronous spatial temporalities emerging from a multiplicity of situations, oppressions and relations *in, against and beyond* the violent ongoing process of abstraction, homogenization and synchronization that underpins the accumulation of capital.

Ernst Bloch's philosophy of praxis

Despite hope and prefiguration belonging together, hope is rarely mentioned in the theory or practice of prefiguration. One plausible explanation for this is that the concept of hope is confined to philosophy, ethics and religion, and – while it may be recognized as motivating – hope does not seem to befit radical activists' prefigurative politics, which aim to enact in the present the change desired in the future. In his three-volume *The Principle of Hope*, Bloch takes the concept of hope outside the religious and ideological realms into an original philosophy of praxis (Rehmann, 2020). Hope is not wishful but wilful (Levitas, 1997). Hope is neither a passive expectation nor a fantasy nor a paralysing ideological discourse, but the vital impulse behind an action, behind the active process of discovering the world. The latter is not predetermined, but rather 'undecided material' (Bloch, 1986, p 199). As argued elsewhere (Dinerstein, 2015, pp 58–9), Bloch contends that the utopian function of hope has historically inspired the creation of architectural, social, medical, political, cultural, literary and musical utopias. These concrete utopias demonstrate that humanity is in search of itself, humanity is unfinished, and it is possibility: 'Humanity … does not have possession of itself simply as it is. Rather, it "is something that has yet to be discovered"' (Daly, 2013, p 172, quoting Bloch). The discovery of the world's content is not contemplative or passive; it is active. Here, Bloch purposely distinguishes between the 'cold' and the 'warm' streams of Marxism that should exist in a dialectical balance: the cold stream is 'the conditional analysis on the whole historical-situational', and the warm stream is the 'liberating intention' (Bloch, 1986, p 209). In this way, Bloch rescues Marx from vulgar economism and linear conceptualizations of revolutionary politics and brings about Marx's 'prefigurative critique of political economy' (Dinerstein, 2016).

Interestingly, Bloch's materialist (Marxist) approach begins with 'life' (Dussel, 2013, p 335). From the moment of birth, 'I move. From early on, we are searching. All we do is crave, cry out. Do not have what we want' (Bloch, 1986, p 21). The cry out is *not* a scream of 'sadness, a scream of horror, above all a scream of anger, of refusal' (Holloway, 1991, p 69); rather, it is an *expectant* cry out − a scream of hope that seeks to cover *a lack*. This lack and the need to cover it never leave us, so hope will never leave us, and in this sense hope, for Bloch, is anthropological − that is, a genuine feature of what makes us human (Levy, 1997, p 181). Hope is behind the (collective) determination to move outward and forward in search of the realization of what we do not have (yet). As we can see, Bloch was neither a romantic thinker (Habermas, 1969) nor 'mystical, eschatological, idealistic' (Rehmann, 2020, p 75), but an unorthodox open Marxist and a philosopher of praxis. He offers a 'concept of (collective) agency' (Rehmann, 2020, p 78) positioned within, but also challenging, the capitalist world's reality. Above all, Bloch presents us with a non-linear reading of history and time (Tomba, 2019) and a decolonizing (Dietschy, 2017), intercultural (Hahn, 2007) and prefigurative (Dinerstein, 2015) critical perspective.

Bloch's concept of possibility: the not-yet and the ontology of becoming

Possibility is a key concept in Bloch's philosophy and to the debate around prefiguration. Possibility does not reside in our imagination, but exists in the undecided material of the world. For Levy, Bloch shows that 'hope is not merely a projection of reason', a mental creation of human thought, 'but an expression of what is really possible' (Zipes, 1997, p 9). The function of philosophy is to perceive 'the real as process' (Bloch, 1971, p 4). Theorizing for Bloch is to *venture beyond* the given. Bloch's 'speculative materialism' (Moir, 2020) is explicitly committed to radical change and aims to overcome philosophy's lack of a 'true concept of reality as an unfinished and autopoietic process' (Thompson, 2015, pp 52–3). For Bloch, facts are 'simply processes' (1986, pp 196–7), so we can infer that those other potential forms of social existence (non-capitalist, anti-patriarchal and anti-colonial) always exist within the unfinished materiality of the world. Reality is utopian 'in the sense of being literally not (yet) "there" in a finished form' (Moir, 2018a, p 205). The alternative resides in matter itself, 'and human beings, as matter becomes conscious, can realise it' (Moir, 2018b, p 124). Bloch proposes that matter is 'being in movement' − that is 'being that is not yet manifest; it is the ground and substance in which our future ... is carried out' (1971, pp 38–9). The *Novum* (the name that Bloch gives to the new) is 'fermenting in the process of the real itself' (Bloch, 1986, p 197); interestingly, the *Novum* which is not yet defines the real character of reality: 'there is no true realism without the true dimension of the openness' of the world (Bloch, 1986, pp 237–8), which aids the anticipation of other possible not-yet (inexistent or oppressed) realities that are lurking underneath the surface of the objective reality of colonial, heteropatriarchal capitalism.

Bloch's non-positivistic and non-ossified concept of reality enables us to assume that prefiguration not only depends on activists' political commitment to radical change but also requires a capacity to 'educate hope' – that is, a predisposition to challenge objective reality as the only *possible* reality. An 'objective' reality is always a temporary solidification of an ongoing struggle *over* the establishment and meaning of the objective reality. To prefigure means to contest the inevitability of the objective reality and to struggle for an alternative reality. It was not probable that the indigenous peoples of Chiapas would rise up in 1994, producing the most significant epistemological, theoretical and political revolution of the 20th century. It is only a posteriori that we can argue that this event was plausible. Most of the time, there are no 'objective' conditions for our struggles to flourish. All we have is 'anticipatory illuminations' providing far-reaching visions to trigger a process of prefiguration, moved by hope, even when we don't have yet the words to describe what we are searching for. Bloch posits that to resist, change and prefigure another world (or worlds) – that is, prefiguration – is a *necessity* (Monticelli, 2021). Why? Because humans and humanity are both unfinished and becoming. Bloch's ontology of not-yet-being, or of becoming, amends our understanding of ourselves and the (capitalist) world: in addition to being or existing, we are also not-yet-beings in the process of becoming, and so is the world. We are, Thompson explains, 'a temporary resting place for a greater process of collective ontological becoming, in which the processual nature of nature itself makes existence into a gigantic experiment of its own becoming – an *Experimentum Mundi*, as [Bloch] called it' (2015, p 55).

Learning hope: from abstract to concrete utopia

Bloch's distinction between abstract and concrete utopias is crucial for prefigurative politics, for prefiguration cannot rely on abstract ideals. Bloch advises that only *imagining* a better society is a weakness, for we must have the strength to realize it (1986, p 1034). Bloch criticizes utopian thought that is not anticipatory (Levitas, 2008, p 43) and establishes a fundamental difference between abstract and concrete utopias. Following Geoghegan (1996, p 38), abstract utopia is created before the emergence of the revolutionary subject (in the historical sense), and it performs as a collective imagination that will be realized in the future when the expected conditions arise, following the party's plan (in the critical sense). Instead, concrete utopia is a collective act of venturing beyond, here and now. Bloch's concrete utopia, as Levitas (1997, p 70) highlights, 'is not simply a "correct" version of abstract utopia, but a praxis-oriented category'. Concrete utopia is 'praxis' (Geoghegan, 1996, p 38). Bronner observes: 'Utopia in Bloch's philosophy is no longer "nowhere", as an Other to real history. It is a constituent element of all human activity and, simultaneously, historical. ... The question becomes how to articulate and realize the hopes unconsciously shared by humanity' (1997, p 166). We must educate hope to move from dreaminess to concrete action (*docta spes*). To educate hope, following Levitas (2008), is to examine the abstract elements of our concrete praxis and remove them.

Bloch was not concerned with the 'feasibility' of utopia, which is disturbed by its probability or viability (see Wright, 2010). The adjective in 'concrete utopia' denotes the anticipation of the not-yet reality. As we have seen, for Bloch, real possibility is not necessarily objective or probable; it is not to be expected scientifically. But what is really possible is 'everything whose conditions in the sphere of the object itself are not yet fully assembled; whether because they are still maturing, or above all because new conditions ... arise for the entry of the real' (Bloch, 1986, pp 196–7). Our dreams and expectations are maturing in the present, waiting to be concretized without empirical signs showing their existence. However, hope cannot be ruled out a priori. No objection to the possibility of the alternative can be raised as long as the world contains unclosed possibilities that are not realized. We can object to (bad) utopias for being 'abstractly extravagant' and 'badly mediated', but concrete utopias mediate in the creation of the *Novum* (Bloch, 1986, p 197).

Situating prefigurative praxis: capitalism as indifference, homogeneization and synchronization

Where does the possibility to create concrete utopias dwell amid the expansive and homogenizing movement of global capital? Prefigurative struggles stand within, against and beyond a global system characterized by the exploitation and subordination of human activity and human and non-human life to money – that is, 'the supreme social power through which social reproduction is subordinated to the power of capital' (Clarke, 1988, p 1). The system is based on the *indifference* 'toward any specific kind of labour [which] presupposes a very developed totality of real kinds of labour, of which no single one is any longer predominant' (Marx, 1993, p 103). While workers and individual capitalists have different preferences, capital does not; and it expands by transforming all specific forms of work into abstract labour (Cleaver, 2002). Abstract labour refers to a socially necessary labour time and attains an unpalpable form of existence in the exchange of commodities, *regardless* of the form of expenditure of the concrete labour that created them (Dinerstein and Pitts, 2021, p 9; see also Dinerstein and Pitts, this volume). The implication of this process is not just economic;

it means that what is *recognized* in a system governed by money is not concrete labour – that is, the expenditure of human energy – but abstract labour – a 'social form' abstracted from the concrete *experience* of work. It is abstract labour that creates the capitalist 'social synthesis' (Sohn-Rethel, 1978; see also Holloway, 2010; Trenkel, 2014). Abstract labour amounts to the 'weaving of capitalism', an ongoing process of abstracting from human activity the form through which capitalism weaves its web of social cohesion (Holloway, 2010, p 157; see also Dinerstein and Pitts, this volume). The 'weaving of capitalism' through abstract labour is achieved through a violent process of homogenization to make 'abstract labour to constitute a totality' (Holloway, 2010, p 143) that is represented by the universal character of money. The expansion of indifference towards homogenization also requires synchronizing different activities at a planetary scale. Being essential for the survival of capital, synchronization means the combination of different temporalities: slavery *and* free labour exist side by side and 'are always *re-synchronised* through the violence of the state' (Tomba, 2013b, p 405).

Decolonizing prefiguration: understanding the multiversum

A critical engagement with prefigurative praxis begs the question of *how* to understand different struggles and how to connect them into a web of global solidarity. Most scholars, activists, artists and practitioners embrace the Zapatistas' proposal that

> Many words are walked in the world. Many worlds are made. Many worlds make us. There are words and worlds that are lies and injustices. There are words and worlds that are truthful and true. In the world of the powerful there is only room for the big and their helpers. In the world we want, everybody fits. The world we want is a world in which many worlds fit. (EZLN, 1996)

In their recent 'Declaration … for life' of 1 January 2021 (EZLN, 2021), the Zapatistas highlight again the value of defending diversity to fight destruction as one of the two interconnected elements of contemporary global resistance:

> the fight for humanity is global. Just as the ongoing destruction does not recognize borders, nationalities, flags, languages, cultures, races; so the fight for humanity is everywhere, all the time [as is] the conviction that there are many worlds that live and fight within the world; any pretence of homogeneity and hegemony threatens the essence of the human being: freedom. The equality of humanity lies in the respect for difference. In its diversity resides its likeness. (EZLN, 2021)

One way of understanding difference is through the notion of 'pluriversality' used by decolonial and post-development scholars. Pluriversality (Mignolo, 2013; Escobar, 2018, 2021; Kothari et al, 2019) offers a critique of modernity and accounts for the impossibility of universality. Pluriversality means that the world contains diverse forms of doing, being, knowing and becoming that have been obliterated, oppressed and subsumed under one alleged *universal* form: modernity. The establishment of modern Northern-Western knowledge as universal took place in a long, bloody process of domination and subjugation of alternative knowledge. Pluriversality addresses questions regarding which practices are deemed prefigurative – and by whom – and defines the limits of prefiguration's present conceptualizations. Marxist critics of pluriversality charge the concept with situating prefigurative struggles outside or beside capitalism and note its lack of explanatory power for how capitalism works. The pluriversal, argues Moore (2022), is a romantic, anti-dialectical and abstract term that rejects dialectical thinking and does not recognize the totalizing force of global capital.

Like pluriversality, Bloch's concept of the multiversum gestures towards the decolonial (Dietschy, 2003, 2017; Hahn, 2007). However, it is superior to pluriversality in many respects. The multiversum – which enabled Bloch to explain fascism (Rabinbach, 1977) and to create an 'explanatory model of plural temporality' to elucidate the formation of Nazism in Germany (Morfino, 2017, p 137) – not only points to the plural character of the global world but also, mainly, refers to diversity as an expression of the *non-contemporaneity* that is hidden in a unilinear (universal) capitalist time (Hahn, 2007, p 141).

In one of the sections of *Heritage of our Times*, Bloch writes: 'Not all people exist in the same Now. They do so only externally, through the fact that they can be seen today. However, they are thereby not yet living at the same time with others. They instead carry an earlier element with them' (1991, p 97). Bloch used the idea of non-contemporaneity, also called non-synchronicity or non-simultaneity (Schwartz, 2005), to propose the need for an alternative vision of time and history:

> Instead of the linearity, we need a broad, flexible, totally dynamic multiversum, a continuous and frequently linked counterpoint with historical voices. In this way, and to do justice to the gigantic extra-European material, it is no longer possible to work linearly, without sinuosity, in series (order), without a complex and new variety of time. ... Thus, we need a framework of a philosophy of the history of non-European cultures. (Bloch, 1970, p 143)

Here, as Tomba (2019) suggests, Bloch is attuned to Marx's late work. Marx read Kovalevski's discussion of landownership, worked on his *Ethnological*

Notebooks (1880–81) and exchanged ideas with Russian populists. Vera Ivanovna Zasulich's question about the significance of the *obshchina* for revolutionary change triggered Marx's reflection on the Russian situation and the problem of the directionality of evolutionary change (see Hudis, 2018). In the 1882 preface to the *Manifesto of the Communist Party*, Marx and Engels enquired about the *obshchina* as a potential seed for revolutionary development in Russia.

> The Communist Manifesto had, as its object, the proclamation of the inevitable impending dissolution of modern bourgeois property. But, in Russia, we find … more than half the land owned in common by the peasants. Now the question is: can the Russian obshchina, though greatly undermined, yet a form of primaeval common ownership of land, pass directly to the higher form of Communist common ownership? (Marx and Engels, 1882)

Marx realized that other non-capitalist forms were not residual but contemporary forms of resistance with a specific temporality. They also contained the possibility of new forms of emancipation and liberation. Considering Marx's late developments, and inspired by Bloch, Tomba deploys Bloch's concept of the multiversum to reject linear historical time and to propose a new historiographical paradigm. According to Tomba, 'to be understood, the world market requires a historiographical paradigm that is able to comprehend the combination of a plurality of temporal strata in the violent synchronizing dimension of modernity' (2013b, p 409). He suggests that 'the different forms of exploitation should be thought in the historical-temporal multiversum in which they are intertwined in the contemporaneity of the present' (Tomba, 2013a, p 156).

The relevance of grasping history as a non-linear and non-synchronized multiversum and understanding capitalism as the 'juxtaposition of a plurality of historical times, where slavery is contiguous to high-tech production' (Tomba, 2013b, p 409) for seizing the power of the prefigurative praxis cannot be overemphasized. First, this opens a path towards the decolonization of prefigurative struggles by revealing their alternative temporalties subordinated to universal, modern, colonial time of global capital. Second, it situates myriad prefigurative struggles with their different temporalities in the real-abstract dialectical dynamics of the movement of global capital. Hence, prefigurative struggles are non-synchronous and juxtaposed, navigating contradictions and shaping to not-yet realities in the form of concrete utopias against and beyond an imposed reality of 'progress' (Bloch, 1970). The dialectical contradictions that emerge from the processes of prefiguration are also multiple. Bloch's analysis of Germany – that is, 'the classical land of non-contemporaneity' (Bloch, 1991, p 106) – suggests that '[a] society is therefore not a homogenous space permeated by a single time that would constitute the playing field of a simple contradiction' (Morfino, 2017, p 126). Capitalist society is characterized by 'multi-level dialectics' (Bloch, 1977) instead of a 'simple dialectic' where there is a linear development of historical time (Morfino, 2017, p 127). One of the significant implications of the multiversum approach to prefiguration is that we can widen the spectrum of radical subjectivity and embrace a non-linear direction of time against and beyond the 'directionally dynamic movement of capital itself' (Arboleda, 2020, p 231). Once the latter is regarded as an abstract contemporaneity (Diestchy in Pineda Canabal and Diestschy, 2018) – that is, an oppressed multiversum of temporalities, modes and experiences of rich human sensuous activity, disappearing under the time of capital, the 'time of domination' (Holloway, 2010) – other forms of being and becoming that do not fit within the modern capitalist time become recognizable. The question is how to educate and organize hope so that we can recognize and connect different struggles in their own terms and with their own temporalities, in an alternative form of *weaving* social cohesion against and beyond indifference, homogenization and synchronization that characterize the workings of global capital.

Indigenous non-contemporaneity and the Zapatistas

Bloch's philosophy of hope and his conceptions of non-contemporaneity, non-synchronicity and the multiversum enable us to align prefiguration with a non-linear vision of time shared by non-indigenous prefigurative praxis and indigenous cosmologies, and at the same time give prefiguration a material grounding in the dynamics of global capitalism. For Bloch, past, present and future are not simply aligned in progressive stages, but dialectically related. Future possibilities exist in a latent state, unrealized in the present; in the present, we can find 'the signs of foreshadowing that indicate the tendency of the direction and movements of the present into the future' (Kellner, 1997, p 81). The future is not necessarily located ahead; as with the indigenous conceptualization of time, it could be in the 'past', as there is contingency and the past contains unrealized possibilities.

Zapatismo is one possible concrete form of prefiguring dignified lifeworlds. In this temporality of prefiguration, there are individual, communitarian and family acts of awakening by means of a thinking–feeling praxis by which we feel with our minds and think with our hearts simultaneously and collectively: 'historical acts of *xWaychinel Lum-K'inal* and the awakening of *ch'ulel* are collective and individual acts, in which people's hearts and minds are the first space-territory where the seeds of struggle and liberation emerge or "in-surge"' (López Intzín, 2019). The wisdom of indigenous ancestral practices has been revitalized in a new light, as in the Zapatista case. They are not stuck in the past. The past is not behind; it has not 'passed' but remains present as memory (Vázquez, 2016). The past should be translated as memory, and indicates a different understanding and experience of time than linear progressive modern time. For indigenous peoples living in their communities, the act of defending *la tierra* (the land) is a 'political responsibility', a revolutionary act against the modern ontology where 'the present and presence are the sole locus of the real' (Vázquez, 2011, p 38). The ancestors have a *real* presence on the land for

> there is no *post* or *pre* in this vision of history that is not linear or teleological but rather moves in cycles and spirals and sets out on a course without neglecting to return to the same point. The indigenous world does not conceive of history as linear; the past-future is contained in the present. (Rivera Cusicanqui, 2012, p 96)

With the multiversum, we can also comprehend 'precedence' (Vázquez in Brittany Chávez and Vázquez, 2017, p 41). Precedence alludes to conceiving of the body as 'not confined by the temporality of presence, by its materiality'. Vázquez writes: 'I want to think of the possibility of crossing from the individualised body of presence to the embodiment of the relational and the ancestral' as a form of hope. Precedence 'speaks of a mode of being in the world in time, it is the mode of being through relational temporalities' (Vázquez in Brittany Chávez and Vázquez, 2017, p 41).

Non-contemporaneity, suggests Diestchy, 'is a necessity of prefiguration. It is not possible to relegate the subordination and exclusion that indigenous people continue suffering to a colonial past' (Dietschy in Pineda Canabal and Diestchy, 2018, p 425) without producing a 'time-based discrimination' (Vázquez, 2009). In other words, in the 'politics of non-contemporaneity' (Schwartz, 2005), the expulsion and invisibilization of the indigenous people cannot be regarded as archaic and unrelated to modern 'abstract contemporaneity of capitalism' because, as Diestchy suggests, 'the formation and reproduction of the contradictions of an abstract capitalist contemporaneity engenders the production of non-contemporaneity and subalternity' (Dietschy in Pineda Canabal and Diestchy, 2018, p 425) that spring from the diverse forms of subsumption of life under capital (Menozzi, 2021).

The Zapatistas' *hope* is non-contemporaneous to other forms of prefigurative praxis. The multiversum enables us to comprehend the Zapatista praxis where the new is intertwined with ancestral customs rooted in alternative knowledge and the memory of a still present 'past'. However, it is crucial *not* to essentialize 'indigeneity' (Ioris, 2020) and regard it as a category of political economy with deep historical roots yet subjected to changes produced by oppression 'recognition' and institutionalization via multiculturalism policy. The Zapatistas' self-government councils (the Juntas de Buen Gobierno), created in 2003, brought Mayan traditions, habits and customs into innovative indigenous movements and new forms of self-determination. The principle of 'command while obeying' – one of the fundamental principles that guide the Zapatistas' community life and the Zapatista National Liberation Army – is based on Mayan traditions of decision-making in the indigenous *ejidos* (indigenous land); it is an ancestral custom of self-government practice by the Tzeltal, Tzotzil, Ch'ol, Mam, Zoque and Tojolabal peoples in Mexico.

In 2021, the Zapatistas altered linear historical time. That year – the year that marked the 500th anniversary of the conquest of the Americas and the 200th anniversary of Mexico's independence from Spain – a delegation of the Zapatista movement travelled to Europe to 'invade' the continent, aiming to reverse the colonial process that started in 1492 with a conquest of the Americas by the Spanish crown. On 22 May 1521, Spanish forces led by Hernan Cortés attacked the Great Temple of Tenochtitlán – the Aztec capital and the Mexico City of today – during a religious service, destroyed the city and, after that, obliterated eight million inhabitants of Abya Yala (Latin America), producing the biggest holocaust in global history. On 22 June 2021, the Zapatistas' first delegation, travelling in Squadron 421 (with a crew of four women, two men and one *unoa otroa*), finished their journey from Mexico to Vigo, Spain, after almost 50 days at sea. In this symbolic political action, the movement proved that they were not conquered despite all attempts to destroy them.

The Zapatistas brought a message of solidarity to Europe, which they renamed the Slumil K'ajxemk'op (Rebel Land), inviting those who struggle to sign and adopt their Declaration for Life (EZLN, 2021). This recent declaration is inspired by the 'defence of life' proposed by Zapatista women at the International Gathering of Women who Struggle (Chiapas, March 2018) (Gies, 2018). More than 7,000 women from all over the world travelled to this gathering in Chiapas to discuss the necessity of fighting capitalism and patriarchal violence and the need to create a new world at once: 'We agree to live, and for us to live is to struggle ... so we agree to each struggle in our own way, place, and *time*' (Gies, 2018, emphasis added). They concurred that the possibility of life on this planet depends on eradicating this violence. In the written invitation to the Second International Gathering of Women who Struggle, published in September 2019, the Zapatista women wrote:

> What if, *compañera* and sister, we learn not only to scream out of pain but to find the way, place, and time to scream a new world into being? Just think, sister and *compañera*, things are so bad that in order to stay alive, we have to create another world. (EZLN, 2019)

Conclusion

I have argued that Bloch's principle of hope, his speculative materialism and his concept of the multiversum can enrich our understanding of prefigurative praxis. Hope takes us into the material capitalist realm of struggle to discover *real* possibility and rethink how the revolutionary transformation of the world occurs through creating concrete utopias. Educating hope means that to prefigure alternatives, we must consider ourselves and the world to be in the process of *becoming*, rather than in a state of being, enabling us to match our collective hopes with the political multilayered contradictions and tendencies that exist in the global capitalist world. We can reject abstract utopias and embrace the struggle to engage in concrete radical praxis within historical and geographical contexts by educating hope. I highlighted the need to decolonize prefiguration in order to grasp the connection between the working of capital and prefigurative struggles that combine ancestral and new practices and question modern linear time. I suggested that the multiversum corrects the shortcomings of the notion of pluriversality, which informs a radical praxis that brings about diverse knowledges and cosmologies but does not explain how prefigurative politics disrupt and venture beyond capitalism. I presented global capitalism as a violent homogenizing and synchronizing expansive force which collapses non-synchronous forms of exploitation into one universalizing temporality (Tomba, 2013a, 2013b). To grasp the power of prefiguration, the latter ought to be regarded as part of a multiversum of different temporalities. Hope is then the impulse and vital energy behind the struggles against and beyond the 'abstract contemporaneity of capitalism' (Diestchy in Pineda Canabal and Diestchy, 2018), towards the creation of concrete utopias that realize the not-yet realities – with their overlapping temporalities – emerging from, against and beyond the material forces that govern capitalism in our convoluted planet.

References

Arboleda, M. (2020) *Planetary Mine: Territories of Extraction under Late Capitalism*, London and New York: Verso.

Bloch, E. (1970) 'Differentiations in the concept of progress', in *A Philosophy for the Future*, trans J. Cumming, New York: Herder and Herder, pp 112–41.

Bloch, E. (1971) *On Karl Marx*, trans J. Maxwell, New York: Herder and Herder.

Bloch, E. (1977) 'Nonsynchronism and the obligation to its dialectics', *New German Critique*, 11: 22–38.

Bloch, E. (1986) *The Principle of Hope*, Cambridge, MA: MIT Press.

Bloch, E. (1991) 'Non-contemporaneity and obligation to its dialectic', in *Heritage of Our Times*, trans Neville and Stephen Plaice, Cambridge: Polity Press, pp 97–148.

Boggs, C. (1977) 'Marxism, prefigurative communism and the problem of workers' control', *Radical America*, 11(6): 99–122.

Brittany Chávez, D. and Vázquez, R. (2017) 'Precedence, trans★ and the decolonial', *Angelaki*, 22(2): 39–42.

Bronner, S. (1997) 'Utopian projections: in memory of Ernst Bloch', in J.O. Daniel and T. Moylan (eds) *Not Yet: Reconsidering Ernst Bloch*, London and New York: Verso, pp 165–74.

Clarke, S. (1988) *Keynesianism, Monetarism and the Crisis of the State*, Aldershot: Edward Elgar.

Cleaver, H. (2002) 'Work is still the central issue!', in A.C. Dinerstein and M. Neary (eds) *The Labour Debate: An Investigation into the Theory and Reality of Capitalist Work*, Aldershot: Ashgate, pp 135–48.

Daly, F. (2013) 'The zero point: encountering the dark emptiness of nothingness', in P. Thompson and S. Žižek (eds) *The Privatisation of Hope: Ernst Bloch and the Future of Utopia*, Durham, NC: Duke University Press, pp 164–202.

Dietschy, B. (2003) 'En la penumbra del tiempo: las exploraciones de Ernst Bloch sobre la no conteporaneidad' [In the twilight of time: Ernst Bloch's explorations of non-contemporaneity], *Intersticios*, 18: 133–66.

Dietschy, B. (2017) 'Multiversum, Ernst Bloch a la rencontré de la pensée décoloniale' [Multiversum, Ernst Bloch meeting decolonial thought], *Séminaire: Penser les décolonisations* [Seminar: Thinking Decolonizations], Université Catholique de Louvain, 20 June.

Dinerstein, A.C. (2015) *The Politics of Autonomy in Latin America: The Art of Organising Hope*, Basingstoke: Palgrave Macmillan.

Dinerstein, A.C. (2016) 'Denaturalising society: concrete utopia and the prefigurative critique of political economy', in A.C. Dinerstein (ed) *Social Sciences for an Other Politics: Women Theorising without Parachutes*, Basingstoke: Palgrave Macmillan, pp 49–64.

Dinerstein, A.C. (2017) 'Concrete utopia: (re)producing life in, against and beyond the open veins of capital', *Public Seminar* [online], 7 December, available from: http://www.publicseminar.org/2017/12/concrete-utopia/

Dinerstein, A.C. and Pitts, F.H. (2021) *A World beyond Work? Money, Labour and the Capitalist State between Crisis and Utopia*, Bingley: Emerald Publishing.

Dussel, E. (2013) *Ethics of Liberation: In the Age of Globalization and Exclusion*, Durham, NC: Duke University Press.

Escobar, A. (2018) *Designs for the Pluriverse: Radical Interdependence, Autonomy, and the Making of Worlds*, Durham, NC: Duke University Press.

Escobar, A. (2021) 'Reframing civilisation(s): from critique to transitions', *Globalizations* [online], 30 November, available from: https://doi.org/10.1080/14747731.2021.2002673

EZLN (1996) 'Fourth Declaration of the Lacandon Jungle' [online], 1 January, available from: https://schoolsforchiapas.org/library/fourth-decl aration-lacandona-jungle/

EZLN (2019) 'Invitation to the Second International Gathering of Women Who Struggle', *Enlace Zapatista* [online], 21 September, available from: https://enlacezapatista.ezln.org.mx/2019/09/21/invitation-to-the-second-international-gathering-of-women-who-struggle/

EZLN (2021) 'Part one: A declaration … for life', *Enlace Zapatista* [online], 1 January, available from: https://enlacezapatista.ezln.org.mx/2021/01/01/part-one-a-declaration-for-life/

Figueroa Helland, L. and Lindgren, T. (2021) 'What goes around comes around: from the coloniality of power to the crisis of civilisation', *Journal of World-Systems Research*, 22(2): 430–62.

Geoghegan, V. (1996) *Ernst Bloch*, London and New York: Routledge.

Gies, H. (2018) 'The Zapatistas' First International Gathering of Women Who Struggle', *Countercurrents.org* [online], 22 March, available from: https://countercurrents.org/2018/03/the-zapatistas-first-international-gathering-of-women-who-struggle/

Graeber, D. (2011) *Revolutions in Reverse: Essays on Politics, Violence, Art, and Imagination*, New York: Autonomedia.

Habermas, J. (1969) 'Ernst Bloch—a Marxist romantic', *Salmagundi*, 10/11: 311–25.

Hahn, P. (2007) 'A "não-simultaneidade" e "multiversum" contra um Totum cultural: uma possível aproximação de Ernst Bloch com a filosofia intercultural', in *Revista Interculturais*, São Leopoldo: Nova Harmonia, pp 139–49.

Holloway, J. (1991) 'In the beginning was the scream', *Common Sense*, 11: 69–78.

Holloway, J. (2010) *Crack Capitalism*, London and New York: Pluto Press.

Hudis, P. (2018) 'Non-linear pathways to social transformations: Rosa Luxemburg and the post-colonial condition', *New Formations*, 94: 63–81.

Icaza, R. and Vázquez, R. (2013) 'Social struggles as epistemic struggles', *Development and Change*, 44(3): 683–704.

Ioris, A. (2020) 'Indigenous labor and land resources: Guarani–Kaiowa's politico-economic and ethnic challenges', *Resources* [online], 9(7): Art 84, available from: https://www.mdpi.com/2079-9276/9/7/84

Kellner, D. (1997) 'Ernst Bloch, utopia, and ideology critique', in J.O. Daniel and T. Moylan (eds) *Not Yet: Reconsidering Ernst Bloch*, London and New York: Verso, pp 80–95.

Kothari, A., Salleh, A., Escobar, A., Demaria, F. and Acosta, A. (eds) (2019) *Pluriverse: A Post-Development Dictionary*, New Delhi: Tulika/AuthorsUpFront.

Levitas, R. (1997) 'Educated hope: Ernst Bloch on abstract and concrete utopia', in J.O. Daniel and T. Moylan (eds) *Not Yet: Reconsidering Ernst Bloch*, London and New York: Verso, pp 65–79.

Levitas, R. (2008) 'Pragmatism, utopia and anti-utopia', *Critical Horizons*, 9(1): 42–59.

Levy, Z. (1997) 'Utopia and reality in the philosophy of Ernst Bloch', in J.O. Daniel and T. Moylan (eds) *Not Yet: Reconsidering Ernst Bloch*, London and New York: Verso, pp 175–85.

López Intzín, J. (2019) 'Zapatismo and Tseltal philosophy: *ch'ulel* and the dream of another becoming', trans M. Olavarría and M. Ramírez-Cancio, *Resistant Strategies* [online], available from: https://resistantstrategies.hemi. press/zapatismo-and-tseltal-philosophy-chulel-and-the-dream-of-anot her-becoming/

Maeckelbergh, M. (2016). 'The prefigurative turn: the time and place of social movement practice', in A.C. Dinerstein (ed) *Social Sciences for an Other Politics: Women Theorising without Parachutes*, Basingstoke: Palgrave Macmillan, pp 121–34.

Marx, K. (1993) *Grundrisse: Foundations of the Critique of Political Economy*, London: Penguin.

Marx, K. and Engels, F. (1882) 'Manifesto of the Communist Party', *Marxists Internet Archive* [online], available from: https://www.marxists.org/arch ive/marx/works/1848/communist-manifesto/preface.htm#preface-1882

Menozzi, F. (2021) 'Marxism in plural times: decolonizing subsumption', *Rethinking Marxism*, 33(1): 111–33.

Mignolo, W. (2013) 'On pluriversality' [online], 20 October, available from: http://waltermignolo.com/on-pluriversality/

Moir, C. (2018a) 'Ernst Bloch: the principle of hope', in B. Best, W. Bonefeld and C. O'Kane (eds) *The Sage Handbook of Frankfurt School Critical Theory*, Los Angeles and London: Sage, pp 199–215.

Moir, C. (2018b) 'In defence of speculative materialism', *Historical Materialism*, 27(2): 123–55.

Moir, C. (2020) *Ernst Bloch's Speculative Materialism: Ontology, Epistemology, Politics*, Leiden and Boston: Brill.

Monticelli, L. (2021) 'On the necessity of prefigurative politics', *Thesis Eleven*, 167(1): 99–118.

Monzó, L. (2019) *A Revolutionary Subject: Pedagogy of Women of Colour and Indigeneity*, New York: Peter Lang Publishing.

Moore, J. (2022) 'Anthropocene, Capitalocene & the flight from world history: dialectical universalism & the geographies of class power in the capitalist world-ecology, 1492–2022', *Nordia Geographical Publications*, 51(2): 123–46.

Morfino, V. (2017) 'On non-contemporaneity: Marx, Bloch and Althusser', in V. Morfino and P. Thomas (eds) *The Government of Time: Theories of Plural Temporality in the Marxist Tradition*, Chicago, MI: Haymarket Books, pp 117–47.

Murray, D. (2014) 'Prefiguration or actualisation? Radical democracy and counter-institutions in the Occupy movement', *Berkeley Journal of Sociology* [online], 3 November, available from: http://berkeleyjournal.org/2014/11/prefiguration-or-actualization-radical-democracy-and-counter-institution-in-the-occupy-movement/

Nail, T. (2020) *Marx in Motion: A New Materialist Marxism*, New York: Oxford University Press.

Pineda Canabal, A. and Dietschy, B. (2018) 'En Recuerdo de Ernst Bloch: Entrevista con Beat Dietschy' [In memory of Ernst Bloch: an interview with Beat Dietschy], *Escritos*, 26(57): 409–26.

Quijano, A. (2008) 'Coloniality of power, Eurocentrism, and Latin America', *International Sociology*, 15(2), 215–32.

Rabinbach, A. (1977) 'Unclaimed heritage: Ernst Bloch's heritage of our times and the theory of fascism', *New German Critique*, 11: 5–21.

Raekstad, P. (2018) 'Revolutionary practice and prefigurative politics: a clarification and defence', *Constellations*, 25(3): 359–72.

Rehmann, J. (2020) 'Ernst Bloch as a philosopher of praxis', *Praktyka Teoretyczna*, 1(35): 75–94.

Rivera Cusicanqui, S. (2012) '*Ch'ixinakax utxiwa*: a reflection on the practices and discourses of decolonization', *South Atlantic Quarterly*, 111(1): 95–109.

Schwartz, F. (2005) 'Nonsimultaneity: Ernst Bloch and Wilhelm Pinder', in F. Schwartz (ed) *Blind Spots: Critical Theory and the History of Art in Twentieth-Century Germany*, New Haven and London: Yale University Press, pp 103–35.

Sohn-Rethel, A. (1978) *Intellectual and Manual Labour*, Atlantic Highlands, NJ: Humanities Press.

Thompson, P. (2015) 'Ernst Bloch, *Ungleichzeitigkeit*, and the philosophy of being and time', *New German Critique*, 42(2[125]): 49–64.

Tomba, M. (2013a) *Marx's Temporalities*, trans P.D. Thomas and S.R. Farris, Chicago: Haymarket Books.

Tomba, M. (2013b) 'Pre-capitalistic forms of production and primitive accumulation: Marx's historiography from the *Grundrisse* to *Capital*', in R. Bellofiore, G. Starosta and P. Thomas (eds) *In Marx's Laboratory: Critical Interpretations of the* Grundrisse, Leiden and Boston: Brill, pp 393–412.

Tomba, M. (2019) *Insurgent Universality: An Alternative Legacy of Modernity*, New York: Oxford University Press.

Trenkel, N. (2014) 'The crisis of abstract labor is the crisis of capitalism', *Libcom.org* [online], 9 January, available from: https://libcom.org/library/crisis-abstract-labor-crisis-capitalism-norbert-trenkle-krisis-group

Vázquez, R. (2009) 'Modernity coloniality and visibility: the politics of time', *Sociological Research Online* [online], 14(4): Art 7, available from: https://www.socresonline.org.uk/14/4/7.html

Vázquez, R. (2011) 'Translation as erasure: thoughts on modernity's epistemic violence', *Journal of Historical Sociology*, 24(1): 27–44.

Vázquez, R. (2016) 'Relational temporalities: from modernity to the decolonial', *CPD/BISA Workshop on 'Exploring Epistemic Violence'*, Queen Mary University of London, 22 February.

Wright, E.O. (2010) *Envisioning Real Utopias*, London: Verso.

Zipes, J. (1997) 'Traces of hope: the non-synchronicity of Ernst Bloch', in J.O. Daniel and T. Moylan (eds) *Not Yet: Reconsidering Ernst Bloch*, London and New York: Verso, pp 1–13.

4

Rethinking Prefiguration: Between Radical Imagination and Imaginal Politics

Aris Komporozos-Athanasiou and Chiara Bottici

Introduction

What is the link between prefiguration and imagination? This chapter offers a conceptualization of the 'radical imagination' as the capacity to produce ideas and visions of the future that materially condition an increasingly uncertain present. Imagining the future is not synonymous with fantasizing; how and what societies imagine defines the horizon of what seems possible, and thus bears real consequences for our collective ability to act in the present. In this sense, the radical imagination is an essential element of prefiguration and extends much further than the realm of society. Capitalizing on the future's unknowability is the zeitgeist of today's financialized economy – capitalism's own prefigurative act. In what follows, we draw on the work of Cornelius Castoriadis to theorize this revolutionary role of the imagination. We propose a view of prefiguration that articulates the 'radical' in 'imagination' – a necessary step towards realizing the possibilities for articulating alternatives to today's financialized economy and society.

It is precisely this 'generative function' of the imagination that makes it radical – its crucial yet under-recognized role in producing, mediating and structuring our lived social realities. Today, mainstream (regressive, ethnonationalist, populist) politics collapses future promises to a sense of generalized precariousness and blurs the boundaries between reality and fiction (Komporozos-Athanasiou, 2020, 2021). Against this backdrop, channelling a radical and productive imagination points to a type of prefiguration that is not merely an illusionary escape from political reality, but rather a blueprint for a radical future. Radical imagination must therefore be understood as a steam engine, rather than a mirror, of reality – a point of contact rather than a separation of fantasy from reality. As such, more than an individual faculty or a collective social imaginary, we situate the radical imagination within the imaginal sphere: the site for producing images, understood as (re)presentation, that are also presences in themselves (Bottici, 2014). Whereas traditional political philosophy understands imagination as an individual faculty we possess, theorists of the social imaginary emphasize how any individual product of the imagination is always shaped by the social context that gives it meaning. In contrast to both of these understandings, 'imaginal' simply denotes what is made of images, which can be the result of both an individual imagination and a social imaginary. Furthermore, the concept of imaginal does not make any a priori ontological assumptions as to the status of images, and thus their reality *versus* their unreality; it is, rather, a much more malleable tool for empirical analysis, particularly in contexts – such as financial capitalism – where the most illusory risks are also the most real.

Critical scholarly engagements with prefiguration and utopia have strived to overcome this separation between the practical–real(ized) and the fantastical–imagined; from Ruth Levitas' (2013) *Utopia as Method*[1] and E.O. Wright's (2010) *Envisioning Real Utopias* to Rutger Bregman's (2017) *Utopia for Realists*, a string of arguments calls for taking utopianism seriously in the increasingly dystopian present, characterized by regressive nativism and protractive political crisis the world over. The imaginal driving this dystopian present is nowhere more prominent than in the fictitious operation of financialized capitalism. As has recently been argued (see, for example, Davies, 2018), science fiction is no longer the exclusive playground for utopian artistic experimentation and daring filmmaking; rather, finance itself comes to encompass some of science fiction's 'real utopianism' (to use Wright's term): technologically enabled financial modelling and algorithmic trading are continuously expanding domains of investment in virtual and imagined value, paving the way for limitless growth (Komporozos-Athanasiou, 2021). Processes of forecasting the future and staking its uncertainty guide the operation of today's financial markets, in which speculative capital and fictional expectations work tirelessly to imagine future states that orientate economic, as well as social and cultural, values (Beckert, 2016). This process has clear political consequences, making the link between politics and the imaginal so tight that images no longer merely mediate our 'doing' of politics, but rather risk doing politics in our steads (Bottici, 2014).

In this chapter, we begin by discussing the work of Cornelius Castoriadis, a prominent theorist of the human and social imagination who remains surprisingly unacknowledged in anglophone scholarship. In doing so, we bring Castoriadis' notion of the radical imagination into dialogue with theories of the imaginal, and with Marx's philosophy of history, to illustrate its generative and material capacities across both economy and society. Our central argument is that to realize the full potential of prefiguration, we must consider the ways in which financial capitalism wields its own imagination *in tandem with* the possibilities for articulating alternative counter-imaginaries, thereby reclaiming capitalism's own appropriation of our imaginal world.

The imagination as intrinsically social

To illuminate the conceptual link between prefiguration and imagination, we heed Castoriadis' thesis that the radical imagination can only be investigated through a parallel investigation of the notion of the social-historical imaginary. In particular, Castoriadis' (1987) *The Imaginary Institution of Society* decisively contributes to the passage from the paradigm of imagination as an individual faculty to that of the imaginary as a social context. Despite the inspiration he draws from both Aristotle and Kant, his shift towards the notion of the social imaginary stems precisely from his perception that the available vocabulary is inadequate. By looking back to the history of philosophy, he emphasizes the extent to which most theorists have tried to cover over, or at least limit, the radical character of imagination. In contrast to such a tendency, only Aristotle and Kant rightly emphasize the *constitutive* role of imagination – so much so that Castoriadis attributes to them nothing less than the 'discovery of the imagination' (Castoriadis, 1997c). However, both Aristotle and Kant remain entrapped in an ego-logical philosophy of the subject that portrays the capacity to imagine as an individual faculty that we carry around as though it were a briefcase we take out as needed. This prevents us from perceiving the intrinsically social nature of imagination. As he writes in an emblematic passage:

> [T]here is nothing more deprived of imagination than the transcendental imagination of Kant. And, of course this position is inevitable so long as the problem of imagination and of the imaginary is thought solely in relation to the subject, within a psycho-logical or ego-logical horizon. … If the transcendental imagination set itself the task of imagining anything whatsoever, the world would collapse immediately. This is why, later on, the 'creative imagination' will remain, philosophically, a mere word and the role that will be recognized for it will be limited to domains that seem ontologically gratuitous (art). A full recognition of the radical imagination is possible only if it goes hand in hand with the discovery of the other dimension of the radical imaginary, the social-historical imaginary, instituting a society as source of ontological creation deploying itself as history. (Castoriadis, 1997c, p 245)

This passage is of crucial importance and deserves detailed analysis. To begin, let us note that Castoriadis' notion of the imaginary has nothing in common with Lacan's, despite the hegemony the latter maintains in most academic debates. Castoriadis distances himself from Lacan very early on by observing that the latter reduces the imaginary to the specular – to the 'image *of* something' (Castoriadis, 1987, p 3) – as rooted in Lacan's theory of the mirror phase, which leads him to conceive of the imaginary as constitutively alienating. On the contrary, Castoriadis' notion of the imaginary is not the 'image *of* something'; rather, as he puts it at the beginning of *The Imaginary Institution of Society*, the imaginary 'is the unceasing and essentially *undetermined* (social-historical and psychical) creation of figures/forms/images, on the basis of which alone there can ever be a question of "something"' (Castoriadis, 1987, p 3, emphasis in original).

The imaginary is therefore social-historical by definition, since, for Castoriadis, society is nothing other than alteration, time and history itself (Castoriadis, 1987, pp 167–215). Inherited ontology and logic have always tried to hide this fundamental identity between society and history for one fundamental reason: every society needs to present itself as a given, as always already *instituted*; it cannot recognize its own being as always *instituting*, because this means accepting the possibility of pure chaos, of social order perpetually standing on the fringes of the abyss (Castoriadis, 1987, p 167). Inherited modes of thinking have displayed only forms of logic incapable of thinking the undetermined. 'Society is not a thing, not a subject, and not an idea – nor is it a collection or system of subjects, things and ideas' (Castoriadis, 1987, p 167). This may be a banality, but it is worth remembering, as it shows how our inherited language is incapable of thinking the undetermined and, thus, the social-historical itself (here expressed by the fact that we always speak of 'a' society or 'this' society) (Castoriadis, 1987, p 167).

'Remaining Marxist' or 'remaining revolutionary'

Accordingly, Castoriadis prefers to speak of the 'social-historical' (in particular, see Castoriadis, 1987, pp 167–215). Society is nothing but history itself, which, in turn, is temporal alteration produced in and through society. The question of history, for Castoriadis, 'is the question of the emergence of radical otherness or of the absolutely new' (Castoriadis, 1987, p 172). As a result, Castoriadis, who had been a leading figure of libertarian Marxism in the 1960s, distances himself from orthodox Marxism. His critique of Marx – especially in articulating a radical political imagination – is shared by eminent scholars of prefiguration, such as Ernst Bloch (whose theorizing of utopia seeks to depart from orthodox Marxism). But Castoriadis goes much further, vehemently rejecting Marxist determinism and stating that by starting from revolutionary Marxism, he finally faced a situation where he had to 'choose between remaining Marxist and remaining revolutionary' – between faithfulness to orthodoxy and faithfulness to a project of radical social change (Castoriadis, 1987, p 14).

The centrality of Castoriadis' experiences of Marxism and Marxist militancy are clearly observable in the structure of *The Imaginary Institution of Society*, in which the concept of the social imaginary is developed through an internal critique of Marxism. Castoriadis perceived in Marx – and in Marxism more generally – a fundamental tension between two incompatible perspectives and modes of explanation. On the one hand, the emphasis on class struggle points to the possibility of making history, in the deep sense of creating something new. On the other hand, Marx's economic determinism, which reduces history to the conflict between the material productive forces of society and the existing relations of production, endangers the possibility of thinking of history as the radical creation of something new (Castoriadis, 1987, pp 30–1).

What Castoriadis ultimately perceives in the historical evolution of orthodox Marxism is not a synthesis between these two tendencies, but rather a 'triumph of determinism over class struggle' (Castoriadis, 1987, p 30). Castoriadis asks: Is the essential factor in the evolution of capitalism the technological revolution and the effects of the economic laws that govern the system? Or is it the struggle of classes and social groups? In reading *Capital*, we see that the first response is correct. Once its sociological conditions are established, once what can be called the 'axioms of the system' are posited in historical reality (that is, the degree and specific type of technical development, the existence of accumulated capital, a sufficient number of proletarians and so on) and under the continuous impetus of an autonomous technical progress, capitalism evolves solely in terms of the effects of the economic laws it contains, and which Marx had formulated. Class struggle comes in nowhere (Castoriadis, 1987, p 30).

In this respect, Marx's economic determinism does not differ from all other philosophies of history, which, by reducing history to a predetermined logic – dialectical, divine or natural – destroy the possibility of thinking of history as the alteration and emergence of the new. 'The Marxist knows where history must go', observes Castoriadis (1987, p 31); in this regard, he does not differ much from any other philosophical attempts to cover over the instituting dimension of society, the fact that society itself is history – that is, alteration. However, we believe this emphasis on alteration is, paradoxically, a great Marxist heritage in Castoriadis' own thinking. The idea of a 'revolutionary praxis', of 'a conscious transformation of society by the autonomous activity of men', is indeed – by Castoriadis' own admittance – the 'most profound and durable contribution made by Marxism' (Castoriadis, 1987, p 62), albeit one that was potentially curtailed by some of Marx's followers and their economic determinism.

Thus, whereas within some Marxist frameworks the problems of imagination and the social imaginary are treated in terms of the function they perform in a society, Castoriadis turns this perspective upside down; to speak about a function presupposes the work of imagination/imaginary, not the other way around. Along with Marxism, Castoriadis distances himself from all forms of reductionism that tend to veil the instituting dimension of society – functionalism being the very first to fall under his attacks (Castoriadis, 1987, p 115). Against the latter, Castoriadis points out that every act, both individual and collective, without which no society could survive – labour, consumption, love, war and so on – is impossible outside of a social imaginary (Castoriadis, 1987, p 117). All functions performed within any society are, in fact, 'functions of something' – that is, they are functions only insofar as their ends can be defined. But these ends, which vary from society to society as well as from one epoch to the other, can only be defined at the level of those social significations without which no social function or need could ever be defined. This is the level at which the social imaginary operates.

Every individual body needs food to reproduce itself, but the very practices of eating assume different functions in different contexts, according to the imaginary significations within which they are performed. Every society continually defines and redefines its needs, and no society can ever survive outside of the imaginary significations that constitute and are constituted by it. In this sense, imaginary significations also imbue everyday life with a prefigurative quality by actively cultivating 'alternatives'. Taking the example of the slow food and degrowth movements, for instance, Francesca Forno and Stefan Wahlen (this volume) show how all manner of human activity can be thought of as constantly prefiguring everyday life 'by redrawing and questioning the balance of forces through inventive negotiations with the system making up social reproduction'. In Castoriadis' terms, the institution of a society presupposes the institution of imaginary significations that must, in principle, be able to provide meaning to whatever presents itself.

There are, Castoriadis notes, limits to the social imaginary. First, it must always start from the material that it already finds there. Therefore, the limits posed by nature are primary. For example, societies define the meaning of nourishment, but they must start from the need for it. Second, some limits are posed by rationality, by the coherence of the symbolic edifice. Finally, other limits are imposed by history – by the fact that every symbolism is built on the ruins of the preceding symbolic constructions – so that even to break radically with such constructions, one must begin with them as premises (Castoriadis, 1987, p 125).

Realizing the radical imagination

The way in which Castoriadis addresses the question of the limits to the social imaginary demonstrates that his view does not imply a too general conception of imagination. The idea that there are limits intrinsic to the social imaginary derives from Castoriadis' creative reappropriation of Freud's notion of *Anlehnung* (leaning on), thus pointing to the intrinsic anchorage to any work of the imagination. Furthermore, Castoriadis also tries to make space for the individual within this theory. He explicitly observes that the major threat to the instituted society is its own creativity; the society that created individuals is, at the same time, created by them. As we saw in the lengthy passage quoted earlier on (see 'The imagination as intrinsically social'), the radical imaginary has two dimensions: the social-historical imaginary and the radical imagination. Indeed, the merit of Castoriadis' approach is to point out that the *instituting* social imaginary is always at the same time *instituted*, which means no society could ever exist if the individuals created by the society had themselves not created and reproduced it.

Society can only exist concretely through the fragmentary and complementary incarnation and incorporation of its institution and its imaginary significations in the living, talking and acting individuals of that society – which also demarcate the 'political space' of everyday prefiguration emerging out of the 'cracks' of such incarnation and incorporation. Athenian society is nothing but the Athenians, Castoriadis points out; without them, it is only the 'remnants of a transformed landscape, the debris of marble and vases, indecipherable inscriptions and worn statues fished out of the Mediterranean' (Castoriadis, 1991, p 145). But the Athenians are only Athenians by means of the *nomos* of the *polis*. In this relationship between an instituted society on the one hand – which infinitely transcends the totality of the individuals who 'compose' it, but can exist only by being 'realized' in the individuals it produces – and these individuals on the other, we experience an unprecedented type of relationship that cannot be thought of under the categories of the whole and its parts, the set and its elements or, even less, the universal and the particular (Castoriadis, 1991, p 145).

By speaking of a 'radical imagination' together with a social imaginary, Castoriadis (1987) suggests these categories reciprocally imply each other. Even more so, as he put it in his aforementioned quote, full recognition of the radical imagination implies the recognition of the other dimension of imagination – that is, of the social imaginary. The concept of *radical* imagination has the function of stressing that, as Aristotle maintained, together with an imitative and reproductive or combinatory '*phantasia*', there is also what can be called a primary imagination. This consists of the faculty of producing 'images in the largest possible sense of the term (that of "forms", "*Bilder*"), that is images without which there would not be any thought at all, and which, therefore, precede any thought' (Castoriadis, 1987, p 336; 1997d, pp 320–1).

As a consequence, Castoriadis' notion of a radical imagination helpfully emphasizes that imagination does not imply the non-existence of the objects of imagination, even though we can also have images that do not correspond to anything in the external world. Images (or 'figures') are our way of being in the world (and a necessary part of prefiguring that world). Indeed, one could even say that no world is given for us that is not imagined. According to Castoriadis, imagination came to be associated with the idea of fictitiousness and unreality because it can create ex nihilo – not *in nihilo* or *cum nihilo* (Castoriadis, 1987, p 221).

Because the traditional Western ensemble logic is based on the identity assumption *ex nihilo nihil*, it cannot help but conceive of imagination as essentially non-existence. To this identity and set logic – which could never account for the fact that when 'x = x', it is always 'x = non-x' – Castoriadis counterposes the logic of magmas. The concept of magma points to the fact that significations are not 'determinate beings', but rather webs of references or bundles of referrals (*faisceaux de renvois*) (Castoriadis, 1987, p 347). While these are always determinable, they are never completely determinate (Castoriadis, 1987, p 221). Hence, to investigate the nature of the radical imaginary in its two constitutive dimensions, we need an alternative logic that is able to think the undetermined.

Radical imagination, moreover, points to the question of power as fundamental to the constitution of autonomous society. In additional to the ex nihilo creative capacity of imagination, its radicality lies in the recognition of indeterminacy. This is a key issue for our understanding of radical imagination today – and, indeed, a further point of departure from Marxist orthodoxy. In an era of prescribed solutions to crises and tired emancipatory narratives, a Castoriadian imagination points to a truly alternative way of engaging with the future's indeterminacy – that is, as a first step to acknowledging its openness, an endeavour familiar to many of those writing within utopian and prefigurative studies. But perhaps more importantly, such acknowledgement implies taking ownership of radical openness, pointing to the emancipatory potential of prefiguration – our future may be indeterminate, but it is nonetheless *our own* indeterminate future (Komporozos-Athanasiou, 2021).

In sum, the expression 'radical imagination' has the function of conveying two key ideas. In the first place, 'radical' points to the generative and material function of imagination: its capacity to produce reality 'in the present' through projecting visions, figures and meanings of the future. In so doing, the radical invokes here the concept of creation, or the fact that imagination is prior to the distinction between real and fictitious. In other words, it is because radical imagination exists that 'reality' exists for us, and that it exists as it exists – and, therefore, one can add, it exists tout court (Castoriadis, 1997a, p 321).

Second, and relatedly, 'radical' refers to the modern project of autonomy (Castoriadis, 1987, 1991). Castoriadis recovers such a project, but tries to address it within a theory of imagination informed by psychoanalysis, and thus by the observation that individuals are the imaginary products of socialization. Psychoanalytically, imagination is said to be radical in the sense that it can always potentially question its own products, since it can never be completely mastered. Far from being a source of errors and falsity, imagination is seen as a means for critique, and critique is identified as the condition of autonomy – of the possibility to give oneself one's law – whereas Castoriadis roots the radicality of our capacity to imagine in the unmasterable nature of the unconscious, which can be understood as being one and the same as the psyche itself (Castoriadis, 1987, pp 101–7). What is the psyche if not the uninterrupted stream of images, an imaginal space that escapes established dichotomies such as those between the real and the unreal, the social and the individual (Bottici, 2014)?

It is precisely because the concept of radical imagination escapes such binary thinking that it enables us to rethink prefiguration as an imaginal practice outside of such dichotomies. The future that is prefigured in/through prefigurative politics is, indeed, beyond any simple opposition between real vs unreal, social vs individual. Prefiguration foregrounds experimental practices, alternative modes of 'producing' value in the economy, and the importance of small scale and 'here and now' politics that embody future change in the present (Monticelli, 2018); it thus collapses the dichotomous boundary between future and present. Prefiguration, in this sense, can be seen as an effective defence strategy deployed by radical social movements against financialized modes of production and being, through the creation of spaces that allow 'openness' and the enactment of a collective imagination (Holloway, 2002). As Monticelli (2018, p 511) puts it, for prefigurative movements, 'social change is achieved through a "plural configuration of practices" and iterative processes of experimentation, re-organisation, and re-imagination' (Yates, 2015).

Conclusion

These ideas have important implications for our understanding of contemporary capitalism, and specifically the possibilities for radical prefiguration against the dominance of finance over the public and private realms of everyday life. Epitomized by the immersive, accelerated and future-orientated fervour of speculative markets, finance poses new risks for prefigurative thinking and practice – above all, through the threat of co-opting our prefigurative imaginations of the future. Financial capitalism's fictitious operation moves further than unrealized fantasies, wagering an eerily real future reigned by risk speculations and debt dependencies. Herein lie some questions that we can no longer afford to ignore. How is the radical and speculative imagination of finance transforming our lived realities – prefiguring, in this sense, capitalism's own future? How do the worlds of fiction and reality coalesce to speculate dystopian or utopian value in financialized capitalism? And what are the implications of financial imagination for articulating prefigurative alternatives to such dominant future projections?

In exploring these questions, we suggest it is necessary to keep in mind the inseparability of the imaginary and the real, the imaginal and the social, the utopian and the dystopian. More attention should be paid to the latent links between financial capitalism's imaginative renewal, its foreclosure of (alternative) future imaginaries and the possibilities for developing new solidarities against the intersections of neoliberal, financial and colonialist imaginations. The task ahead of us is none other than reclaiming the 'radical' in 'imagination' itself. As we have argued in this chapter, prefiguration is a key component of such a task, because it foments a counter-spectacle within our financialized imaginary. In a time when financial imaginaries constantly project us towards a future always yet to come, towards the spectacularization of a profit perpetually searched for and postponed, prefigurative politics works as a homeopathic strategy; a cure of the mega-spectacle of finance with the little spectacular action of living together differently; yet another small dose of spectacle, but this time in order to say that the future is now – and it is ours.

Note

1   Tellingly, the title of Levitas' book, *The Imaginary Reconstitution of Society*, is a direct reference to Castoriadis' *The Imaginary Institution of Society*, foregrounding the corollary role of the imagination in utopian theory and practice.

References

Beckert, J. (2016) *Imagined Futures*, Cambridge, MA: Harvard University Press.

Bottici, C. (2014) *Imaginal Politics: Images Beyond the Imagination and Beyond the Imaginary*, New York, NY: Columbia University Press.

Bregman, R. (2017) *Utopia for Realists: How We Can Build the Ideal World*, London: Hachette.

Castoriadis, C. (1987) *The Imaginary Institution of Society*, Cambridge: Polity Press.

Castoriadis, C. (1991) 'Power, politics, autonomy', in D.A. Curtis (ed) *Philosophy, Politics, Autonomy: Essays in Political Philosophy*, Oxford: Oxford University Press, pp 143–74.

Castoriadis, C. (1997a) 'Institution of society and religion', in D.A. Curtis (ed) *World in Fragments: Writings on Politics, Society, Psychoanalysis and the Imagination*, Stanford, CA: Stanford University Press, pp 311–30.

Castoriadis, C. (1997b) 'Radical imagination and the social instituting imaginary', in D.A. Curtis (ed) *The Castoriadis Reader*, Oxford: Blackwell, pp 319–37.

Castoriadis, C. (1997c) 'The discovery of the imagination', in D.A. Curtis (ed) *World in Fragments: Writings on Politics, Society, Psychoanalysis and the Imagination*, Stanford, CA: Stanford University Press, pp 246–72.

Castoriadis, C. (1997d) 'Radical Imagination and the social instituting imaginary', in D.A. Curtis (ed) *The Castoriadis Reader*, Oxford: Blackwell, pp 321–37.

Davies, W. (ed) (2018) *Economic Science Fictions*, Cambridge, MA: MIT Press.

Holloway, J. (2002) *Change the World Without Taking Power*. London: Pluto Press.

Komporozos-Athanasiou, A. (2020) 'Re-imagining the future in finance capitalism', *Journal of Cultural Economy*, 13(3): 261–4.

Komporozos-Athanasiou, A. (2021) *Speculative Communities: Living with Uncertainty in a Financialized World*, Chicago, IL: University of Chicago Press.

Levitas, R. (2013) *Utopia as Method: The Imaginary Reconstitution of Society*, Houndmills: Palgrave Macmillan.

Monticelli, L. (2018) 'Embodying alternatives to capitalism in the 21st century', *tripleC: Communication, Capitalism & Critique*, 16(2): 501–17.

Wright, E.O. (2010) *Envisioning Real Utopias*, London: Verso.

Yates, L. (2015) 'Rethinking prefiguration: alternatives, micropolitics and goals in social movements', *Social Movement Studies*, 14(1): 1–21.

5

Prefiguration and Emancipatory Critical Pedagogy: The Learning Side of Practice

Antonia De Vita and Francesco Vittori

Introduction

The intersection of the current debate around prefiguration (Maeckelbergh, 2011; Dinerstein, 2012; Mason, 2014; van de Sande, 2015; Cooper, 2017) with education offers an interesting entry point from which to approach the orientation, in our own time, of imaginaries and practice in educational and social situations marked by injustice and exclusion. Our intention in this chapter is to discuss, in theoretical terms, how ideas and principles from critical pedagogy might enrich certain examples of prefigurative visions.

Critical pedagogy argues that the education of adults and young people (in formal and informal contexts) can be emancipatory, offering a collection of real-world mediations with which to achieve social justice through a sustained, critical approach to all forms of oppressive systems – including the systems of neoliberalism (Burbules and Berk, 1999; Aliakbari and Faraji, 2011; Mayo, 2015). Critical pedagogy has a profound relevance to the contemporary world, both as a current of philosophical enquiry and as an educational and formative outlook that is inextricably linked to political practice. In its commitment to the creation of 'an open, social, democratic education capable of problematizing social issues and questions in a time of commoditization' (Mayo and Vittoria, 2017, p 8), it has clear areas of overlap with prefigurative visions of society. Specifically, both critical pedagogy and prefigurative visions share the intention to transform society through participative, inclusive and non-hierarchical activities that run counter to a vision of education commodified by the forces of capitalism. As such, weaving together these two perspectives seems, to us, to be a significant step towards re-establishing the importance and relevance of education as a creative emancipatory praxis.

In recent decades, social movements and real-world initiatives inspired by feminism, environmentalism, the fight against racism and respect for human rights have served as laboratories for increasingly intersectional modes (Luchies, 2014) of critical thought and practice – and are prime examples of informal contexts of critical education. When adults freely choose to build contexts of learning, education and self-education around instances of social and/or ecological justice, critical consumption and new lifestyles, they are adopting an educational methodology to create new practices of citizenship and develop praxis, in the sense of concrete actions that transform reality (De Vita and Bertell, 2018; Bertell et al, 2020). Sharing a prefigurative vision with other people instigates processes of personal and collective self-determination and growth – 'conscientization' processes in which the means are entirely consistent with the ends and which enable the autonomous development of strategies and methods with which to engage in real-world contexts.

An insistence on education, as a means consistent with the goal of transforming society, is an unmistakeable presence in the work of theorists of prefiguration, such as Timothy Luchies (2014), who envisioned opposition to oppression as a form of pedagogy:

> I reframe anti-oppression as a logic of struggle, more specifically as a pedagogical project, in order to bring its collective and cumulative operation into view. This shift in perspective reveals networking as an often-neglected condition for effective anti-oppression practice. It also provides some insight into how we might use the idea of prefiguration to further integrate an intersectional politics into anarchistic movements. (Luchies, 2014, pp 100–1)

Anti-oppression is thus advanced as a collection of tactics that share the goals of identifying and excising the violence inherent in the structures of society and generating forms of responsibilization on the part of the political community. It is a perspective in which struggle is conceived of as a progressive, multidimensional subversion of all forms of supremacy, implicit in which is a profound historical understanding of forms of dominion at both the global and regional levels. The intersectional nature of anarchic, anti-oppressive pedagogies is indebted to the notion of prefiguration cultivated at the heart of anti-authoritarian movements, in which it serves to create and capitalize on opportunities for activists to build new subjectivities and relationships through a root change in political, social and economic infrastructures.

Critical pedagogy and instances of prefiguration: towards a transformative vision of reality

Critical pedagogy can be directly traced to the north-east Brazilian pedagogist Paulo Freire, as well as other thinkers who progressed his ideas with their own contributions, such as Henry Giroux, Wolfgang Klafki, Michael Apple, Peter McLaren and Ira Shor. Critical pedagogy advances a vision of education as something that contributes concretely to the formation of experiences, practices and ways of understanding that are unlike those of the neoliberal paradigm. Instead, they are based on popular education; on the practices of groups, communities and social movements; on any configuration of educational action undertaken outside, and independently of, the market; and on education that is open to dialogue, difference and diverse conceptions of politics and history. Based on a detailed critique of socio-economic and political models and their impact in educational contexts, critical pedagogy draws meaning and potential from an awareness of the power of education to transform society – an awareness based on a critical analysis of inequalities, marginalization, working conditions, human rights and social relationships (Mayo and Vittoria, 2017, p 15).

With his theoretical explorations in the 1960s and 1970s, which went on to form the basis for innovative and effective methods of adult literacy education developed and disseminated in (particularly) Brazil and Africa, Paulo Freire revisited the theories of the Frankfurt School, giving them new relevance for his own time. Starting with his best-known and most significant work, *Pedagogy of the Oppressed*, Freire's (2000) approach not only offered a practical philosophy capable of perceiving and interpreting the oppression experienced by north-east Brazil's poor and illiterate peasants, but also cultivated in them a consciousness of their own condition – that is, a pathway out of their oppression. Critical pedagogy challenges any form of domination and subordination, and is primarily concerned with the goal of emancipation, to be achieved by educating any people who are under the dominion of a subjugating, marginalizing power, with educational practices serving to create awareness of their oppression and how to escape it.

From north-east Brazil to North America and Western Europe, Freire's ideas remain as relevant as ever. However, the face of oppression has changed. In our time, it often manifests in the violence of the capitalist system – a system that, in its current biocapitalist and biopolitical form, has become anthropophagic, devouring lives as it extracts value from them as a factor of production; a system that feeds on subjectivity, language and relationships, leaving the soul a dried-out husk (Lazzarato, 1997; Foucault, 2008). Critical perspectives thus call out for conscientization – or, rather, a deepening of consciousness (Freire, 2000) – a shift from a naïve to a critical consciousness that can engender transformations in our reality and bring us closer to social justice and the emancipation of subjects and circumstances alike. Critical pedagogy (or, more specifically, Freirean pedagogy) joins the ranks of pedagogical approaches that admit a socio-educational perspective, one designed to develop critical forms of thought and consciousness – as well as a situated self-awareness – as part of a tangible relationship with our world.

> People, as beings 'in a situation', find themselves rooted in temporal–spatial conditions which mark them and which they also mark. They will tend to reflect on their own 'situationality' to the extent that they are challenged by it to act upon it. Human beings *are* because they *are in* a situation. And they *will be more* the more they not only critically reflect upon their existence but critically act upon it. Reflection upon situationality is … critical thinking by means of which people discover each other to be 'in a situation'. (Freire, 2000, p 109, emphases in original).

Following a Freirean approach to conscientization (that is, by investigating the thought-language men and women use to refer to reality), contemporary groups and movements for social change may be required to identify 'generative themes' that have the potential – by enabling the subjects of oppression to be conscientized – to be transformed into liberating, emancipatory themes (Freire, 2000). As Luchies (2014) elucidates, all current anti-oppression movements that embody some sort of prefigurative calling can be said to have drawn, directly or indirectly, on the school of Freirean pedagogy:

> [A]ctivists and community members engage in a form of Freirean pedagogy to build critical consciousness as they identify, analyze, and respond to particular tasks collectively. ...
> Feminist, queer, dis/ability and anti-racist applications of this form of action increasingly dovetail with anti-oppression. While such applications remain exceptions to general anarchistic practice, they are growing in number and influence on the radical Left. Intertwining anti-oppression and prefiguration, activists are building empowering political relationships and spaces through actively confronting systems of oppression and exploitation. There is a broad spectrum of direct-action tactics at the overlaps of varied social movement struggles that are beginning to reflect this transformative impulse. (Luchies, 2014, p 113)

Across the globe, this encompasses a great array of 'ground-up' movements that focus on critiquing capitalism and searching for a sustainable future – addressing, in the first instance, questions of gender and social, economic and environmental crises – and which share both a deeply rooted commitment to education – including self-education (Bertell and De Vita, 2013; De Vita and Vittori, 2015) – and a passion for learning born of a transformative, prefigurative vision of the world (see also the chapters by Raekstad, Monticelli, and Dinerstein, this volume).

Towards a pedagogy of praxis: from hegemony to affinity

For Paulo Freire – as for Antonio Gramsci – there could be no pedagogy without politics. Pedagogy has to take the side of the oppressed; as Gramsci (1917) asserted in his famous declaration 'Odio gli indifferenti' (I hate the indifferent), it cannot exclude itself from picking a side in the struggle for social justice. In this spirit, whoever educates is an exponent of *praxis*, which goes much further than mere *practice*, as the term's Aristotelian origins confirm. Praxis is a process of reflection that permits a certain critical distance from the world of action in order to contribute to transforming that world into one that Freire (2000) describes as 'less ugly, more beautiful, less discriminatory, more democratic, less dehumanizing, and more humane' (2000, p 25).

Gramsci's importance to the development of critical pedagogy is largely related to the concept of hegemony as an educational and pedagogical practice. Gramsci developed this significant, multifaceted construct in dialogue with Marx, taking the dialectical relationship between infrastructure and superstructure as a starting point. Like Gramsci, albeit recognizing the relationship between the economy and systems of consensus, Freire considered this relationship in terms of a dialectic and reciprocal – rather than determinist – process that acknowledges that the cultural, political and educational can also come to bear on the systemic, as well as on questions of production. In a prison notebook from 1932, Gramsci maintains that the pedagogical relationship cannot be restricted to specifically scholastic relationships, because education involves society in its entirety – every subject and every relationship:

> This form of [pedagogical or educational] relationship exists throughout society as a whole and for every individual relative to other individuals. It exists between intellectual and nonintellectual sections of the population, between the rulers and the ruled, élites and their followers, leaders [*dirigenti*] and led, the vanguard and the body of the army. Every relationship of 'hegemony' is necessarily an educational relationship and occurs not only within a nation, between the various forces of which the nation is composed, but in the international and world-wide field, between complexes of national and continental civilisations. (Gramsci, 1971, p 350)

The concept of hegemony as an opportunity for education for all is highly significant and has been widely studied. For Gramsci, it was necessary to distinguish between power and hegemony. Power is based on the simultaneous presence of force and consensus. When force is predominant, the result is domination; when consensus prevails, it is hegemony. Hegemony is an expression of power based on consensus – on the ability to achieve outcomes through persuasion and adhesion to a particular political and cultural project. A hegemonic process, in addition to shaping the collective will, is capable of producing a new apparatus of state and transforming society itself through the development and enactment of a new conception of the world. Gramsci talks of the hegemony of one social group over the whole society of the nation, effected through so-called private organizations such as the church, unions, schools. The importance of a hegemony lies in how it gives direction to politics and in its ability to orientate society by involving all relevant participants: institutions and civil society groups. Hegemony is, therefore, the capacity to assert – through everyday practices and shared beliefs – a perspective from which a complex system of control can emerge, which might enable the ideologies of a certain social class to operate across the entirety of civil society.

The Gramscian concept of hegemony, and the logic derived from it, made a significant contribution to the political imaginary of the 20th century. Yet, as the conceptual formulations and tangible examples of contemporary social movements demonstrate, it is an imaginary that has lost much of its influence, both over practice and over the theories that inspire movements to plan for social change. In *Gramsci is Dead*, Richard J.F. Day (2005) offers a useful means of interpreting this evolution from a vision of social transformation informed by the concept of hegemony to one inspired by 'affinity'. Taking this logic as his starting point, and from there examining the many (and often innovative) examples of autonomous organization across the world, Day outlines how postmodernity's radical struggles – anti-sexism, anti-racism, anti-capitalism, indigenous rights, alterglobalism and so on – all indicate that 'cosmopolitical liberation under a single sign is a modernist fantasy' (2005, p 154) – and, at heart, totalitarian in nature. In contrast, the increasingly influential affinity approach is based on horizontal (rather than vertical) modes of organization and decision-making, whose inspiration is evidently progressive. The affinity approach proposes a new reading of anarchism filtered through a number of post-structuralist and post-Marxist influences. For Day, in seeking to *reverse* the relationship between dominated and dominator by acquiring state power, Marxist revolutionaries have followed the logic of hegemony (see also Raekstad, this volume). In hoping to *overturn* the relationship between dominated and dominator by acquiring state power, liberal and post-Marxist forms of reformism have obeyed the same logic of hegemony, albeit in a different mode. In other words, the contribution of socialist and social democratic parties in the West is not indicative of a desire to take state power, but these parties do seek to influence its operation, through processes of pluralist cooperation and conflict (Giddens, 1998).

> What is most interesting about contemporary radical activism is that some groups are breaking out of this trap by operating non-hegemonically rather than counter-hegemonically. They seek radical change, but not through taking or influencing state power, and in so doing they challenge the logic of hegemony at its very core … the shift away from hegemonically orientated 'movements', and towards *non-branded strategies and tactics* … what I call an affinity for affinity, that is, for non-universalizing, non-hierarchical, non-coercive relationships based and mutual aid and shared ethical commitments. Examples would include certain indigenous communities in North America … as well as some strands of transnational feminism and queer theory. My basic argument in this book is that all of these groups and movements, strategies and tactics, are helpful in understanding—and furthering— the ongoing displacement of the hegemony of hegemony by an affinity for affinity. (Day, 2005, p 9, emphasis in original)

Inherent to contemporary pedagogies of praxis and social change, therefore, is a belief in the radical transformation of the forms of politics and of education, as well as in the possibility of envisioning social relationships that the system of power cannot assimilate or suppress.

The shift from a political outlook that aspires to hegemony to one based on affinity is one way to describe the transformation of political modes and forms in this transitory age. It may be that prefigurative movements have begun to orientate themselves along these lines, given that many 'ground-up' social movements are conducting, in the present, what we might describe as rehearsals of the future. But what is the sought-after future that we might seek to manifest today?

In this regard, and using an Italian example – the Bilanci di Giustizia – we now explore how a movement for lifestyle change to achieve greater social justice between the Global North and Global South has, in recent decades, given tangible form to this paradigmatic shift along the path of affinities, and how it has thus sought to prefiguratively express its specific vision of the future.

Bilanci di Giustizia: an example of informal learning

'*Quando l'economia uccide … bisogna cambiare!*' (When the economy kills … something needs to change!) This was the slogan of the National Assembly that Beati i costruttori di pace (Blessed the Peacemakers)[1] called in Verona in 1993. In the course of the meeting, many arguments and testimonies presented the need to change an economic system that generates violence, as well as how – through which theories, tools and practices – this might be achieved. A range of varied and significant initiatives were subsequently instigated, including the Bilanci di Giustizia (Budgets of Justice, or Balance Sheets of Justice), which emerged over 20 years ago. In the late 1990s and early 2000s, many other liberalist, Marxist, humanist, neo-Marxist and Catholic-inspired explorations of deliberative democracy, political consumerism and social forums came together in the global justice movement's transnational mobilizations (della Porta, 2003). In common with the early days of these organizations, an element of prefiguration was quick to take root in the praxis of the Bilanci di Giustizia. The movement decided to develop new practices involving changing lifestyles – beginning with participants' own consumption habits – to be more sustainable and/or self-sufficient. Using 'balance sheets' to record expenditure and identify where certain forms of spending could be shifted in favour of greater (environmental, social and economic) justice, participants were able to both deepen their awareness and quantify the extent to which their actions could contribute to medium- to long-term change (De Vita and Vittori, 2015).

The Bilanci movement is a collective enterprise that – even today – involves hundreds of women, men and families who have committed to modifying their everyday consumption at a structural level in the interests of 'justice'. As the German economist Gerhard Scherhorn suggests: 'the significance of material goods lies in immaterial goods, but the abundance of material goods eliminates immaterial goods. Indeed, only we ourselves can produce the latter: they are our social relationships, our spirituality, our creativity. It is these things that determine quality of life' (quoted in Valer and Sachs, 2000, pp 19–20). Practices of reduced consumption and moderation regarding material goods must be incorporated into a wider, symbolic, cultural landscape. Scherhorn clarifies the links between goods and 'the good' (between the material and the immaterial, between wealth and poverty) and between abundance and scarcity, as well as the potential for women and men to generate 'quality of life' through social relationships and their capacity to make these relationships – and their lives – both profound and creative. The Bilancisti (adherents to the Bilanci project) distilled their practices from this capacity to generate happiness through changes in lifestyle, demonstrating that they both engage with and shape the needs of the contemporary age. Gaggioli and Valer (2011) reveal that the primary motivation for such transformations is often participants' desire to encourage their own family to adopt lifestyles that embody values of justice, harmony with nature and solidarity, and which translate into a constructive, forward-thinking plan for the present and future alike. It is perhaps this aspect – a plan for the future, enacted in the present – that best defines the construct of 'transformative learning' (Boström et al, 2018), particularly if we consider the intergenerational value transmission that prompted the earliest Bilancisti's children to form their own autonomous activity – the Fuorirotta (off course).

One thing that unites the numerous stories told to us over more than three years of research and co-research with the association (August 2014–December 2017),[2] is the positive connotations of the term *sobrietà* ('moderation' or 'simplicity'), which is frequently associated with both happiness and the wisest approach to one's relationship with things. The picture painted is of a pathway to a new understanding of *sobrietà* where simplicity and moderation are no longer viewed as privation or rejection, but rather as a sort of rediscovered creativity in regard to things and relationships. The interest in practices associated with critical consumption and alternative lifestyles is prompted by their ability to reveal the extent to which focusing on economic considerations can eclipse other models of, and pathways to, wellbeing. The rediscovery of the 'limit', with regard to the conscientious use of goods, opens up fresh possibilities for the very concept of the limit, which can now be transformed from *limit-as-restriction* to *limit-as-impetus*. Such experiences fall into the class of social movements and practices that favour what we might call 'different economies'. These movements and practices advocate lifestyles and concepts that, building from a critique of economism, (re)activate – in an educational mode – participative processes relating to developing social bonds, connections and new forms of active citizenship, including by creating spaces for adult self-education and learning.

The results of our study (Bertell et al, 2020) present numerous significant points to consider. Pivotal to our reflections in this chapter are the processes of learning, self-education/self-learning and political participation activated by the Bilanci communities, and how these intersect with processes of individual and collective change, critical approaches and prefiguration. As we have seen, the objective of the Bilanci movement was to demonstrate that global change can begin with the individual's own experience: configuring this alternative way of doing politics in which the starting point is the concreteness of everyday actions and the real-world practice of what has been discussed at the level of the collective.

Critiquing neoliberal institutions and international agreements, and undertaking activism in favour of peace and the protection of workers' rights in the Global South, were embodied in practices in the local context the 'citizens' operated in. In the case of the Bilanci, this transformative element gave rise to workshops, and what we might describe as the Bilancista school, as a way of transmitting this marriage of praxis and theory to others. However, the social changes that followed the disappointments of alter-globalization activism (della Porta, 2003), along with the economic crisis that beset Western democracies in 2008–09, created an unfavourable climate to fully concretize this idea of an imagined and practised future. What we can say is that the criticisms and questions these experiences proposed have brought to light distortional aspects of the global economic system. Here, we need only observe how practices of self-production and/or co-production (of food, for example) became more widespread in countries like Italy (and elsewhere), and the penetration achieved – even at local levels – by alternative food networks (Brunori et al, 2011). We can thus trace the origin of these new initiatives to both this process of demobilization (2003–05) and the economic crisis (2008–09) (Graziano and Forno, 2012; Bosi and Zamponi, 2015).

In any case, this understanding of lifestyle as the starting point for change is clearly associated with education and self-education: a potential for learning that is realized on the basis of the individual's personal motivation, but for which the support of the group – of other people – is fundamental. Through the participation of adults who organize themselves into groups in an informal, spontaneous fashion, the Bilancisti have formulated pathways to awareness in relation to many different aspects of critical living and consuming. A passion for doing, making, studying and developing one's theoretical understanding indicate one of the movement's core methodological approaches: self-education, in the form of self-production workshops, which feature an intriguing potential that harks back to the rediscovery of knowledge that was so central to Illich's (1973) theories.

All the same, it is also true – at least as far as we, as researchers, have been able to learn – that the group has not yet found a way to move beyond either individual action or action at the level of the collective. In terms of connections of affinity, we often see relationships between couples or co-inhabitants in such cases. The notion of affinity brings into focus a key dimension of the Bilancista journey – that is, the transmutation of 'I' into 'we', in the sense of a couple or group. Furthermore, one of the few, but significant, ways in which the future emerges as a consideration among the older Bilancisti is the understanding – echoed by the younger generation of the Fuorirotta group – that the family nucleus implies a responsibility on the part of the parents for the education of the children.

The movement has reached an apparent impasse, due to its almost complete absence of a programme for the future. Despite this, younger generations, who are increasingly responsive to environmental, societal and civic issues – from the increasingly apparent climate emergency to the gradual global advance of the New Right – have reclaimed the movement's entire cultural and activistic patrimony – that is, the discourse, practices and processes adopted in the construction of individual and collective identities and actions. Such a reclamation has, inevitably, generated a forward-thinking response.

Conclusion

While movements like the Bilanci di Giustizia might be said to have run aground on the question of the future, more explicit efforts to engage with the future have seen the emergence – almost out of nothing – of other examples of mobilization. We might surmise that the implicit legacy of the Bilancista school – and of numerous other training grounds of democracy – has included playing some role in this new global wave of protests, strikes and demonstrations. Indeed, after a long hiatus, a tangible desire to push forward with intersectional action and discourse is once again discernible within contemporary global mobilizations (Luchies, 2014). We thus find that, while contemporary movements and mobilizations – such as Fridays for Future, Ni Una Menos, Extinction Rebellion and Black Lives Matter – are adapting to a contemporary reality in which participation has become a more complex and fine-grained proposition, they nonetheless also aspire to what we might describe as 'owning the past'. They have also influenced movements that, historically, have been dedicated to more purely materialist concerns, such as the workers/union movement.[3] The prefigurative praxis of these new movements is clearly discernible; indeed, it is intentionally embodied, not only at a symbolic level but also – and above all – in the forms and language they adopt. We need only consider the media impact of Greta Thunberg, or the Chilean women who took to the streets in November 2019 to the cry of 'El violador eres tú' (The rapist is you), or the African American women and their comrades marching in American cities following the murder of George Floyd – a plurality of discourses and symbols that suggest a convergence of movements working towards a future that acknowledges a plurality of realities. This could not be more in keeping with the idea, discussed throughout this chapter, of 'affinity for affinity', in which intersectional conceptions, critiques and metaphors begin to overlap, each nourishing and feeding into the others. It is through these processes that the struggle for social change is carried forward, anchored not (as before) in propagating the cultural hegemony of the oppressed but rather in the relationships that various social categories bring into the light – indeed, bring into *being* – by sticking together, developing relationships, cultivating in the other a respect for biodiversity and making concrete, in the present, the vision of a possible alter-hegemonic future.

To conclude, in this chapter we have attempted to illuminate the prefigurative dimensions of critical pedagogy. We have done so by preserving a focus on the contributions of Paulo Freire and Antonio Gramsci, who – by harnessing processes of conscientization and literacy education (Freire) and processes of hegemony (Gramsci) – demonstrated possible paths out of a condition of oppression and subalternity. Both these thinkers present education as the coherent means to an end – one that, in itself, resembles no less than the emancipation of the categories of society that capitalist hegemony and Western normativity excludes or discriminates against. The different phases of conscientization and the configuration of hegemony can only take place, in concrete terms, when people are able to effect the processes of individual and collective learning in the contexts in which they live – that is, when they begin to self-educate in the interests of self-determination (see also Raekstad, and Komporozos-Athanasiou and Bottici, this volume).

The pedagogical shift that social movements are affecting all around the world – from a transformational vision of reality, inspired by a hegemony model, to a perspective that is far more orientated towards relationships and networks of affinity – makes the intersectionality of the anti-oppression struggle visible. For the latest generation of movements, this concern for the forms and modes of collective action has become the core of a formative and educational operation; the processes activated, in pursuit of their struggle's objectives, are the subject of profound and creative inquiry. As we find in the case of the Bilanci di Giustizia, concern for, and development of, 'practices for justice' are intimately connected with the very idea of justice the movement was pursuing decades ago as part of its prefigurative vision.

What we are witnessing today is a change in this prefigurative vision. The universalistic project of transforming the world, both within and outside the state, is now preceded by an intersectional vision. In this vision, spaces of overlap and interchange between different struggles are brought to the fore, and greater attention is afforded to new forms and modes of doing/making politics and society as part of a fabric of relationships with the living environment, in the sense of the so-called 'practicability of life' (Bertell, 2019).

Taking shape, in the process, are a vision and an accompanying imaginary of transformation and social change that – through interconnections and intersections – are able to create 'in common' spaces and opportunities. Such commonalities, however, arise from the meeting of the different rather than the meeting of similar, despite us being accustomed to thinking – and, indeed, practising – the latter. We are witnessing only the first dawn of this incipient process, but it perhaps presents the best opportunity to draw out – from a confused picture formed of myriad separate experiences – new modes of creating, by communal action, a world in common.

Notes

[1] Beati i costruttori di pace is a voluntary association founded in Padua in 1985 by the diocesan priest Albino Bizzotto. Among the principal activists was Alex Zanotelli, the Combonian missionary who founded the Rete di Lilliput (Lilliput Network), which became a mainstay of the 'new global' movement and the 2001 G8 protests in Genoa. The association's primary concerns include anti-militarism, disarmament, the rejection of

war – including the use of warfare to advance a new Western imperialism – and sustainable degrowth. See http://www.beati.eu/

[2] In total, we conducted four focus groups (involving a total of 70 individuals), 25 in-depth interviews (which were analyzed from a grounded theory perspective) and two community-of-inquiry sessions (involving a total of 25 individuals). We also collected 1,000 questionnaires. (See Bertell et al, 2020.)

[3] See https://www.repubblica.it/economia/2020/03/23/news/coronavirus_sciopero_lombardia-252057177/

References

Aliakbari, M. and Faraji, E. (2011) 'Basic principles of critical pedagogy', *2nd International Conference on Humanities, Historical and Social Sciences IPEDR*, 17: 77–85.

Bertell, L. (2019) 'ECOautonomous work for "practicability of life": experiences of work and production in different economy movements in Italy', *Miscellanea Anthropologica et Sociologica*, 20(3): 11–24.

Bertell, L. and De Vita, A. (eds) (2013) *Una città da abitare: rigenerazione urbana e processi partecipativi*, Roma: Carocci editore.

Bertell, L., De Vita, A., Forno, F. and Rossi, C. (eds) (2020) *Pratiche e visioni del cambiamento e dell'apprendimento: dalla riduzione dei consumi a nuove ipotesi di convivenza*, Cores Working Paper 1.

Bosi, L. and Zamponi, L. (2015) 'Direct social actions and economic crises: the relationship between forms of action and socio-economic context in Italy', *Partecipazione e conflitto*, 8(2): 367–91.

Boström, M., Andersson, E., Berg, M., Gustafsson, K., Gustavsson, E., Hysing, E., Lidskog, R., Löfmarck, E., Ojala, M., Olsson, J., Singleton, B.E., Svenberg, S., Uggla, Y. and Öhman, J. (2018) 'Conditions for transformative learning for sustainable development: a theoretical review and approach', *Sustainability*, 10(12): Art 4479. https://doi.org/10.3390/su10124479

Brunori, G., Rossi, A. and Malandrin, V. (2011) 'Co-producing transition: innovation processes in farms adhering to solidarity-based purchase groups (GAS) in Tuscany, Italy', *International Journal of Sociology of Agriculture & Food*, 18(1): 28–53.

Burbules, N.C. and Berk, R. (1999) 'Critical thinking and critical pedagogy: relations, differences, and limits', in T. Popkewitz and L. Fendler (eds) *Critical Theories in Education: Changing Terrains of Knowledge and Politics*, New York: Routledge, pp 45–65.

Cooper, D. (2017) 'Prefiguring the state', *Antipode*, 49(2): 335–56.

Day, R.J.F. (2005) *Gramsci is Dead: Anarchist Currents in the Newest Social Movements*, London and Ann Arbor, MI: Pluto Press.

De Vita, A. and Bertell, L. (2018) 'Education and work in movements for different economies: new envisaged scenarios and grass-roots political practices', *Journal of Theories and Research in Education*, 13(1): 151–69.

De Vita, A. and Vittori, F. (2015) 'Learning practices, self-education and social re-connection: the case of "*Bilanci di Giustizia*"', *Formazione, Lavoro, Persona,* V(14): 225–39.

della Porta, D. (2003) *I new global: Chi sono e cosa vogliono i critici della globalizzazione*, Bologna: Il Mulino.

Dinerstein, A.C. (2012) 'Interstitial revolution: on the explosive fusion of negativity and hope', *Capital & Class*, 36(3): 521–40.

Foucault, M. (2008) *The Birth of Biopolitics: Lectures at the Collège de France, 1978–1979*, New York: Palgrave Macmillan.

Freire, P. (2000) *Pedagogy of the Oppressed* (30th anniversary edn), trans M.B. Ramos, New York and London: Continuum.

Gaggioli, L. and Valer, A. (2011) *Prove di felicità quotidiana: istruzioni per l'uso*, Milan: Terre di mezzo.

Giddens, A. (1988) *The Third Way: The Renewal of Social Democracy*, Cambridge: Polity Press.

Gramsci, A. (1917) 'Odio gli indifferenti', *La città futura*, 11 February.

Gramsci, A. (1971) *Selections from the Prison Notebooks of Antonio Gramsci*, ed and trans H. Quentin, London: Lawrence & Wishart.

Graziano, P.R. and Forno, F. (2012) 'Political consumerism and new forms of political participation: the *Gruppi di Acquisto Solidale* in Italy', *The Annals of the American Academy of Political and Social Science*, 644(1): 121–33.

Illich, I. (1973) *Tools for Conviviality*, New York: Harper & Row.

Lazzarato, M. (1997) *Lavoro immateriale: forme di vita e produzione di soggettività*, Verona: Ombre corte.

Luchies, T. (2014) 'Anti-oppression as pedagogy; prefiguration as praxis', *Interface: A Journal for and about Social Movements*, 6(1): 99–129.

Maeckelbergh, M. (2011) 'Doing is believing: prefiguration as strategic practice in the alterglobalization movement', *Social Movement Studies*, 10(1): 1–20.

Mason, K. (2014) 'Becoming Citizen Green: prefigurative politics, autonomous geographies, and hoping against hope', *Environmental Politics*, 23(1): 140–58.

Mayo, P. (2015) *Hegemony and Education under Neoliberalism: Insights from Gramsci*, New York: Routledge.

Mayo, P. and Vittoria, P. (2017) *Saggi di pedagogia critica oltre il neoliberismo*, Firenze: Società Editrice Fiorentina.

Valer, A. and Sachs, W. (2000) *Bilanci di Giustizia: famiglie in rete per consumi leggeri*, Verona: Editrice missionaria italiana.

van de Sande, M. (2015) 'Fighting with tools: prefiguration and radical politics in the twenty-first century', *Rethinking Marxism*, 27(2): 177–94.

PART II

Prefigurative Politics in Practice

6

Prefiguration and the Futures of Work

Ana Cecilia Dinerstein and Frederick Harry Pitts

Introduction

The world is a product of work. Work makes us social and makes us human – although it is not, of course, exclusively human; spiders and bees also work (Marx, 1976), and many species possess 'basic senses entirely outside the human repertoire' (Harvey, 2002, p 20). But there is a significant difference between the work of the spider and the bee, on the one hand, and the work of the human worker, on the other – namely, the capacity to imagine, plan and execute an idea that, while initially residing in her imagination alone, can be transformed into reality. It is thus only the human 'architect' who can be 'insurgent' and 'struggle to open spaces for new possibilities, for future forms of social life' (Harvey, 2002, p 20). Only the human architect can 'prefigure' alternatives to the present through work. Largely neglected or avoided by prefiguration scholars and activities, how we conceive of work and capitalism shapes how we understand the praxis of prefiguration.

A common contemporary radical imaginary (see Pitts and Dinerstein, 2017) that set in during the post-crisis period suggested that the problem with capitalism is that it makes us dependent on exploited 'work' (Weeks, 2011; Graeber, 2018), and that the solution is therefore to prefigure postwork alternatives with the potential to create a path to a post-capitalist society (Mason, 2015; Srnicek and Williams, 2015). Up until the cusp of the outbreak of the COVID-19 pandemic, postwork advocates generated a significant debate, mainly in the United Kingdom and other countries in the Global North. As argued elsewhere, a set of shared understandings underpinned the diverse scholarship and activism that fall under the banner of 'postwork' (Dinerstein and Pitts, 2021). These can be summarized as follows: (a) the development of information technology is accelerating, and is allied with crisis tendencies in the current phase of capital accumulation; (b) dynamics of automation and new cooperative commons are enabling a postwork society of abundance and leisure; and (c) implementing a universal basic income is the way to maintain the link between money and subsistence in a world in which the wage relation weakens (Pitts et al, 2017). These shared understandings are reminiscent of a utopia envisioned in the period following the deep economic crisis of the 1970s, which was based on the dream that the dynamics of automation, released by capitalist crisis, would enable society's progressive liberation from capitalist work (Pitts, 2016). Bestselling books (Mason, 2015; Srnicek and Williams, 2015; Bastani, 2019) brought these debates to prominence beyond academia, and – at a time when Left populism seemed to be in the ascendancy with Jeremy Corbyn and Bernie Sanders – successfully translated postwork thinking into an agenda digestible, if not immediately implementable, by centre-Left policymakers and the liberal media (Dinerstein and Pitts, 2021, p 48). Elements of the UK Labour Party's policymaking were inspired by these perspectives, expressed in plans for basic income pilots and modelling exercises that mirrored those developed at centre-Left think tanks and research institutes elsewhere in the world (Pitts and Dinerstein, 2017; Lombardozzi and Pitts, 2020).

In this chapter, we suggest that a post-capitalist society will not come through the suite of options offered by that iteration of the post-crisis left, which sought to escape work alone (principally via automation and universal basic income), as opposed to escaping the social relations that characterize capitalist society. The association between transcending capitalist social relations and transcending work misses what is specific about capitalism: 'the subordination of human life to the logic of money, sustained by the separation between the producers and the means of production as the precondition for its existence' (Dinerstein and Pitts, 2021, p 90). What is specific about capitalism is not capitalism's productive activity, but rather the social conditions that underpin a society where we must work to live in the first place, and the specific 'social forms' the results of production assume in the market and society. 'Form', here, should be confused with neither formality nor a form of social relations. Rather, form is central to Marx's discussion in *Capital* (1976, p 164), and facilitates the understanding of the inner connections (and mediations) of class struggle. The notion of form points to the historical condition of 'transitoriness' in how labour exists in and against capital, and capitalist social relations exist through categories of social domination (Dinerstein, 2018, p 537). These social forms are political (the state), economic (value) and legal (the law). They constitute 'real abstractions' through which capitalism exists and is reproduced. We thus contest both the common interpretation that the problem with capitalism is work, and the proposed solution of prefigurative forms featuring less or no work. In taking work as the basis of capitalism as an exploitative system, postwork utopian alternatives are not so much incorrect as incomplete. In contemporary society, work is not just work (an activity undertaken to produce something), but *capitalist* work (labour). This chapter explores the implications of this insight for how we understand prefiguration and the futures of work. First, we explain how *specifically capitalist* relations of social reproduction precondition work, and the relevance of this for prefigurative politics. We then set out how work in a capitalist society is mediated by abstract social forms, and the relevance of this for how we create prefigurative alternatives to the unfolding futures of work. Subsequently, we reflect on the impact of these insights on the wider question of how prefiguration is understood in theory and practice. We conclude the chapter by considering the importance of these discussions for contemporary notions of a forthcoming postwork society.

Work and the significance of social reproduction for prefigurative politics

Labour – that is, work in a capitalist society – is characterized by its conditions of possibility in antagonistic relations of social reproduction. Social reproduction is 'a broad term for the domain where lives are sustained and reproduced' (Zechner and Hansen, 2015). As such, a social reproduction perspective sees the 'conditions of possibility of labour-power' and the 'manner in which labour power is biologically, socially and generationally reproduced' as key to capitalist society, characterized by workers' separation 'from the means of their subsistence (or social reproduction)' (Ferguson and McNally, 2015).

Marx writes that 'the worker belongs to capital before he has sold himself [sic] to the capitalist' (1976, p 723). This relationship begins 'not with the offer of work, but with the imperative to earn a living' (Denning, 2010, p 80). This relates to an ongoing process of primitive accumulation, whereby workers are *continually* dispossessed of the common means of meeting their needs, and in which new enclosures spring up daily (Dalla Costa, 1995). This process is reproduced constantly to keep workers in a situation whereby they must sell their labour power to live. Workplace exploitation, then, is not a singular moment of domination (Bhattacharya, 2015). The violent denial of the human need to subsist here precedes the compulsion to labour. This standpoint suggests that capitalism is characterized as much by what supports a 'society of work' as by work itself, and that the work relationship is not the only relationship that must be undone to abolish capitalism. It is labour power, and its reproduction by a range of actors and activities, that count – not labour and its performance by workers alone.

What does such an understanding of social reproduction suggest for the envisioning of prefigurative alternatives to, and futures of, work? In the context of work's conditioning by social relations and social forms, its futures lie in the hands of those struggling for new mediations of social reproduction amid its crises. The 'crisis of social reproduction' manifests in a situation in which employment is (and will be) unable to support subsistence across wide sections of the Global North and Global South (Caffentzis, 2002). Under the shadow of this political and economic shift, the crisis of social reproduction takes root where the rupture between employment and social reproduction is most intense, and especially where the temporal and spatial organization of work escapes the limits of formal working time and space. This forces the issue of how to organize productive and reproductive activities, undertaken for survival, back onto urban communities. Thousands of people are organizing autonomously around housing, food, land, education, health, care and culture. This is 'a crisis and widespread vulnerability ... that has opened an incredible number of struggles around social, economic, resource and survival, which have put the struggle for life in the centre of politics' (Zechner and Hansen, 2015).

Struggles around social reproduction signal an intersectional class struggle waged beyond workplaces and into neighbourhoods and communities, both urban and rural. These forms of struggle are our starting point for discussing prefiguration and the futures of work (Dinerstein and Pitts, 2018, 2021). By recasting the relation of work, social reproduction and new forms of class struggle with their 'concrete utopias' (Dinerstein, 2015), this approach points to the inadequacy of abstract utopias and restates the significance of praxis-orientated utopias (Levitas, 1997) in understanding how social movements navigate capitalism's contradictions and anticipate alternative futures for work. 'Struggles around social reproduction', highlight Zechner and Hansen (2015), 'allow for a renegotiation of what is considered work, or what is valued as such'. Today, the politics of social reproduction are already reinventing work and forms of reproducing life in this way, rather than waiting for the correct state policy or technological advance to come along. These interventions are transforming the political too, challenging existing matrices of power, coloniality and patriarchy and their sociopolitical horizons. They are organizing alternatives in the form of autonomous forms of cooperative and dignified work, democracy, land, care for human and non-human life, indigenous autonomy, pedagogies and education. Innumerable collective actions, emerging from the fissures of a system in crisis, are dedicated to not only making demands of governments but also developing 'concrete utopias' (Dinerstein, 2015) in urban and rural territories (see also the chapters by Dinerstein and Clarence-Smith, this volume).

These struggles have significant prefigurative potential to reveal 'the tendencies of the future (the Not Yet) upon which it is possible to intervene so as to maximize the probability of hope vis-à-vis the probability of frustration' (Santos, 2004, p 241). Importantly, these struggles challenge the predominant view of the prefiguration of the future of work. This predominant view claims that alternatives to capitalist social relations can be realized through escaping work and/or organizing alternative forms of work, thereby missing what is specific about capitalism – that is, not capitalism's productive activity, but rather the social conditions that underpin a society where we must work to live in the first place, and (as we see in the next section) the specific social forms the results of production assume in the market and society as a whole. Considering how automated technologies are already impacting on the practice and experience of work, this type of prefiguration process – which confuses *capitalist work* with *work in a capitalist society* – could create a less dignified, more impoverished mode of existence than the one we already have (Dinerstein and Pitts, 2021).

Social form, work and prefigurative alternatives

Labour is also conditioned by the abstract social forms through which it, and its results, are mediated. For Marx (1976), capitalist work – that is, labour – exists in two forms: 'concrete labour' and 'abstract labour'. Concrete labour is defined as concrete activity. But in capitalism, concrete labour is mediated by, and becomes socially realized through, its opposite: abstract labour (Dinerstein and Neary, 2002). Abstract labour signifies 'a social formation in which the process of production has mastery over man, instead of the opposite' (Marx, 1976, p 175). The abstract aspects mediate the concrete; the abstract aspect is dominant (Elson, 1979). Thus, while concrete labour is concrete activity, it is only recognized as abstract labour. Abstract labour is less palpable and consists of the exchange of commodities, regardless of the specific way in which concrete labour was expended in the creation of those commodities. What constitutes the substance of value, then, is not concrete labour (the expenditure of human energy) but abstract labour (a social form abstracted from the concrete experience of work). As mentioned in the introduction to this chapter, a 'social form' is a specific form assumed by the abstract and mediated, but nonetheless real, social domination on which capitalism is based. Capital dominates through legal, political and economic forms. In this case, the social form is abstract labour, which is one of the forms of existence of capitalist work, together with concrete labour. While capital exploits labour power in practice, concrete work is only socially validated when abstracted from the sensuality and sensibility of the work itself. Work, or concrete activity, is recognized only in the form of abstract labour, expressed in money. Abstract labour homogenizes particular labours into socially necessary human labour time, which posits equivalence between commodities and is thus the 'form of existence' that work assumes in capitalism – that is, the historically specific form of existence of human practice. This means that in capitalism, concrete labour is mediated by, and becomes socially realized through, its opposite – abstract labour – regardless of the concrete form the exploitation of labour takes (see Marx, 1976). For Dinerstein and Neary,

> there is a real ground to labour, but the ground to labour is not material: the ground is a social relation. In such a situation, labour is not recognised, validated or rendered equivalent as a result of any intrinsic capacity or social need, but only to the extent that it forms a part of this social generality. (Dinerstein and Neary, 2002, p 234)

The violent homogenization of all concrete labour into abstract labour (and the indifference this entails) enables the creation of the social synthesis (Sohn-Rethel, 1978) that mediates social relations under capitalism. Following Holloway, 'there is a systemic closure that gives the social cohesion a particular force and makes it very difficult to break', a 'close-knit character of social cohesion' we can call a *'social synthesis'* (Holloway, 2010, p 52, emphasis in original). The significance of abstract labour is that

> the social synthesis by way of abstract labor constitutes the general frame of reference for all social relations in capitalism and determines its historical trajectory at the level of its basic dynamic. This does not mean that everything is determined by the logic of labor and commodities in the strict sense. Yet this reified mediation basically constitutes the form of social relations, creating hierarchies and relations of social domination. (Trenkel, 2014)

Abstract labour thus amounts to the 'weaving of capitalism' (Holloway, 2010, p 87). The abstraction of concrete human activity into abstract labour – that is, socially necessary labour time – constitutes the form through which capitalism weaves its web of social cohesion (Dinerstein, 2012). Form implies a concept of totality that is *not* closed and impenetrable, as Marxist traditional theory suggests; rather, it refers to 'real abstractions' (Sohn-Rethel, 1978), or the real form of existence of social relations and their mediations of the capital relation. The capitalist form of existence of human activity, or capitalist work, is mediated, subordinated to the value-producing process and thus forced to exist in a 'mode of being denied' (Gunn, 1987).

What does such an understanding of social form suggest for the envisioning of prefigurative alternatives and futures of work? The question of form is of utmost importance for the prefiguration of alternatives because we are dealing with a specific form of mediation of human activity that transforms the power of people into the power of things (such as money). This abstract mediation of work in a capitalist society compromises the prefiguration of alternative forms of work. Prefiguration's practical point of departure is the alienated character of people's individual and collective capacity to live otherwise. Importantly, the alienation of workers occurs not only in the workplace, through the labour process, but also through abstract social forms (like money) that mediate and perpetuate work's alienated existence. Any prefigurative struggle seeking to articulate an alternative must go in and through these forms, because they mediate and shape our resistance and prefigurative collective actions. As a result of this, to say 'no' and to affirm an alternative is a process inevitably criss-crossed by tensions, contradictions, disappointments and setbacks resulting from existing material and institutional conditions, within which we struggle to prefigure better futures of work.

In facing up to the contradictory character of political subjectivity and class struggle in a world dominated and mediated by real abstractions, it is necessary to escape both 'naïve immediatism and subjectivism' and the 'fatalism and quietism' implied in more determinist perspectives (Starosta, 2017, p 376). What lies beyond the abstract forms of social mediation specific to capitalist society is not an unmediated existence; rather, it is a progressively more developed form of that mediation (Starosta, 2017, p 387). Human activity – work, in short – is the producer of 'perverted forms' of existence; in other words, 'labour is against itself in the form of capital' (Dinerstein, 2015, p 46). The subjectivity of labour is transformed and mediated by the (objective and subjective) real abstractions that govern capitalist society (Dinerstein, 2002). It is therefore insufficient to simply defend 'concrete' existence against the abstraction of our concrete labour into value or money – that is, to defend a 'simple and unmediated' form of 'human practice' or 'human dignity' that resists transformation into objective economic categories (Starosta, 2017, pp 388–9). Rather than defend the concrete and thus escape real abstractions (mediations), then, we need to reinvent the forms of mediation through which antagonistic social relations play out.

We would thus distance our approach from those who favour one-sided advocacy of the concrete (as part of a wider critique of abstract social forms) in their critique of capitalism and delineation of utopias. There is, undoubtedly, a danger in pitting concrete labour against abstract labour instead of seeing them as two expressions of capitalist work. Social/labour struggles cannot escape mediation; as such, prefigurative struggles for alternatives should ultimately be understood as a struggle over the *form* within which the subjectivity of labour is mediated. This manifests as a struggle over a diverse array of social mediations, including not only the state, the law, policy and money, but also forms of political participation – labour organization and rights and so on. As such, delineating prefigurative alternatives for the future of work does not propose to escape all forms of mediation for a concrete immediacy. Rather, it confronts contradictions and – when possible – seeks out moments of *de*-mediation and *re*-mediation that inhere not only 'in and against' but 'in, against and beyond' the mediation of struggles in the real abstraction of capital, value and state (Dinerstein, 2015, pp 21–2).

All capitalist mediations – the law, money, the state – are exposed to class struggle; as such, they are prone to enter crisis and to produce such fleeting moments of de- and re-mediation (Bonefeld, 1987; Gunn, 1987). Bonefeld highlights that 'due to the organisational existence of labour within capital [,] the mediation of the capital–labour relation is permanently driven into crisis–contradiction–de-mediation and further transcendence' (1987, p 68). In short, 'the presence of labour within capital constantly de-mediates the mediation of capitalism' (Bonefeld, 1987, p 68). Moments of de-mediation are instances of intense struggle that result in the temporary opening, and potential transformation, of the social, economic and legal forms or mediations. During moments of de-mediation, collective actors can recognize themselves as subjects of resistance and mediations are transformed by the struggle – indeed, during these moments, everything is possible. De-mediation is an instance of the de-fetishization of the capitalist relation and the social forms that mediate and perpetuate colonial and patriarchal capitalism (Dinerstein, 2015, p 70) – for example, a financial or political crisis. Usually, the state reobtains order, but this is never as it was before the crisis. Class struggle during the crisis can thus transform social forms in order to *re*-mediate social relations, examples being the introduction of a new state policy or changes in legislation following an intense period of mobilization.

The theory and praxis of refuting confronting mediation do not lead us down the path to a pure immediacy – which is impossible in a world that subsists, and is reproduced, through real abstractions – but rather ask us to struggle in, against and beyond capitalist mediations, thus leaving the question of new mediations open to praxis. In the process of de-mediation and remediation, the most dramatic changes can take place. And by struggling over the forms of mediation that class struggle assumes, labour struggles break through and open prefigurative possibilities that cannot be thought in advance.

Marx's *prefigurative* critique of political economy

The previous sections exposed struggle and contradiction as essential elements of prefiguration, foreshadowing alternative futures in the here and now. This dimension of struggle in the prefiguration process has been neglected by neo-anarchist scholar–activists theorizing radical change. Regarded as a central tenet of autonomous movements, such as Occupy Wall Street, the term 'prefigurative politics' has recently been deployed to explain the strategy of social movements to enact, in the present, the society we want to see in the future (Maeckelbergh, 2011, this volume). Prefigurative politics can also mean the experience of creating horizontal and democratic organizations and relations that can serve a broader political process, or that embody the new, thus potentially generating revolutionary consciousness (Raekstad, 2017).

For us, meanwhile, prefiguration is a collective process of steering through the contradictions of the capital relation in specific, historically contextualized struggles, which today are mainly around issues of social reproduction. Social struggles create 'surplus possibilities' (Gibson-Graham, 2006), or what one of us calls 'excess' (Dinerstein, 2015). Excess emerges from the process of translation of our radical praxis into the grammar of order led by the state (Dinerstein 2015). As argued elsewhere, 'translation' refers to the processes, mechanisms and dynamics through which autonomous organizing is either integrated, invisibilized or politically obliterated. The question of translation begs the question of untranslatability: 'what is that which remains untranslatable, outside the scope of translation? What is excluded from its movement of incorporation?' (Vázquez, 2011, p 36). Excess is then an untranslatable aspect of the prefigurative praxis that is still unnamed and could even be – paraphrasing Bloch – undecided material, but constitutes both a threat to capital and a source of inspiration for the movements. These possibilities are untranslatable into conventional social sciences epistemology. As Neary (2019) puts it, 'the power of the focus on Marx's value-form is not simply to suggest an alternative form of social epistemology but a radical epistemology of the social'. This radical epistemology enables a 'prefigurative critique of political economy' that, with Ernst Bloch, reads Marx's critique of political economy in *the key of hope*, so as to grasp prefiguration as a radical praxis against and beyond the value-form (Dinerstein, 2016, this volume). Thus, we see prefiguration not as the result of the process of creating a new society in the present, but as the result of a struggle with, against and beyond the mediations of the capitalist social relations. The alternative forms of mediating social reproduction could not have been thought before subjects involved themselves in prefigurative collective actions, focusing on and dealing with precisely those real abstractions that mediate the creation of possibilities both in and beyond capitalist reality. The excess that emerges from the process of steering through real abstractions (or mediations) is highly likely to disappoint; however, even in its failure, it has an inevitable impact on the *form* of the mediation – be that the state, money or the law.

Conclusion

This chapter has suggested that while work is still central, it is not *the* central social relationship that defines capitalism. We have argued that any attempt to prefigure a post-capitalist society based on alternative organizing processes that address only work and stop short of addressing the abstract social forms assumed by the antagonistic social relations that constitute capitalist society will obstruct rather than facilitate the development of an alternative. The basis of capitalism, as an exploitative system, is not work per se; rather, it is the concrete social relations that make work possible in a capitalist society (resting on the social reproduction of human life as labour power) and the abstract social forms in which work is mediated as abstract labour (money, commodities, value). Work's conditioning by its context within these social relations and social forms complicates and compromises prefigurative futures of work. To address work, then, one needs to address the conditions of possibility that make it what it is in a capitalist society, and the forms through which work is alienated in and abstracted from a world where humans are governed by the objectifications of their own doing: markets, money, the law and the state.

That we must work presupposes relations of distribution that relate less to labour than to life itself. Work in a capitalist society produces economic forms that mediate relations with the means of life. A post-capitalist alternative cannot be prefigured through new forms of work alone, nor through its escape, but only through addressing these dimensions together. Experiments in food, care, land, work and housing, led by social movements and organizations worldwide, highlight the possibility of defying capitalism in a broader, more resourceful way by exploring different forms of the social reproduction of life. By intervening in and 'commoning' our access to the things we need, cooperative projects seemingly unrelated to the contemporary world of work may, in fact, pose the most radical challenge to it. These projects develop not outside or 'post' capitalism, but within it, through struggles – often bloody ones. People's concrete utopias are taking heaven by storm, surprising us every day with alternative practices, ideas and horizons that exist in the here and now, realizing a not-yet reality in an unfinished world, the content of which is undecided (Bloch, 1986). They are criss-crossed by tensions and contradictions, disappointments and setbacks, but it is here that we can find the promise of a future – one beyond capitalism, if not necessarily one that is 'postwork'.

References

Bastani, A. (2019) *Fully Automated Luxury Communism*, London: Verso.

Bhattacharya, T. (2015) 'How not to skip class: social reproduction of labour and the global working class', *Viewpoint Magazine* [online], 5, available from: https://viewpointmag.com/2015/10/31/how-not-to-skip-class-social-reproductionoflabour-and-the-global-working-class/

Bloch, E. (1986) *The Principle of Hope*, Cambridge, MA: MIT Press.

Bonefeld, W. (1987) 'Marxism and the concept of mediation', *Common Sense* [online], 2: 67–72, available from: http://commonsensejournal.org.uk/issue-2

Caffentzis, G. (2002) 'On the notion of a crisis of social reproduction: a theoretical review', *The Commoner*, 5: 1–22.

Dalla Costa, M. (1995) 'Capitalism and reproduction', in W. Bonefeld, R. Gunn, J. Holloway and K. Psychopedis (eds) *Open Marxism 3*, London: Pluto Press, pp 1–15.

Denning, M. (2010) 'Wageless life', *New Left Review*, 66(Nov/Dec): 79–97.

Dinerstein, A.C. (2002) 'Regaining materiality: unemployment and the invisible subjectivity of labour', in A.C. Dinerstein and M. Neary (eds) *The Labour Debate: An Investigation into the Theory and Reality of Capitalist Work*, Aldershot: Ashgate, pp 226–39.

Dinerstein, A.C. (2012) 'Interstitial revolution: the explosive fusion of negativity and hope', *Capital & Class*, 36(3): 513–32.

Dinerstein, A.C. (2015) *The Politics of Autonomy in Latin America: The Art of Organising Hope*, Basingstoke: Palgrave Macmillan.

Dinerstein, A.C. (2016) 'Denaturalising society: concrete utopia and the prefigurative critique of political economy', in A.C. Dinerstein (ed) *Social Sciences for an Other Politics: Women Theorising without Parachutes*, Basingstoke: Palgrave McMillan, pp 49–63.

Dinerstein, A.C. (2018) 'John Holloway: the theory of interstitial revolution', in B. Best, W. Bonefeld and C. O'Kane (eds) *The Sage Handbook of Frankfurt School Critical Theory*, Los Angeles: Sage, pp 533–49.

Dinerstein, A.C. and Neary, M. (2002) 'Anti-value-in-motion: labour, real subsumption and the struggles against capitalism', in A.C. Dinerstein and M. Neary (eds) *The Labour Debate: An Investigation into the Theory and Reality of Capitalist Work*, Aldershot: Ashgate, pp 226–39.

Dinerstein, A.C. and Pitts, F.H. (2018) 'From post-work to post-capitalism? Discussing the basic income and struggles for alternative forms of social reproduction', *Journal of Labor and Society*, 21(4): 471–91.

Dinerstein, A.C. and Pitts, F.H. (2021) *A World Beyond Work? Labour, Money and the Capitalist State between Crisis and Utopia*, Bingley: Emerald.

Elson, D. (1979) 'The value theory of labour', in D. Elson (ed) *Value: The Representation of Labour in Capitalism*, London: CSE Books/Humanities Press, pp 115–80.

Ferguson, S. and McNally, D. (2015) 'Social reproduction beyond intersectionality: an interview', *Viewpoint Magazine* [online], 5, available from: https://viewpointmag.com/2015/10/31/social-reproduction-beyondintersectionality-an-interview-with-sue-ferguson-and-david-mcnally/

Gibson-Graham, J.K. (2006) *A Postcapitalist Politics*, Minneapolis and London: University of Minnesota Press.

Graeber, D. (2018) *Bullshit Jobs: A Theory*, London: Allen Lane.

Gunn, R. (1987) 'Marxism and mediation', Common Sense [online], 2: 57–66, available from: http://commonsensejournal.org.uk/issue-two/

Harvey, D. (2002) *Spaces of Hope*, Edinburgh: Edinburgh University Press.

Holloway, J. (2010) *Crack Capitalism*, London: Pluto Press.

Levitas, R. (1997) 'Educated hope: Ernst Bloch on abstract and concrete utopia', in J.O. Daniel and T. Moylan (eds) *Not Yet: Reconsidering Ernst Bloch*, London and New York: Verso, pp 65–79.

Lombardozzi, L. and Pitts, F.H. (2020) 'Social form, social reproduction and social policy: basic income, basic services, basic infrastructure', *Capital & Class*, 44(4): 573–94.

Maeckelbergh, M. (2011) 'Doing is believing: prefiguration as strategic practice', *Social Movement Studies*, 10(1): 1–20.

Marx, K. (1976) *Capital: Volume I*, London: Penguin.

Mason, P. (2015) *Postcapitalism: A Guide to Our Future*, London: Allen Lane.

Neary, M. (2019) 'Chain reaction: critical theory needs critical mass – contradiction, crisis and the value-form', *Social Epistemology Review and Reply Collective* [online], 8(9): 31–41, available from: https://social-epist emology.com/2019/09/16/chain-reaction-critical-theory-needs-critical-mass-contradiction-crisis-and-the-value-form-mike-neary/

Pitts, F.H. (2016) 'Beyond the fragment: the postoperaist reception of Marx's fragment on machines and its relevance today', School of Sociology, Politics and International Studies Working Paper Series, 02-16, Bristol: University of Bristol.

Pitts, F.H. and Dinerstein, A.C. (2017) 'Corbynism's conveyor belt of ideas: postcapitalism and the politics of social reproduction', *Capital & Class*, 41(3): 423–34.

Pitts, F.H., Lombardozzi, L. and Warner, N. (2017) 'Speenhamland, automation and the basic income: a warning from history?', *Renewal: A Journal of Social Democracy*, 25(3/4): 145–55.

Raekstad, P. (2017) 'Revolutionary practice and prefigurative politics: a clarification and defense', *Constellations*, 25(3): 359–72.

Santos, B. (2004) 'The World Social Forum: toward a counter-hegemonic globalisation (part I)', in J. Sen, A. Anand, A. Escobar and P. Waterman (eds) *The World Social Forum: Challenging Empires*, New Delhi: Viveka Foundation, pp 235–45.

Sohn-Rethel, A. (1978) *Intellectual and Manual Labour*, Atlantic Highlands, NJ: Humanities Press.

Srnicek, N. and Williams, A. (2015) *Inventing the Future*, London: Verso.

Starosta, G. (2017) 'Fetishism and revolution in the critique of political economy: critical reflections on some contemporary readings of Marx's *Capital*', *Continental Thought and Theory*, 1(4): 365–98.

Trenkel, N. (2014) 'The crisis of abstract labor is the crisis of capitalism', *Libcom.org* [online], 9 January, available from: https://libcom.org/library/crisis-abstract-labor-crisis-capitalism-norbert-trenkle-krisis-group

Vázquez, R. (2011) 'Translation as erasure: thoughts on modernity's epistemic violence', *Journal of Historical Sociology*, 24(1): 27–44.

Weeks, K. (2011) *The Problem with Work: Feminism, Marxism, Antiwork Politics and Postwork Imaginaries*, Durham, NC: Duke University Press.

Zechner, M. and Hansen, B.R. (2015) 'Building power in a crisis of social reproduction', *ROAR Magazine* [online], 0, available from: https://roar mag.org/magazine/building-power-crisis-social-reproduction/

7

Prefiguration and Utopia: The Auroville Experiment

Suryamayi Aswini Clarence-Smith

Introduction

Fellow-travelling with utopian practice broadens the conceptual and experimental scope of enacting prefiguration and thereby, through multiple avenues, enables prefigurative actors to achieve their goal of transforming societies. Based on auto-ethnographic research in Auroville, India – the largest intentional community in the world – I introduce this potential 'prefigurative utopianism' – that is, utopian practice enacted through prefigurative processes. The time is ripe for such an exploration. The utopian is now understood as an anticipatory and transgressive praxis that seeks to transform the present for the better – rather than an imagined and static perfect future state – no matter how imperfect the conditions (Bloch, 1986; Sargisson, 2000; Wright, 2010). I will explore this (r)evolution in conceptualization in the first section of this chapter. There are obvious parallels between utopianism and prefiguration, whose actors are characterized as 'intentionally prefigurative of the "other world(s)" they would like to see' (Maeckelbergh, 2009, p 4), using organizational means that reflect their desired ideals so that 'the struggle and the goal, the real and the ideal, become one in the present' (Maeckelbergh, 2011, p 4).

And yet, prefigurative scholarship concentrates almost exclusively on political practice. In the second section of this chapter, I therefore consider what the prefigurative canon stands to gain from engaging with the diversity of transformative experiments that utopian practice encompasses. Next, I chart the development of the intentional community movement towards

106

a prefigurative enactment of utopian practice, drawing on the specific case study of Auroville to propose how certain forms of utopian practice – those that embody utopian ideals through strategic and reflexive experimentation – are to be recognized as prefigurative.

Utopianism in evolution

Lyman Tower Sargent, the long-standing and present-day bibliographer of utopian scholarship, identifies 'three faces of utopianism' through which diverse expressions of this concept have been articulated (2010, p 7). One is literary: descriptions of fictitious (although sometimes familiarly situated) societies that present better alternatives to contemporary ones. Another is utopian social theory, which examines the various roles of utopianism in society. The third, utopian practice, is the only articulation that actually attempts to transform people and societies for the better.

In the last three decades, utopianism has been radically re-evaluated and redefined in all three of these avenues. Rather than being synonymous with perfection, fixity and the intangible, what constituted the utopian became internally diverse, changeable, imperfect, reflexive, self-critical, embedded within and dynamically engaged in evolving progressive alternatives to present conditions. Utopian fictions, such as Marge Piercy's (1976) *Woman on the Edge of Time*, newly portrayed utopian societies that were not based on perfect, uniform, fixed blueprints, offering space instead for difference, nonconformity, contestation and subversion – literary utopias that Moylan theorized as 'critical' and Sargisson as 'transgressive' (Firth, 2018).

Rather than defining and delivering blueprints for utopian society, utopian social theory came to focus on the role of utopianism in bettering existing societies; in 'the education of desire' for a better way of life (Levitas, 2011). Key to this shift away from perfection and towards perfectibility – from form to process – was German Marxist utopian philosopher Ernst Bloch's seminal work *The Principle of Hope*, translated into English in 1986. According to Bloch, utopia is not fixed or preconceived, but rather dynamic and anticipatory; the role of the utopian is to continually reach into future potential while remaining connected to the possibilities embedded in existing reality (1986, p 172).

This forms the basis of the conceptual differentiation Bloch makes between 'abstract' and 'concrete' utopia (see Bloch, 1986; Levitas, 1997), which has significant implications for how we evaluate utopian – and, eventually, 'prefiguratively utopian' (Clarence-Smith, 2019) – practice. An abstract conceptualization of utopia has no inherent connection with reality, and has contributed to the narrative that utopian practice is a groundless and futile endeavour; in Bloch's words, '[p]ure wishful thinking, which has discredited utopias for centuries, both in pragmatic political terms and in all other expressions of what is desirable; just as if every utopia were an abstract one' (1986, p 145). By contrast, a concrete utopia articulates, and is anticipatory of, the development of 'tendencies' or 'latencies' existing in the present (Bloch, 1986, p 223; see also Dinerstein, 2017).

This understanding of a concrete utopia has been key to identifying a utopian praxis, and to defining a broad range of collective practices engaged in such praxis as being utopian. A concrete utopia is rooted in and transformative of the present – however compromised and contradictory an evolutionary process – and actively mediates between aspiration and present conditions. Such utopias include, most notably, 'hope movements' (social mobilizations for autonomy that arise from popular aspirations for alternative paradigms to statist and neoliberal development agendas) (Dinerstein and Deneulin, 2012) and economic experiments that prefigure alternatives to capitalism: 'real utopias' (Wright, 2010), 'nowtopias' (Carlsson and Manning, 2010) and 'current utopias' (Martell, 2018) such as cooperatives, time banks, participatory budgeting practices, reconverted factories, free alternative universities, urban gardens and do-it-yourself collectives (see Monticelli, this volume and also Monticelli, 2018).

In recent years, a variety of social phenomena that actively seek to effect positive social change – protests, practices and performances across realms from the arts to politics – have increasingly been framed as utopian practice (Dinerstein and Deneulin, 2012; Cooper, 2014). Historically, the locus of utopian practice has been intentional communities; these remain significant given their potential to experiment with transforming societies as whole entities, albeit at a micro level. Recently, scholars have also started adopting the concept of prefiguration to describe these, given that they are a radical, embodied exercise in redefining society according to alternative values – of the present, for the future (Farias, 2017; Monticelli, 2018; Clarence-Smith and Monticelli, 2022).

Utopian practice and prefiguration

In my work, I further the collective theorization of utopian practice outlined in this chapter by qualifying it as prefigurative (Clarence-Smith, 2019). I do so given that the practice of prefiguration is one in which a collective emulates in the present the attitudes, social relations, culture and organization it envisions for the future, through 'experimental and experiential' means (van de Sande, 2015, p 189). Scholarship on prefiguration emerged from and has remained focused on political practice, with a few recent diversions, notably into economic and environmental practices (Mason, 2014; Monticelli, 2018). I believe prefigurative action and conceptualization stands to significantly gain in breadth and bearing from bridging with utopian practice given that the latter encapsulates a vast range of human activity – from art and technology to governance, economy and education – that seeks to transform human society (Cooper, 2014; Clarence-Smith, 2019).

The restrictive scope of strategic political practice is perhaps why prefiguration is barely even conceptually associated with utopianism. A few scholars of prefiguration mention in passing that prefigurative action embodies 'utopic' or 'utopian' alternatives (see Juris, 2008; Yates, 2015), but rare are those who actually engage with contemporary theorizations of utopian practice in doing so (Dinerstein and Deneulin, 2012; Monticelli, 2018). Political practice alone, however, is not going to construct an alternative society, while the actors of prefigurative politics are driven precisely by the prospect of living in one. My father, who joined Auroville in 1975, was one of the young protestors who barricaded the streets of London in the late 1960s and early 1970s; but unlike his friends at the time, who focused on 'the revolution', his burning question was: what are we going to do once we win? In Auroville, a multifaceted work in progress towards a new society, he found his answer. By remaining as exclusive as it is today, the conceptualization and ensuing ethnographic focus of scholarship on prefiguration does a disservice to its underlying project and potential (Clarence-Smith, 2019).

I do not propose that prefigurative practice should de facto be considered utopian, or that utopian and prefigurative practices should be indiscriminately conflated. What I do propose is that we consider certain forms of utopian practice to be prefigurative – namely, experimental attempts to embody utopian alternatives to existing practices and forms of relating and organizing, which are strategic in that they engage in and propel an evolution towards these alternatives (Clarence-Smith, 2019). Ethnographic examples of the latter are explored here in the context of the intentional community Auroville.

Towards a prefigurative utopianism: intentional communities

An 'intentional community',[1] an umbrella term that encompasses a vast array of historical and contemporary communal experiments, is defined as a 'group of five or more adults and their children, if any, who come from more than one nuclear family and who have chosen to live together to enhance their shared values or for some other mutually agreed upon purpose' (Sargent, 2010, p 9). Such communities have come into existence for many different reasons, and they have taken various forms throughout history. They have been religious, spiritual and secular in nature. They include groups that are strongly bounded, such as Buddhist or Christian monastic orders, and others that are open, such as educational communities (for example, the Findhorn Foundation). Some, like Auroville, aspire to be institutionally complete, developing their own educational, economic and governmental institutions; others, such as co-housing cooperatives, arise to fulfil a specific socio-economic need. Although the majority are established in rural areas, they exist in urban settings too; co-housing cooperatives are a common feature of major cities, such as London and San Francisco, and Christiania – a commune in Copenhagen – is one of the largest in the world. They include anarchist communes and communities planned or supported by governments, most notably the kibbutz movement. The first record of an intentional community can be found in St Paul's fifth-century letters, and according to the Fellowship for Intentional Community's (nd) directory, thousands of intentional communities exist across the world today.

The history of intentional communities is marked by a progression from abstract to concrete – and, eventually, prefigurative – utopian practice. The communities established in the 19th century are considered to be the 'first wave' of utopian intentional communities (Schehr, 1997); these were based on the prescriptions of European utopian social theorists[2] (notably Robert Owen, Charles Fourier and Henri de Saint-Simon) and literary utopias (such as Etienne Cabet's [1848] *Voyage en Icarie* and Edward Bellamy's [nd] *Looking Backward, 2000–1887, Or, Life in the Year 2000 AD*). Marx and Engels (1848) condemned these abstract and theoretical utopias for not being grounded in reality, not taking into account the material conditions of the time and, therefore, being unrealistic and futile – a common criticism of utopian practice (Engels, 1880; Paden, 2002). Under various combinations of external and internal pressures – such as power struggles and economic sustainability – most disbanded, disintegrated or changed form (Pitzer, 1997; Clarence-Smith, 2019).

The framing of subsequent intentional communities as utopian has been contentious for their members because of the prevalent identification of the concept of utopia with a fixed, abstract ideal of perfection – which many intentional community members feel they are far from – and its association with a detailed, predetermined blueprint, towards which much sound criticism has been levelled (see Kateb, 1963).

The 'second wave' of intentional communities (Schehr, 1997) – the 'hippie communes' of the 1960s and 1970s counterculture movements – largely did not seek to model microsocieties; nor did they articulate explicit, overarching utopian visions of society. They were more experimental, egalitarian and anarchist in nature, adopting feminist-inspired models of collective decision-making based on consensus. More recently, ecovillages, which experiment with various dimensions of sustainability (environmental, economic, social and so on), have emerged as a 'third wave' of intentional communities (Clarence-Smith, 2019). The term 'ecovillages' came into use in 1995 with the founding of the Global Ecovillage Network,[3] an organization that promotes the interconnection and visibility of these communities and their sustainable practices in an effort to catalyse a global shift in lifestyles.

Interestingly, the three most successful intentional communities today (in terms of size, longevity and recognition) – Auroville in India, Findhorn in Scotland and Damanhur in Italy – were each founded by charismatic leaders with spiritual understandings of humankind and the world. However, these conceptions were not translated into blueprints for society. Inspired by shared visionary ideals, members of all three communities experiment with alternative forms of governance, economic organization, educational pedagogies, healthcare, ecological practices and more. These communities are exceptional in the breadth of their activities, institutions and services compared with other intentional communities, and similarly sized – or even larger – conventional townships. As such, they have succeeded in creating institutionally complete alternative societies – the project of the first wave of blueprint utopian communities – albeit practised in the experimental, emergent, feminist, anarchist and egalitarian spirit and culture of the second wave.

Based on her research on contemporary intentional communities – primarily Findhorn – Sargisson emphasizes that these are neither based on nor 'construct a blueprint for the ideal polity' (2000, p 3); to the contrary, there is 'no fullstop to the process of politics in this utopianism. ... It is, above all, resistant to closure and it celebrates process over product' (2000, p 3). In response to internal and external criticisms that such communal experiments are not utopian because they cannot claim to be 'perfect', Sargisson – in keeping with the afore-mentioned contemporary utopian scholars, who have contributed to the radical reformulation of the 'utopian' – maintains that inadequacy lies not in the extent to which these communal experiments are realized, but rather in the 'mistaken reading of utopias as perfection-seeking, blueprinting and desirous of perfection and finality' (2000, p 11). Instead, she characterizes utopian practice in Findhorn as 'transgressive', 'internally subversive' and 'flexible to resistance and order' (Sargisson, 2000, p 2).

While Auroville was founded with clearly articulated utopian ideals, its praxis was envisaged as an experimental and – importantly – evolutionary engagement with these ideals, one that would facilitate a progressive transformation of humanity and human society. This conception is in keeping with Bloch's 'concrete utopia' (1986, p 223), while the concept of prefiguration helps us understand how this is articulated in practice. In the next section, I use various ethnographic examples to explore how Auroville's utopian practice is prefigurative in nature.

Auroville: charting out a prefigurative utopianism

While 'to prefigure is to anticipate or enact some feature of an "alternative world" in the present' (Yates, 2015, p 4), and most intentional communities focus on a particular aspect of collective living, the premise of the Auroville project is to prefigure society *as a whole*. This is based on the Integral Yoga philosophy and practice of Indian yogi and independence movement leader Sri Aurobindo, which upholds that 'all life is yoga' and that society can be progressively transformed in accordance with a spiritual evolution of the world and of humankind (Sri Aurobindo, 1999, p 8). The community has engaged with pioneering, organizing and socially reproducing an institutionally complete, spiritually prefigurative society ever since its founding in 1968 – the year in which the revolutionary slogan 'another world is possible' was born – inspired by values of 'unending education', 'constant progress' and 'human unity' (The Mother, 1968).

Today, Auroville is by far the largest, and among the longest-standing, intentional communities in the world. It is also the most developed in terms of an autonomous alternative society, perhaps by virtue of its size and longevity. Over 50 years old, with a culturally diverse population of approximately 3,000 people of 60 different nationalities[4] – more than twice the size of the second-largest intentional community in the world, Damanhur in Italy (Damanhur, nd) – Auroville has its own schools, enterprises, farms, forests, eateries, renewable energy sources, health centres, performance venues, libraries, research institutes, communal governance and conflict-resolution services, all existing on ecologically restored land in Tamil Nadu, a few kilometres north of the coastal town of Puducherry.

It is important to note that Auroville does have founding ideals (and even a model for a city plan) that provide the basis on which it enacts a prefigurative utopianism (as do other contemporary influences, most notably the environmental movement). 'The Mother',[5] Sri Aurobindo's spiritual counterpart, launched the experimental township when she was in her nineties. She articulated the founding ideals in a short four-point charter (1968), provided a guiding document for individual members (1971) and produced an essay based on a dream she had of an ideal society (1954). In answer to questions by early community members, The Mother made specific recommendations for certain aspects of the community's collective organization – notably in the sphere of economy (see The Mother, 1977) – but never detailed a societal 'blueprint' for Auroville to realize, as this would be contrary to the evolutionary and experimental nature of the project.

With a mandate to evolve (into) a more conscious society through experimentation, and a set of founding ideals, Auroville is teeming with micro-institutions, microenterprises, associations and projects that seek to prefigure modes of collective organization, as well as individual and social practices that progressively concretize and facilitate the embodiment of the community's ideals. These range from common-account cooperatives (which foster conscious consumption) to communal decision-making forums and educational programmes (which integrate spiritual practices, such as meditation) to social enterprises (which encourage ecologically conscious living).

Given Auroville's longevity, its communal organization and institutions – notably governance, economics and education – are now institutionalized to a certain extent; however, reformulation and new initiatives are also common, due to the community's overarching experimental and evolutionary ethos and praxis. This flexible and open-ended practice, which Sargisson theorizes as part of a 'transgressive' utopianism (2000, p 11), echoes the 'inherently experimental and experiential' nature of prefigurative practice (van de Sande, 2015, p 189). In the next section, I investigate in more detail how Auroville explores and enacts a 'prefigurative utopian practice' in two key fields – governance and economy – based on ethnographic observation and analysis. That said, I consider a broad wealth of practices enacted in Auroville to be 'spiritually prefigurative' of its utopian ideals, notably educational, artistic, decision-making and work practices (see Clarence-Smith, 2021).

Prefigurative politics in Auroville

The radical political culture that emerged in the 1960s and 1970s foregrounded feminist, anarchist, non-hierarchical, collectivist practices of consensus decision-making. Like many other intentional communities of this era, this was the form and ethos adopted in Auroville. Since its early years, the community has espoused direct democratic forms of governance, developing forms and processes of political administration that empower participation and consensus-based decision-making. These include community-wide 'general meetings', which constitute the community's ultimate decision-making forum, and a broad, rhizomatic spectrum of dozens of community groups responsible for the management of various aspects of community life, such as farming, forestry, community services, commerce, education and relationships with outside identities. In addition, spontaneously formed groups regularly arise around various communal concerns and new initiatives.

Auroville's anarchist political mode is key to its prefiguratively utopian nature, differentiating it from historical utopian communities that were predicated on blueprints. Even today, while many intentional communities embrace non- hierarchical forms of political organization, some are strictly hierarchical (Firth, 2018, p 497). Similar models of anarchist decision-making have been used to organize thousands of participants in prefigurative social movements, such as Occupy Wall Street and the global justice movement, with 'general assemblies' and 'spokes-councils' formed of representatives of groups organizing various aspects of direct actions (Graeber, 2013, p 136). However, an intentional community practice encompasses a far wider range of activities than direct actions, and is inscribed in time; Auroville is significantly older than even the longest-standing social movements, such as the Zapatistas' civil resistance (active since 1983).

To this day, many community members uphold this anarchist mode – considered to be the cutting edge of prefigurative political practice (see Maeckelbergh, 2009; Graeber, 2013) – as a governance ideal. However, others question whether this mode is satisfactorily prefigurative in the Auroville context, concerned that the community's political practice does not engage with its overarching intention of spiritual prefiguration. Clouston (2003) notes that

> At one time it was said that the Residents' Assembly's fundamental function is to arrive at an agreement. This statement is good, but not sufficient. It is not an instrument of agreement and disagreement. The starting-point is wrong. It is to mature, constantly, the sense of all of us as a collectivity, devoted to the Divine's will.

To help address this, in recent years, several of the community's political forums have experimented with spiritualized collective decision-making practices. These have included using spiritual prompts, primarily quotes from The Mother, and particularly from *The Auroville Charter*, to inform deliberations; moments of silent meditation; and even an institutionalized role of 'Silent Presence-Keeper' – someone who maintains a meditative state throughout a meeting or assembly (Vidal, 2018; Clarence-Smith, 2019, 2021). But these are contested due to concerns over both their efficacy and a ritualization of the non-prescriptive spiritual practice of Integral Yoga (Clarence-Smith, 2019, 2021). Interestingly, spirituality-inspired practices, such as moments of silence and meditation, have also been incorporated into prefigurative social movements such as Occupy (see Chari, 2016; Rowe, 2016).

Prefiguring a utopian economy in Auroville

Auroville's founder, The Mother, gave broad directives on the matter of the economy (*The Auroville Charter, A Dream* and *To Be a True Aurovilian* all refer to economic ideals for the township); she also outlined some specific economic arrangements, in response to questions from Aurovilians, in the early years of the community (see Guigan, 2018). It was thus clear from Auroville's inception that its economic organization would be critical for prefiguring a spiritualized society. This grounding of a utopian project in the material conditions of life is characteristic of what Marxist utopian scholars define as 'real' (Wright, 2010) or 'concrete' (Bloch, 1986; Dinerstein, 2017, this volume; Monticelli, this volume) utopias.

Throughout the community's history, Aurovilians have experimented with various alternative socio-economic forms of association and practices that sought to embody the ideals of a communal economy, with no private property and no exchange of money between community members, each of whom would contribute to the collective in one of three ways – 'work, kind[6] or money' (The Mother, 2003, p 261) – and whose basic needs would, in turn, be provided for by the community. These have included common accounts, cooperatives, participatory budgeting, communal housing and alternative currencies.

While some of these experiments failed, many have proved strategic in prefiguring an 'Auroville economy' (in the idealized sense). Interestingly, this is true even for some of the failed experiments; lessons learned from attempts at common accounts eventually led to the successful institutionalization of 'basic needs' cooperative community-funded services: a grocery; the Pour Tous (For All) Distribution Centre; and Nandini, a clothing, linens and tailoring centre. All running costs are met by Auroville's communal fund (financed by its own enterprises, community members and external donations), while members pool monthly contributions to bulk purchase items, from which they are free to take whatever they feel they need, although their consumption is tracked and addressed if excessive (Clarence-Smith, 2019). Some members intentionally contribute in excess of their usage to subsidize those with greater needs and less means, inspired by economic ideals of communality and solidarity. Similarly, in two recent Aurovilian housing projects (Citadines and Sunship), approximately half of the apartments were allocated for free to people with insufficient means, paid for by some members making premium contributions, thus successfully implementing a solidarity model of wealth-sharing to provide for the basic need of shelter.

Conclusion

As evidenced in the case study of Auroville, a prefigurative conception and practice of utopia empowers an experimental yet strategic, reflexively evolving embodiment of an alternative utopian society. In this chapter, I have proposed that we consider certain forms of utopian practice to be prefigurative – namely, experimental attempts to embody utopian ideals and alternatives to existing practices and forms of relating and organizing, which are strategic in that they engage in and propel an evolution towards these alternatives. In doing so, I have invited a bridging of these two strands of scholarship, as well as a broadening of the current conceptual and experimental scope of prefiguration to include any practice that enacts attitudes, modes and relations with the strategic intention of constructing alternative, so-called 'utopian', societies. Such practices may include educational approaches that seek to foster attitudes, values, skills and experiences conducive to developing more diverse, progressive and holistic societies; economic praxes that demonstrate alternatives to capitalist values, behaviours and organizing; and artistic performances that provide opportunities to embody transcendent forms of relating. Intentional communities are hotspots in which we may observe a high density and diversity of such enactments, but these are also spread throughout social movements, community centres, schools, and public and activist spaces across the world. Folding these into a joint canon of prefigurative utopianism stands to reinforce both utopian and prefigurative practices and to empower the societal transformations that each strive to realize.

Notes

[1]   Alternate terms include communes, utopian communities, communal utopias, cooperative communities and ecovillages.
[2]   Here, one must note that non-European utopian philosophy, social theory and practice are under-represented in the canon of utopian studies.
[3]   https://ecovillage.org
[4]   These figures are based on Census data for March 2021, available from: https://aurovi lle.org/contents/3329, accessed 20 April 2021.
[5]   Born Mirra Alfassa, and first referred to as 'The Mother' by Sri Aurobindo in recognition of her spiritual attainment and embodiment of a divine consciousness.
[6]   'Kind' here is meant in the sense of material offerings.

References

Bellamy, E. (nd) *Looking Backward, 2000–1887, Or, Life in the Year 2000 AD*, London: William Reeve.

Bloch, E. (1986) *The Principle of Hope: Volume 1*, Oxford: Basil Blackwell.

Boggs, C. (1977) 'Marxism, prefigurative communism and the problem of workers' control', *Radical America*, 11(6): 99–122.

Breines, W. (1989) *Community and Organization in the New Left 1962–68: The Great Refusal*, New Brunswick, NJ: Rutgers University Press.

Cabet, E. (1848) *Voyage En Icarie*, Paris: Au Bureau du Populaire.

Carlsson, C. and Manning, F. (2010) 'Nowtopia: strategic exodus?', *Antipode*, 42(4): 924–53.

Chari, A. (2016) 'The political potential of mindful embodiment', *New Political Science*, 38(2): 226–40.

Clarence-Smith, S.A. (2019) *Towards a Spiritualised Society: Auroville, an Experiment in Prefigurative Utopianism*, PhD thesis, University of Sussex.

Clarence-Smith, S.A. (2021) 'Auroville, an experiment in spiritually prefigurative utopianism', in L.T. Sargent and R. Baccolini (eds) *Transgressive Utopianism: Essays in Honour of Lucy Sargisson*, Oxford: Peter Lang, pp 139–58.

Clarence-Smith, S.A. and Monticelli, L. (2022) 'Flexible institutionalization in Auroville: a prefigurative alternative to development', *Sustainability Science* [online], available from: https://doi.org/10.1007/s11625-022-01096-0

Clouston, D. (2003) 'How to govern utopia', *Auroville Today*, 301.

Cooper, D. (2014) *Everyday Utopias: The Conceptual Life of Promising Spaces*, Durham, NC: Duke University Press.

Damanhur (nd) 'What is Damanhur?' [online], available from: www.daman hur.org/en/what-is-damanhur

De Prat de Lamartine, A.M.L. (2016) 'Utopie d'aujourd'hui, réalité de demain', ['Utopia of today, reality of tomorrow'], *Georges Bertin* [online], available from: https://www.georges-bertin.com/utopie-daujourdhui-real ite-de-demain/

Dinerstein, A.C. (2017) 'Concrete utopia: (re)producing life in, against and beyond the open veins of capital', *Public Seminar* [online], 7 December, available from: http://www.publicseminar.org/2017/12/concrete-utopia/

Dinerstein, A.C. and Deneulin, S. (2012) 'Hope movements: naming mobilization in a post-development world', *Development and Change*, 43(2): 585–602.

Engels, F. (1880) 'The development of utopian socialism', in *Socialism: Utopian and Scientific* [online], available from: https://www.marxists.org/archive/marx/works/1880/soc-utop/ch01.htm

Epstein, B. (1991) *Political Protest and Cultural Revolution*, Berkeley, CA: University of California Press.

Farias, C. (2017) 'That's what friends are for: hospitality and affective bonds fostering collective empowerment in an intentional community', *Organization Studies*, 38(5): 577–95.

Fellowship for Intentional Community (2021) 'Community directory' [online], available from: https://www.ic.org/directory/listings/

Firth, R. (2018) 'Utopianism and intentional communities', in M. Adams and C. Levy (eds) *Palgrave Handbook of Anarchism*, Basingstoke: Palgrave McMillan, pp 491–510.

Franks, B. (2003) 'The direct action ethic: from 59 upwards', *Anarchist Studies*, 11(1): 13–41.

Graeber, D. (2010) *Direct Action: An Ethnography*, Edinburgh: AK Press.

Graeber, D. (2013) *The Democracy Project: A History, a Crisis, a Movement*, London: Allen Lane.

Guigan, G. (2018) *Auroville in Mother's Words*, Auroville: Auroville Press.

Juris, J. (2008) *Networking Futures: The Movements against Corporate Globalisation*, Durham, NC: Duke University Press.

Kateb, G. (1963) *Utopia and Its Enemies*, New York, NY: Free Press of Glencoe.

Levitas, R. (1997) 'Educated hope: Ernst Bloch on abstract and concrete utopia', in J.O. Daniel and T. Moylan (eds) *Not Yet: Reconsidering Ernst Bloch*, London and New York: Verso, pp 65–79.

Levitas, R. (2011) *The Concept of Utopia*, Oxford: Peter Lang.

Maeckelbergh, M. (2009) *The Will of the Many: How the Alterglobalisation Movement Is Changing the Face of Democracy*, London: Pluto.

Maeckelbergh, M. (2011) 'Doing is believing: prefiguration as strategic practice in the alterglobalisation movement', *Social Movement Studies*, 10(1): 1–20.

Martell, L. (2018) 'Utopianism and social change', *Capital and Class*, 42(3): 435–52.

Marx, K. and Engels, F. (1848) 'Critical-utopian socialism and communism', in *Manifesto of the Communist Party*.

Mason, K. (2014) 'Becoming Citizen Green: prefigurative politics, autonomous geographies, and hoping against hope', *Environmental Politics*, 23(1): 140–58.

Monticelli, L. (2018) 'Embodying alternatives to capitalism in the 21st century', *TripleC: Communication, Capitalism & Critique*, 16(2): 501–17.

Paden, R. (2002) 'Marx's critique of the utopian socialists', *Utopian Studies*, 13(2): 67–91.

Piercy, M. (1976) *Woman on the Edge of Time*, New York, NY: Fawcett Crest.

Pitzer, D.E. (ed) (1997) *America's Communal Utopias*, Chapel Hill, NC: University of North Carolina Press.

Rowe, J.K. (2016) 'Micropolitics and collective liberation: mind/body practice and Left social movements', *New Political Science*, 38(2): 206–25.

Sargent, L.T. (2010) *Utopianism: A Very Short Introduction*, Oxford: Oxford University Press.

Sargisson, L. (2000) *Utopian Bodies and the Politics of Transgression*, London and New York: Routledge.

Schehr, R.C. (1997) *Dynamic Utopia: Establishing Intentional Communities as a New Social Movement*, Westport, CT: Bergin & Garvey.

Sri Aurobindo (1999) *The Synthesis of Yoga*, Puducherry: Sri Aurobindo Ashram.

The Mother (1954) *A Dream*, Puducherry: Sri Aurobindo Ashram.

The Mother (1968) *The Auroville Charter*, Puducherry: Sri Aurobindo Ashram.

The Mother (1971) *To Be a True Aurovilian*, Puducherry: Sri Aurobindo Ashram.

The Mother (1977) *The Mother on Auroville*, Puducherry: Sri Aurobindo Ashram.

The Mother (2003) *Words of The Mother – I*, Puducherry: Sri Aurobindo Ashram.

van de Sande, M. (2015) 'Fighting with tools: prefiguration and radical politics in the twenty-first century', *Rethinking Marxism*, 27(2): 177–94.

Vidal, M. (2018) *Manifesting the Invisible*, MA thesis, École des Hautes Études en Sciences Sociales, Paris.

Wright, E.O. (2010) *Envisioning Real Utopias*, London: Verso.

Yates, L. (2015) 'Rethinking prefiguration: alternatives, micropolitics and goals in social movements', *Social Movement Studies*, 14(1): 1–21.

8

Prefiguration in Everyday Practices: When the Mundane Becomes Political

Francesca Forno and Stefan Wahlen

Introduction

The growth logic of contemporary capitalism digs deeper and grows larger in everyday life. The increasing commodification of social reproduction has transformed everyday life, spreading economic insecurity, fragmentation and disengagement, worsening health and wellbeing, and progressively limiting people's autonomy to choose the lives they want to live. Mushrooming discontent with problems ranging from environmental degradation to growing economic inequalities and social injustice intensifies the need for social change, but the so-called modern repertoire of collective action (Tilly, 1986) – such as national strikes or demonstrations – is less capable of pressurizing powerful actors to deliver such change. As a result, activists have started to search for new spaces and modalities of action. Given this context, it is no surprise that many contemporary struggles focus on 'reclaiming the everyday', experimenting with new tactics that encompass people's lives, consumption habits and leisure activities. In other words, in a system characterized by 'capitalist enclosure' (Chatterton and Pusey, 2020; see also Federici, 2009) – the market's appropriation of non-human ecological systems and local cultural knowledge – everyday life appears to have become a space of resistance.

The purpose of this chapter is twofold. First, it aims to understand the interplay between everyday life and prefiguration. It does this by scrutinizing three key facets of everyday life and discussing which type of everyday practices, under which circumstances, can be considered prefigurative – namely, particular utopian practices that not only envision alternative futures but also enact them. Second, it aims to reflect on how people, individually and collectively, try to articulate and respond to challenges posed by the contemporary capitalist system of production, trade, sale and consumption. It does this by focusing on everyday life as a key locus for change.

We begin with a critical appraisal of conceptualizing 'the everyday'. After this general and theoretical discussion, we highlight how contemporary activism politicizes the everyday. We then use new food movements to explore the role that more personal forms of engagement can play in shaping people's political consciousnesses and motivating them to collective action. Finally, the chapter concludes by discussing the potentials and limits of everyday life practices for prefiguring social change.

Conceptualizing everyday life

Sociological inquiry has long acknowledged how the complexity and indeterminacy of everyday activities silently contribute to making the world (Cicourel, 1964; Garfinkel, 1964; Berger and Luckmann, 1996). 'The everyday' includes both formal and informal 'ways of doing things'. Its inconspicuousness lays the foundation for social relations, activities and reproduction. Felski understands everyday life as 'the essential, taken-for-granted continuum of mundane activities that frames our forays into more esoteric and exotic worlds. It is the ultimate non-negotiable reality, the unavoidable basis for all other forms of human endeavour' (1999, p 15). In other words, everyday life can be anything or nothing. Yet, understanding its implicitness might be a first step towards critiquing the world and engaging in prefiguration. After all, no great social changes are likely to happen if a myriad of ordinary and mundane practices are not combined with an 'imaginative construction of "alternatives"' (Yates, 2015, p 19). In analytical terms, we can distinguish three different but interrelated key facets of everyday life – time, space and modality (Felski, 1999) – all of which are closely linked with prefiguration.

Time

First, the notion of the everyday is closely linked to temporality, rhythm and repetition. Time has multiple dimensions; it is more than merely physical and linear clock time. Time is also inextricably interrelated with people's lived experience. A cyclical dimension of time emphasizes the recurring and repetitive nature of daily activities, underscoring the relationship between prefiguration and the everyday, as manifested in acceleration. In alignment with commodification, capitalist societies increased the standardization of life, with modern timetables promoting collective everyday rhythms. Although potentially time-saving, the development of technical instruments – modern transport, communication, industrial automation and so on – has also resulted in an acceleration of actions that, paradoxically, often lead individuals to perceive that they lack time (Rosa, 2019). As Rosa (2019) argues, the acceleration of everyday activity that follows the economic growth imperative (Latouche, 2009) is currently the primary source of alienation. In other words, contemporary society increasingly considers time as a scarce resource represented by economist logic, rather than considering the lived experience of time in daily routines.

While everyday repetition is often highlighted as monotonous or negative and 'the everyday' designates alienating aspects of human life (the repetitive nature of work, consumption and so on), everyday activity can also be a locus of disruption and creativity (de Certeau, 1984; Lefebvre, 1991) associated with the development of surprising creative potential, continuously unfolding innovation and enacting change. Rather than consisting solely of repetitive and ordinary actions, then, everyday rhythms and routines are constantly traversed by tensions between alienating and creative forces. The high-speed tempo of (micro) changes that lead to manifold forms of alienation (Rosa, 2019) are at the centre of a number of contemporary 'alternatives' that have emerged within either mobilization-related or everyday activities, which can be considered prefiguration. This is the case for the slow food and degrowth movements, as well as individualized practised action (slow travelling, slow living, slow eating and so on). After all, people have never been passive users or subjects of institutions and discourses – quite the opposite, human activity is constantly prefiguring everyday life, redrawing and questioning the balance of forces through inventive negotiations with the social reproduction system.

Space

Second, the everyday is closely linked with the notion of space; indeed, it is the space in which all life occurs. Yet because the everyday is both everywhere and nowhere, it can be a space of submission and normalization as well as one of innovation and resistance. By analysing the contradictions and potentials inherent in the transformation of living conditions under modernization, Lefebvre (1991, p 93) highlights how, within the 'bureaucratic society of controlled consumption', everyday life has become increasingly commodified. Accordingly, a vast array of everyday activities has been moved from the home to the market (for example, cooking or leisure activities). While the process of commodification is intrinsic to the privatization of public space, capitalism has increasingly invaded important aspects of social reproduction (Hochschild, 2012), making individual freedom more and more dependent on economic resources. However, although contemporary societies contain repressive aspects, an element of creative resistance to these structures is enacted to prefigure an alternative future.

Resistance can be enacted though micro-social activities, such as walking, reading and cooking in private family life. Indeed, all everyday spaces are 'free spaces' (Melucci, 1989) that can eschew the main forces of control and of repression. By appropriating the residues of work and time through 'subterranean practices', people can create everyday expressions of freedom, as every gesture (whether of obedience or insubordination) instantaneously constitutes an appropriation of constraints. One space inextricably linked to the everyday, but that seems to have acquired new meaning, is the home. The political character of often unrecognized household activities is increasingly acknowledged in a broad range of attempts to provide alternatives to home-based capital production. For example, the home is the place where food culture and related competencies of choosing, preparing and tasting food are transmitted and preserved, with important consequences for sustainability and the use of resources such as nutrients, water and electricity. A number of movements now choose to buy their food from a local farmer, or even grow their own, with the aim of 'tak[ing] back the economy' (Gibson-Graham et al, 2013) and attempting to provide alternatives to capitalist production. As such, even in a world of endlessly circulating messages used primarily to sell the latest commodities, everyday life (and choices) can become a space for efforts towards 'disalienation' (Lefebvre, 1991). In other words, everyday life affords a space where individuals can address loss of value and meaning, expanding movements' actions beyond street protest and towards individual responsibility-taking actions (Micheletti, 2003) – in the market as well as the home.

Modality

Third, the everyday is linked with modality of action. Practices are enacted depending on the meanings actors attribute to them. Modality can be distinguished as both strategy and tactics. For de Certeau (1984), strategies are used by those within organizational power structures, whether small or large, such as the state, municipality and corporation. Tactics, however, are employed by those who are dominated, such as disempowered groups (migrants, workers, LGBTQI+ people, ethnic groups and so on). Tactics, which also depend on reasonable utilization of time, are practices that come together to disrupt business as usual. They often stem from everyday practices and have no explicit borders; they represent acts of resistance against strategies, and prefigure new forms of power relations.

In a context of increased commodification, social movement actors have made steps towards disalienation in the market, sometimes moving their actions from the streets to the shops (Forno and Ceccarini, 2006).

Individualized collective actions (Micheletti, 2003) have also become a means to express non-economic values. This is important for understanding the modalities of action that prefigure alternatives. Political consumerist acts and alternative lifestyles, such as veganism, can be seen as everyday attempts to seek congruence between the means and the ends of political action (reflected in the phrase 'be the change that you wish to see in the world'). That is to say, the unofficial sphere of everyday life is where processes of social change might begin. As Alberto Melucci (1989) argues, in contemporary society, everyday life is never far removed from collective action and social change. Ultimately, it is in the unofficial networks of everyday social relations and activities that new meaning and identities are formed, providing a basis for the politics of opposition (Melucci, 1989).

Politicizing everyday life

Research on collective action has usually focused on 'visible' action and major social change (Melucci, 1989). Over the last few decades, there has been a significant increase in the number of studies identifying inconspicuous 'everyday life' as significant for understanding citizens' political involvement. Research on different forms of so-called 'lifestyle politics' reflects the growing importance of the everyday as a 'locus for change' in the actions of social movement organizations – for example, market-orientated actions emerging from social and environmental concerns around overconsumption and overproduction (Forno and Ceccarini, 2006; Haenfler et al, 2012; Stolle and Micheletti, 2013; Wahlen and Laamanen, 2015; de Moor, 2017).

Today, alternative everyday practices are among the principal modalities of action of a wide array of social movement organizations. An increasing range of grassroots organizations call on citizens to take action in their everyday practices, whether to build transnational awareness and intensify pressure on corporations or to facilitate the building of alternatives to capitalist production (Wahlen and Laamanen, 2015). Activism embedded in daily life has been central to the spread of both individualized actions, such as 'political consumerism' (Micheletti, 2003) – boycotts, 'buycotts' (for example, 'vote with your dollar' tactics) and lifestyle changes (for example, becoming vegan) – and communitarian efforts, such as communal and ecological ways of producing or living (Forno and Graziano, 2014; Schlosberg and Coles, 2015; Monticelli and della Porta, 2019).

Although different in their scale (or space) of action and attitudes towards consumption (Forno and Graziano, 2014), these efforts emerge from political motivations (Schlosberg and Craven, 2019). Their aim is to transform the present to literally embody prefigurative models of democratic living, in contrast to the economist growth imperative that has increasingly commodified and accelerated daily life. By practising alternative value practices (Centemeri, 2018; Centemeri and Asara, this volume), activists aim to demonstrate that what they do is important – not only in withdrawing support from a structure deemed unjust but also to prefigure, and experiment with, an alternative and desirable society (Yates, 2011; Goodman et al, 2012; Veron, 2016). In other words, considering the everyday as an enacted performance in social practices emphasizes the link between the everyday and politics.

As Haenfler et al stress, the concept of 'prefigurative politics' is closely linked to everyday lifestyle action, 'as it describes activists' attempt to create on a small scale the type of world they envision' (2012, p 4). In this sense, alternative modalities of living and consuming can be interpreted as prefigurative efforts towards disalienation in contemporary consumer society. Deciding to live a communal life, participate in alternative economic networks, adopt a vegan lifestyle, conduct a slower or simpler life and so on directly emphasizes a deeper personal commitment, which synthesizes public and personal responsibility. In this sense, everyday practices can help to prefigure what society could look like in the future, as well as forming part of a broader repertoire of collective action by emphasizing cultivating cultural values for such a future. Everyday practices can thus demonstrate that alternatives are not a distant dream but can be considered in the here and now.

The prefigurative political function of such everyday forms of engagement has also proven particularly important for sustaining collective action in periods of 'latency'. This is because everyday practices help to forge and maintain solidarity between activists, enhancing the possibility of achieving collective goals by providing opportunities to experience the desired ends (Yates, 2015). As an engine of social transformation, prefiguration can perform 'the often-overlooked work of pursuing social change through an emphasis on cultivating cultural values for an alternative future' (Huddart-Kennedy et al, 2018, p 153). In light of an increasing variety of contemporary sustainability agendas, everyday practices also seem to favour encounters and collaborations between different types of actors – activist movements, 'ordinary people', governments (especially local governments) and business – thus moving beyond the traditional public/private divide (Pink, 2012, p 5). Needless to say, such developments should not be misinterpreted as attributing too much responsibility to individuals and communities. Contemporary social movements demonstrate how different fields of activity – home, work, the pub or the streets – cannot be distinguished into separate spaces, as social sites are increasingly interconnected within global value chains.

Reworking food to build eco-glocal futures

Movement organizations encourage everyday practice as a form of direct action (Bosi and Zamponi, 2020) to contrast with the commodification and acceleration of daily life. Alternative everyday practices can challenge commodification and constitute the basis for alternative being and living. Among the various practice-based movement organizations (or lifestyle movement organizations), new food movements have been able to bring about substantive changes to the global food system. By showing that food means more than merely satisfying a daily need at home, these movements have positioned food as a means through which to build a socially and ecologically just future.

By drawing together producers and consumers, local food initiatives – including those labelled 'alternative food networks' – have been surprisingly influential in shaping not only national and international agricultural and food policies but also individual consumer practices. They have been helping to raise awareness of issues, including animal welfare, genetic modification, pesticide and antibiotic residues, land grabs and, most recently, agricultural and food industries' contribution to climate disruption (Kropp et al, 2021). Food movements have targeted contemporary industrialized food systems, showing how advanced capitalist societies are undergoing a food crisis due to a global food system that is highly specialized and dominated by transnational corporations.

Food sovereignty is the cornerstone of a new economy that aims to decommodify nature by dematerializing productive processes and orientating production and consumption towards a more efficient production process – one that uses fewer resources. In other words, provisioning networks enacted by new food movement organizations and community food initiatives – such as community-supported agriculture, solidarity purchasing groups, slow food and ecovillages, to name just a few – have not only offered specific alternatives to the current, unsustainable food system but also embodied a novel style of doing politics across spaces. In all of these grassroots experiences, procuring and provisioning practices rework all three afore-mentioned facets of the everyday: time, space and modality.

Regarding time, new food movements have stressed the need to reconnect with nature's rhythms and rediscover rituals and routines, such as cooking at home (rather than eating out), growing your own food and buying local. The functionality and significance of alternative provisioning practices have highlighted that to transition to sustainability, the speed of life should slow down (for example, slow food). Regarding space, these movements stress that food entails rural–urban and private–public relationships. Empirical examples of this can be found in community-supported agriculture, where consumers and producers attempt to circumvent industrial production and retail, engage in subterranean practices and prefigure a future with a direct relationship between those who provide and those who are in need. This not only has positive financial effects for everyone involved but also, and more interestingly, emphasizes caring for one another. Finally, regarding modality, new food movements prefigure alternative future food systems in which community groups grow or exchange food differently, as in the case of solidarity purchase groups (Forno et al, 2015) and community fridges (Wahlen, 2018). As such, new food movements exemplify how the everyday becomes the locus through which people attempt to regain control over their lives by experimenting with alternatives – ones that reconsider their use of time, space and modality.

Conclusion

If we are to understand the interplay between prefiguration and everyday life, we need to recognize everyday life as a site of the political. As we have seen, the three key facets of everyday life – time, space and modality (Felski, 1999) – resonate with prefiguration in various ways. Everyday temporalities are not only enacted in rhythms and repetition but also constitute a locus for change, extending the past into the future. The economic growth imperative has pushed people to reclaim their everyday lives, envisioning and enacting a different future that contrasts with processes of acceleration and commodification. Everyday space emphasizes political prefiguration's role as a locus of disruption beyond the streets and the ballot box. Prefiguration acknowledges the political character of often unrecognized subterranean practices; for example, the home is the place where food culture and the related skills of choosing, preparing and tasting food are transmitted and preserved, with important consequences for sustainability. Finally, modality can enable prefiguration because it acknowledges the importance of cultural appreciation and appropriation for encouraging disalienation.

The everyday as a site for political action has, however, faced a number of criticisms. In particular, the focus on self-determination and self-changing strategies has been criticized for diverting civic action from real economic and social problems (the so-called 'crowding out' thesis), and for promoting political and ideological formulas that channel social discontent away from targets such as national and international institutions. Using the example of alternative food networks, Goodman et al (2012) stress the limits of lifestyle practices in terms of their transformative potential and efficacy, emphasizing how these experiences are often an expression of the middle and upper classes. As is often highlighted, proponents of such practices have sometimes proven not to be politicized, and to be more interested in preserving their own health and identity. Similarly, it has been argued that sustainable consumption and lifestyles risk remaining a niche phenomenon at the edge of the market, with limited or no impact on how society functions, because they can be easily co-opted by corporate marketing strategies (Dubuisson-Quellier, 2019).

In response to these criticisms, empirical research has shown that alternative ways of living and consuming do not displace other forms of engagement (Adams and Raisborough, 2010). Furthermore, those engaged in alternative consumption and lifestyles tend to also be more active in other forms of political participation, as shown in the case of solidarity-based consumer groups that collectively practise sustainable procuring and provisioning (Forno et al, 2015; Guidi and Andretta, 2015). As the example of new food movements shows, building new, localist food economy networks does not necessitate abandoning lobbying and protesting for (national and transnational) food policy reforms – '[o]ne form of political engagement does not simply replace the other; new materialist political action is not a zero-sum or an either/or' (Schlosberg and Coles, 2015, p 174).

But although empirical research does not support the 'crowding out' thesis, it remains unclear as to whether these practices can change society or merely give rise to niche communities and reinforce traditional class structures. More conceptual work is needed to understand the political nuances of everyday practices that, while they may appear to be 'apolitical', are vital for enhancing people's prefigurative power and resistance – particularly in our increasingly globalized and unsustainable consumer society.

References

Adams, M. and Raisborough, J. (2010) 'Making a difference: ethical consumption and the everyday', *British Journal of Sociology*, 61(2): 256–74.

Berger, P.L. and Luckmann, T. (1966) *The Social Construction of Reality: A Treatise in the Sociology of Knowledge*, Garden City, NY: Anchor Books.

Bosi, L. and Zamponi, L. (2020) 'Paths toward the same form of collective action: direct social action in times of crisis in Italy', *Social Forces*, 99(2): 847–69.

Centemeri, L. (2018) 'Commons and the new environmentalism of everyday life: Alternative value practices and multispecies commoning in the permaculture movement', *Rassegna Italiana di Sociologia*, 64(2): 289–313.

Chatterton, P. and Pusey, A. (2020) 'Beyond capitalist enclosure, commodification and alienation: postcapitalist praxis as commons, social production and useful doing', *Progress in Human Geography*, 44(1): 27–48.

Cicourel, A.V. (1964) *Method and Measurement in Sociology*, New York: Free Press of Glencoe.

de Certeau, M. (1984) *The Practice of Everyday Life*, Berkeley: University of California Press.

de Moor, J. (2017) 'Lifestyle politics and the concept of political participation', *Acta Politica*, 52(2): 179–97.

Dubuisson-Quellier, S. (2019) 'From moral concerns to market values: how political consumerism shapes markets', in M. Boström, M. Micheletti and P. Oosterveer (eds) *The Oxford Handbook of Political Consumerism*, Oxford: Oxford University Press, pp 813–32.

Federici, S. (2009) 'Education and the enclosure of knowledge in the global university', *ACME: An International Journal for Critical Geographies*, 8(3): 454–61.

Felski, R. (1999) 'The invention of everyday life', *New Formations*, 39: 15–31.

Forno, F. and Ceccarini, L. (2006) 'From the street to the shops: the rise of new forms of political actions in Italy', *South European Society and Politics*, 11(2): 197–222.

Forno, F. and Graziano, P.R. (2014) 'Sustainable community movement organisations', *Journal of Consumer Culture*, 14(2): 139–57.

Forno, F., Grasseni, C. and Signori, S. (2015) 'Italy's solidarity purchase groups as "citizenship labs"', in E. Huddart Kennedy, M.J. Cohen and N. Krogman (eds) *Putting Sustainability into Practice: Advances and Applications of Social Practice Theories*, Cheltenham: Edward Elgar, pp 67–88.

Garfinkel, H. (1964) 'Studies in the routine grounds of everyday activities', *Social Problems*, 11(3): 225–50.

Gibson-Graham, J.K., Cameron, J. and Healy, S. (2013) *Take Back the Economy: An Ethical Guide for Transforming Our Communities*, Minneapolis: University of Minnesota Press.

Goodman, M., DuPuis, M. and Goodman, D. (2012) *Alternative Food Networks: Knowledge, Practice and Politics*, London: Routledge.

Guidi, R. and Andretta, M. (2015) 'Between resistance and resilience: how do Italian solidarity based purchase groups change in times of crisis and austerity?', *Partecipazione e conflitto*, 8(2): 443–7.

Haenfler, R.J., Johnson, B. and Jones, E. (2012) 'Lifestyle movements: exploring the intersection of lifestyle and social movements', *Social Movement Studies*, 11(1): 1–20.

Hochschild, A. (2012) *The Managed Heart Commercialization of Human Feeling* (3rd edn), Los Angeles, CA: University of California Press.

Huddart-Kennedy, E., Parkins, J.R. and Johnston, J. (2018) 'Food activists, consumer strategies, and the democratic imagination: insights from eat-local movements', *Journal of Consumer Culture*, 18(1): 149–68.

Kropp C., Antoni-Komar, I. and Sage, C. (2021) *Food System Transformations: Social Movements, Local Economies, Collaborative Networks*, London: Routledge.

Latouche, S. (2009) *Farewell to Growth*, London: Polity Press.

Lefebvre, H. (1991) *The Critique of Everyday Life*, London: Verso.

Melucci, A. (1989) *Nomads of the Present: Social Movements and Individual Needs in Contemporary Society*, London: Century Hutchinson.

Micheletti, M. (2003) *Political Virtue and Shopping: Individuals, Consumerism and Collective Action*, London: Palgrave Macmillan.

Monticelli, L. and della Porta, D. (2019) 'The successes of political consumerism as a social movement', in M. Boström, M. Micheletti and P. Oosterveer, *The Oxford Handbook of Political Consumerism*, Oxford: Oxford University Press, pp 773–92.

Pink, S. (2012) *Situating Everyday Life: Practices and Places*, London: Sage.

Rosa, H. (2019) *Resonance: A Sociology of Our Relationships to the World*, Cambridge: Polity Press.

Schlosberg, D. and Coles, R. (2015) 'The new environmentalism of everyday life: sustainability, material flows, and movements', *Contemporary Political Theory*, 15(2): 160–81.

Schlosberg, D. and Craven, L. (2019) *Sustainable Materialism. Environmental Movements and the Politics of Everyday Life*, Oxford: Oxford University Press.

Stolle, D. and Micheletti, M. (2013) *Political Consumerism: Global Responsibility in Action*, Cambridge: Cambridge University Press.

Tilly, C. (1986) *The Contentious French*, Cambridge, MA: Harvard University Press.

Veron, O. (2016) '(Extra)ordinary activism: veganism and the shaping of hemerotopias', *International Journal of Sociology and Social Policy*, 36(11–23): 756–73.

Wahlen, S. (2018) '"Foodsharing": Reflecting on individualized collective action in a collaborative consumption community organisation', in I. Cruz, R. Ganga and S. Wahlen (eds) *Contemporary Collaborative Consumption*, Wiesbaden: Springer VS, pp 57–75.

Wahlen, S. and Laamanen, M. (2015) 'Consumption, lifestyle and social movements', *International Journal of Consumer Studies*, 39(5): 397–403.

Yates, L. (2011) 'Critical consumption: boycotting and buycotting in Europe', *European Societies*, 13(2): 191–217.

Yates, L. (2015) 'Rethinking prefiguration: alternatives, micropolitics and goals in social movements', *Social Movement Studies*, 14(1): 1–21.

9

Prefiguration and Ecology: Understanding the Ontological Politics of Ecotopian Movements

Laura Centemeri and Viviana Asara

Introduction

In this chapter we discuss prefiguration from the perspective of environmental activism, interweaving the concept of 'ecological prefiguration' with the related debate on 'ecotopia', and point to some of the challenges social movements face in striving towards an ecological society. After reviewing the literature that discusses ecological prefiguration and ecotopia from different disciplinary perspectives, we argue that ecological prefiguration should be approached from an 'ontological politics' perspective. This can help to clarify the transgressive potential of ecotopian initiatives as expressions of a larger movement of everyday environmentalism. Using the example of the transnational permaculture movement, we show how investigating 'value practices' can illuminate the value of ecological prefiguration in creating a more just, sustainable society, but also the limitations it poses when it sidelines more confrontational or contentious approaches to socioecological change.

Critical distancing and direct engagement: different approaches to the study of ecotopian movements

Prefigurative initiatives have been a vital feature of environmental activism since the 1960s at least, probably due to the key role of utopianism in contemporary environmental discourses and practices. Despite the growth of grassroots action since the 1990s, however, social scientists have largely neglected ecological prefiguration until recently.

For geographer David Pepper (1996, 2005, 2007), utopianism – 'critical, creative thinking about alternative social worlds' (Pepper, 2007, p 290) – permeates not only radical but also reformist environmentalism in ways that are commonly marked by idealism – that is, by a 'poor understanding of the structural dynamics of current society and what it will take to change them' (Pepper, 2007, p 290). However, far from criticizing utopianism per se, Pepper stresses that utopian thinking and practice play a crucial role in environmentalism. This is because they provide conceptual and material space for developing the 'transgressive potential' necessary for imagining a future ecological society and 'crossing the boundaries of present society and moving closer to one which is ecologically and socially strongly sustainable' (Pepper, 2007, p 289).

Pepper uses the term 'ecotopia' to denote 'utopian writing, thinking and action in which environmental problems and themes are central rather than incidental' (Pepper, 2005, p 6).[1] His analysis relies on ecotopian writings and academic literature discussing initiatives – which we characterize as 'ecological prefiguration' – that seek to build locally responsible and sustainable economies, such as alternative currencies, local circuits of food and energy production and consumption, alternative agriculture experiments and intentional communities (such as ecovillages – on this topic see Clarence-Smith, this volume). If prefiguration is 'the embodiment, within the ongoing political practice of a movement, of those forms of social relations, decision-making, culture, and human experience that are the ultimate goal' (Boggs, 1977, p 100), what is specific to ecological prefiguration is its emphasis on both *social* and *ecological* relations. In other words, the 'ultimate goal' of ecological prefiguration initiatives is formulated in more-than-human terms; it is the embodiment of forms of coexistence between human beings and other living beings, with the intention of sustaining the transformation towards an ecological society.

Pepper identifies diverse intellectual traditions that fuel radical ecological prefiguration, such as the deep ecology approach (principally American bioregionalism) and anarchist- and socialist-inclined radical environmentalism (exemplified by Murray Bookchin's municipalism).[2] In his opinion, this intellectual eclecticism causes radical ecological utopianism to be riddled with tensions and dilemmas. Indeed, while deep ecology is an ecocentric approach that attributes intrinsic value to nature, collapses the Western philosophical dualism between nature and society and criticizes Enlightenment values, anarchist- and socialist-inclined radical environmentalism adopt a more materialistic analysis of social change – one centred on anti-capitalism and environmental justice (see Piccardi, this volume).

More specifically, Pepper focuses on four dilemmas and tensions of ecotopianism. First, ecotopian thinking encompasses both 'technophilic' and 'technophobic' positions, which sometimes go as far as depicting scenarios of 'future primitivism' or sustaining 'technocratic' tendencies. Second, ecotopianism tends to express itself in rigid social blueprints, based on principles of 'equilibrium' or 'biomimicry',[3] which Pepper sees as regressive because they are grounded in an imagined past – one characterized by harmony between society and nature – rather than in present material realities. Third, ecotopianism argues that all ecological principles should be universally observed and applied, including celebration of the virtues of diversity, which actually translates into 'the right to be culturally and socio-economically different; even to the extent of living ecologically-unfriendly lives' (Pepper, 2007, p 297). Fourth, the ecotopian idea that 'localism forms the source of most appropriate values and behaviour, and giantism and globalisation are often regarded as enemies' risks contributing to 'simplistic, reductionist explanations of environmental problems' (Pepper, 2007, p 303). For Pepper, even when ecotopian practices are motivated by radical intentions, their results are 'reformist' at best; rather than stimulating the 'radical imaginary', he argues, they merely promote small-scale responsible capitalism, which supports non-profit initiatives without really challenging the system. In his view, the potential of these institutions to bring about social change ultimately depends on their capacity to build internally consistent and rigorous reasoning, and their failure to do so explains why they eventually become assimilated into the society they oppose (Pepper, 2007, p 307).

The work of anthropologists Joshua Lockyer and James R. Veteto on ecotopia is in opposition to Pepper's critical distancing approach. Inspired by the writings of socially engaged anthropologists, such as Arturo Escobar and David Graeber, they observe practices from a position 'beyond disengaged cultural critique', instead looking for 'viable possibilities' for moving towards a more just and sustainable society (Lockyer and Veteto, 2013, p 3). Defining ecotopia as 'bodies of ideas and groups of people who are attempting to enact just and sustainable alternatives to existing political and economic hegemonies' (Lockyer and Veteto, 2013, p 6), they focus on what they see as the most relevant 'ecotopian movements' – bioregionalism, permaculture and ecovillages. These movements aim to create 'moral economies grounded in forms of discourse other than dominant Western economic rationality and guided by the compass of justice and sustainability' (Lockyer and Veteto, 2013, p 21). The authors have a positive view of the transgressive potential of these initiatives; they believe that having learned from 'the successes and failures of the 1960s counterculture', they can now try to develop 'more effective strategies for moving toward ecotopia' by building 'bridges across a number of divides – ivory tower from village, Global North from Global South, and nature from culture' (Lockyer and Veteto, 2013, p 4).

The scope of these ecotopian movements is somewhat different. Bioregionalism is mainly an intellectual movement supporting 'a basic understanding that humans and human activities are fundamental components of ecosystems … and that human organization should be guided by natural systems instead of arbitrary political boundaries' (Lockyer and Veteto, 2013, p 6). Permaculture, on the other hand, is a design method: an 'ethically grounded methodological toolkit for putting the bioregional worldview into practice' by providing 'guidelines for developing sustainable human ecosystems' (Lockyer and Veteto, 2013, p 6). Finally, ecovillages are

> intentional human communities that use integrative design, local economic networking, cooperative and common property structures, and participatory decision making to minimise ecological footprints and provide as many of life's basic necessities as possible in a sustainable manner. Ecovillages put bioregional thought and permaculture methodology into practice at the community level in service of the fundamentally ecotopian goal of sustainability. (Lockyer and Veteto, 2013, p 15)

The writings of Pepper and of Lockyer and Veteto exemplify two recurring postures in the scientific debate over the 'transgressive potential' of ecotopian initiatives: 'critical distancing' and 'direct engagement'. On the one hand, Pepper's critical distancing is guided by the idea that the goal of social scientists studying ecotopian movements is to assess their success in triggering political change. In his analysis of what makes a movement successful, Pepper focuses mainly on the level of ideologies, while case studies serve to exemplify a general theory and are selected to support an argument that is supposed to be of general validity. On the other hand, Lockyer and Veteto invite social scientists to engage in socioecological transition initiatives and bring their knowledge and expertise to bear in the service of these social experiments. Their approach is more sensitive to the fact that ideologies inspire concrete actions whose transformative potential can never be fully anticipated, because it is measured in concrete situations of action. The case study, then, is not so much an exemplification as an experiment – one that also involves social scientists, who participate by encouraging forms of reflexivity that have an impact on movements' frames, strategies and imaginary. At the same time, social scientists are challenged in their practices and methods by the need to combine their usual problem-orientated approach with the solution-focused orientation supported by ecological prefiguration initiatives.

Despite different research approaches, however, these authors are united in their conviction that for the transition to an ecological society to take place, a profound transformation is needed in both social discourse and practice.

From ecotopia to the ontological politics of everyday environmentalism

By combining the critical distancing and direct engagement, we can identify two fundamental challenges that ecological prefiguration needs to confront: contravening the hegemonic discourses and power structures it encounters, and rethinking social values and needs consistent with socially and ecologically sustainable livelihoods. As such, the challenge of transitioning to an ecological society is ethical, political and technical, and necessitates simultaneously transforming values, power balances and the material relationship to the environment and non-human beings. For this reason, a critical discussion of ecological prefiguration must consider a perspective of 'ontological politics' (Mol, 1999; see also Escobar, 2018, this volume), which assumes that ' "the real" is implicated in the "political" and vice versa' (Mol, 1999, p 74), because reality is produced and transformed through open and contested practices and interventions that enact ways of existing and of relating human and non-human entities (see also Pellizzoni, 2015).

Ontological politics views reality as being performed in a variety of practices and attends to the pluralism of views or values on reality. It further stipulates that society's complexity stems from an irreducible multiplicity of modes of practical experience of reality, forms of agency and types of objectivity that are intertwined and hierarchized in the institutional forms of common living. Power is therefore understood as operating at the juncture between multifarious practical experiences and the definition of norms and institutions that constitute the social order, making some forms of experience and relationships to materiality and the environment more legitimate than others.

It follows that from an ontological politics perspective, the stake of ecological prefiguration is not so much the anticipation and implementation of an alternative future (whose characteristics would already be known), but rather making visible a potential ontological alternative – one that is already inherent in the present. The activation of this alternative reopens previously ignored possibilities of a radical imagination of the future. Consequently, the transformative potential of ecological prefiguration can be assessed through analyzing and observing the 'alternative value practices' (De Angelis, 2017, p 365; see also Centemeri, 2018) that orientate and materially organize ecotopian initiatives. Here, value practices are the social actions through which people define what is valuable in a given situation and act to attain, and maintain, the condition deemed valuable. This involves both the *discursive* level of value arguments stressed by Pepper (2007) and the *practical* level of modes of valuing considered by Lockyer and Veteto (2013) (see Figure 9.1). The value practices perspective implies moving beyond social sciences' traditional separation between *social values* and *economic value* to focus on the

Figure 9.1: Ecological prefiguration as a form of environmental activism

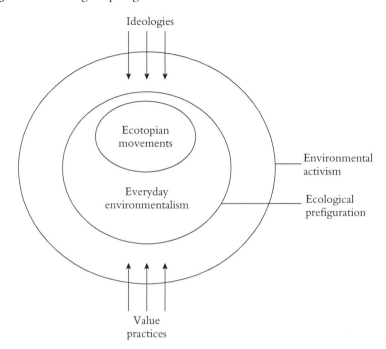

discourses and practices that socially construct what is economically valuable, starting from a multiplicity of social ways of valuing. From this perspective, market prices are the outcome of not only 'the social structure of the market' but also the hegemonic ways of valuing supported by 'institutional rules, networks, and conventions' (Beckert and Aspers, 2011, p 27). In contrast, many ecological prefiguration initiatives openly assume the monetary value of goods and services, as expressed by price, to be an object of deliberation between actors in the chain between producer and consumer.

This focus on value and practice is at the heart of Schlosberg and Coles' (2016; see also Schlosberg, 2019) analysis of ecological prefiguration, which they term as the 'new environmentalism of everyday life' (see Forno and Wahlen, this volume) – a broader concept that includes ecotopian movements and is inspired by research into those movements. This new environmentalism of everyday life includes forms of collective action, such as alternative food networks and energy cooperatives, that prefigure sustainable supply chains as a way to challenge neoliberal capitalism and its 'circulatory power' (Schlosberg and Coles, 2016, p 161). This creates 'flows of technocratic productivity and consumption that increasingly reconstructs the world, human beings, ethics, and political economic institutions in order to maximize further circulations' (Coles, 2012, p 181). According to Schlosberg, 'the objective of this sustainable materialist activism is to reconfigure or *prefigure* a new relationship with the material needs of everyday life and to *institutionalize* it' (2019, p 16, emphasis added), changing the material relationship with the non-human realm (Schlosberg and Coles, 2016, p 171). For Schlosberg (2019), sustainable materialism is a type of activism and politics focused on environmental practices around the basic needs of everyday life, and on the collective development of alternative systems that resist the flows of power and are dedicated to social justice and the functioning and vitality of the non-human realm. Our proposition is to approach this transformation in terms of ontological politics, exploring how alternative value practices developed in prefigurative initiatives can succeed in foregrounding assemblages capable of resisting neoliberal forms of circulatory power.

In the next section, we scrutinize how these concepts and analyses are articulated in the case of the permaculture ecotopian movement. In this ecotopian movement (more clearly than in other movements), the ontological politics dimension that characterizes ecological prefiguration plays a crucial role. Our discussion is based on research conducted mainly in Italy in the period 2015–19 (see Centemeri, 2018, 2019). Findings draw on a triangulation of different research methods: participant observation of permaculture training courses; ethnographic observation of selected permaculture demo sites and permaculture association meetings (national and European levels); interviews with permaculturists (including some of the founding figures of the movement); analysis of documents and literature produced by the movement; and analysis of activities on social media in the case of the Italian permaculture movement. Punctual observations were also conducted in permaculture demo sites in Spain, Portugal, France and Switzerland.

Permaculture: ecotopia meeting ontological politics

The term 'permaculture' is a portmanteau of 'permanent' and 'culture'. Founded in Australia in the 1970s, and spread worldwide during the 1980s and 1990s, the permaculture movement strives for a cultural and material transformation of industrialized societies, starting with devising technical solutions for ecological food production and distribution. Permaculture is an ecotopian movement to the extent that it encourages everyone to act to transform their daily practices and experiment with fairer, more sustainable provisioning systems.

According to Bill Mollison (1988, Chapter 14) – one of the movement's initiators and a supporter of bioregionalism – networking these transformative initiatives should lead to the emergence of new infrastructures and institutions that will make the existing ones obsolete, ultimately leading to a generalized social change – a position that Pepper qualifies as idealistic. However, it is important to note that while bioregionalism remains an important inspiration for permaculture, other political imaginaries, such as degrowth and climate justice, are equally important today. From the point of view of political cultures, permaculture activists perceive the movement as being 'mosaic' – that is, as a movement that values internal difference and is open to collaboration, appropriation and hybridization.

Initially, permaculture – which supports a predominantly small-scale agroecological model of agriculture – was born as a critique of the agricultural model imposed by the so-called 'green revolution', which was based on intensive land use practices with massive inputs of chemicals and energy produced from non-renewable sources.[4] More particularly, the permaculture method consists of a set of ethical and practical principles for designing human settlements in a way that seriously considers and integrates local specificities (ecologically, socially and culturally). This adaptation increases the likelihood of local conditions being maintained over time, with a reduced need for external inputs, particularly in terms of energy. Rather than defining blueprints to be replicated everywhere, permaculture insists on a methodology of process design. This is not restricted to the field of agriculture; rather, it is a design method of socioecological processes. As such, this method can be applied to all areas of daily life – from the design of a house, garden or farm to the design of a teaching course, cooperative, production and distribution chain, network of activism and even protest actions (see Jordan, 2009).

Beyond the differences in practical implementation, what permaculture initiatives have in common is their preference for technical and organizational solutions based on collaboration (rather than exploitation or competition) between humans, animals, plants, materials and natural elements. The ethical foundation of permaculture is summarized in three principles: care of the Earth, care of people and redistribution of surplus (or fair share). These principles combine elements of deep ecology with materialist concerns for social and ecological justice. Permaculture design principles are inspired by observation of how healthy ecosystems function – what Pepper defines as a 'bio/ecomimesis' approach. These principles include: observe and interact; catch and store energy; obtain a yield; apply self-regulation and feedback; use and value renewables; produce no waste; design from patterns to details; integrate, don't segregate; use small, slow solutions; use and value diversity; use edges and value the marginal; and creatively use and respond to change (see Holmgren, 2002).

Permaculture design, therefore, is based on the search for practical solutions to work *with* nature, not against it. This invitation must be understood in the framework of an idea of nature as a process in continuous evolution, in which notions of order and equilibrium refer to dynamic, rather than static, conditions. The debates within the movement today reveal a more complex picture than that drawn by Pepper, who sees ecomimesis as a regressive trend and assumes that the invitation to imitate nature stems from the urge to respect a 'natural' order conceived as stable. Permaculturists, instead, draw inspiration from solutions that can be observed in ecosystems *without* evoking the idea of a natural order; rather, they talk about a constantly moving equilibrium (Rothe, 2014). Moreover, empirical observation also shows that the distinction between technophobes and technophiles is less relevant than the distinction between those who believe that technical solutions alone can induce sociopolitical change and those who believe such solutions should be accompanied by protest and conflict. However, this movement's repertoire of action remains largely non-contentious; it focuses on promoting training courses by creating transnationally networked educational organizations and 'demonstration sites' – concrete examples of 'permanent cultures' ranging from ecovillages to community gardens, farms and 'transition towns' (see Hopkins, 2011).

On the permaculture courses Laura Centemeri attended in Italy, an important part of the training aimed to make participants aware of often ignored ecological relationships and to view animals, plants, other living beings and materials and elements from the perspective of their problem-solving skills. For example, if you wanted to protect a plot of land from excessive wind exposure, a permacultural way to do this would be to design a windbreak barrier using a combination of trees and shrubs that have not only wind-breaking but also nitrogen-fixing capacities, thus increasing soil fertility while enhancing biodiversity. Efforts would also be made to find species that combine the wind-breaking capacity with that of producing fruit for human consumption, berries for animals or even simply refuge areas for animals – preferably beneficial predators. The function of wind protection could also be provided by a structure (for example, a tool shed), which has a specific additional function (storing tools) as well as a beneficial impact on the design problem (wind protection).

It is in this sense that we talk about an 'ontological politics' dimension of permaculture. The discovery of the reality of ecological relationships, and the previously ignored problem-solving skills of non-human beings, is central to triggering imagination and elaborating technical and organizational solutions that respond to human needs by reducing human impacts on ecosystems. This capacity to combine productive activities with processes that repair the 'web of life' indicates an alternative path for agriculture; indeed, according to Jason W. Moore, this alternative points to a possible way out of capitalism and towards a 'socialist world-ecology' (2015, p 200). By 'processes that repair the "web of life"', we mean, for example, permaculture design practices that consider soil fertility to be the result of successful collaborations between a variety of living beings in a relationship of interdependence. Here, soil is considered not as an inert surface but as an interweaving of relationships between living beings – from nematodes and fungi to bacteria and humans. In performing soil as an interweaving of relationships, the permaculturist is called on to collaborate with this multispecies network to achieve goals such as ecological food production. Moreover, the permaculturist seeks to take into account that the soil is not a plot of land with the sole job of producing food; it is also part of a landscape, a place to which memories and affections can be attached, and part of a biosphere and processes involving biodiversity loss or carbon storage. In other words, the permaculturist must consider not only multiple ways of *performing* soil but also multiple ways of *valuing* soil.

In particular, observing value practices in various permaculture demonstration sites in Italy revealed the importance attributed to 'emplaced' modes of valuing the environment. By emplaced, we mean ways of valuing the environment based on the situated experience of being attached to and (inter)dependent on specific people, places and ecosystems (see also Pink, 2009). For example, to explain the organizational choices adopted on her farm in the hills of Genoa, a permaculturist considers multiple evaluation criteria equally, such as: the need to contribute to fighting climate change, the possibility to decide her own working schedule with more autonomy, the desire to dedicate time to herself and her loved ones, the will to create a local food network producing high-quality affordable food, the desire to revive an abandoned place and the memories of its former inhabitants, and the pleasure of enjoying the beauty of the place. In other words, the urge to act for social change is combined with the quest for a mode of living based on taking care of those social and ecological relationships that make a specific place unique in the personal experience.

The question, therefore, is not that of replacing one ontology with another; for example, systematically prioritizing an emplaced perspective over a global one. Both perspectives count for social and environmental sustainability. Rather, it is about recognizing and attributing importance to multiple logics of value and ways of performing reality, and exploring alternative ways of combining – in value practices – both emplaced modes of valuing and logics of value that rely on more standardized evaluation criteria. In permaculture initiatives, social and ecological sustainability appears to be connected with the recognition of this ontological multiplicity and guided by value arguments of care and redistribution. Given these premises, alternative value practices can emerge – ones that try to resist the standardization processes induced by an economy whose only objective is ever-increasing accumulation.

However, the transgressive potential of these alternative value practices is stronger when permaculture initiatives are inserted in mutualistic and collaborative networks, and in processes of mobilization where prefiguration, contestation and strategy are combined in the attempt to transform institutional contexts. For example, permaculture is an important component of the ecological imaginary of the urban movement, which flourished in Barcelona following the experience of the Indignados and the occupation of Plaça Catalunya. Indeed, after the occupation of the square, the decentralization of the Indignados movement to neighbourhood assemblies led to the birth of various prefigurative projects, such as community gardens, social centres and alternative economic initiatives. Permaculture activists were directly involved in these prefigurative experiments, in which the ethical and design principles of permaculture were adopted. In this case, permaculture principles thus contributed to the emergence of alternative value practices, as part of a broader intersectional and radical politics of autonomy and the commons (Asara, 2019, 2020).

Conclusion

To some extent, the example of the permaculture movement shows that the tensions and dilemmas that (according to Pepper) characterize ecotopia are real. More particularly, the urge for the movement to encompass a diversity of visions of an ecological society, as well as a diversity of strategies to move towards it, can act as a restraint on the effectiveness of collective action. Indeed, internal diversity often means that the permaculture movement does not take a strong stance in political debates that can be highly divisive. Even more problematic is the fact that permaculture founders supported a vision of a 'non-polarised and non-contentious politic', based on the assumption that 'it is possible to agree with most people, of any race or creed, on the basics of life-centred ethics and commonsense procedures, across all cultural groups' (Mollison, 1988, p 508). The belief in the 'power of life' to create a spontaneous alignment of political goals underestimates the fact that 'life-centred ethics' can be reactionary and not necessarily emancipatory (see Yates and de Moor, this volume; du Plessis and Husted, this volume).

At the same time, many activists (even if not all) engage in reflection and debate over these tensions. For example, the will to combine local ecological prefiguration initiatives with global mobilizations on environmental issues propels the building of networks and collaborations at different scales. In other words, the reality of ecological prefiguration appears to be much less idealistic than Pepper claimed, even if a certain political naivety is apparent in many (not all) permaculture initiatives.

Furthermore, the multiplication of collaborations appears as an important strategy – one that enables the imaginary of an ecological society to be moulded on a continuous basis, rather than simply anticipated or fixed once and for all. From this point of view, permaculture, as a set of ethical and design principles, appears to be a potential lingua franca or bridging language of ecological prefiguration. It can be mobilized in more or less contentious initiatives, from the anti-capitalist inspired occupation of lands – as in the case of the Zone to Defend in Notre Dame des Landes, France (Bulle,

2018) – to the Transition Network, and from urban community gardens to experimental rural farms.

In this chapter, we have tried to provide some tools with which to analyse the transgressive power of ecological prefiguration initiatives by looking at their value practices as a privileged methodology to reveal their ontological politics. By not separating the analysis of discourse from that of practices, or the analysis of social value from that of economic value, we can better understand the transformative potential of radical ecological prefiguration. As the case of the permaculture movement demonstrates, this potential is strongest where these initiatives succeed in 'contaminating' other movements, building powerful collaborations that can nurture their radical imaginaries and increasing their chance of institutionalization.

Notes

1   The term 'ecotopia' became popular in the 1970s, thanks to Ernest Callenbach's (1975) utopian homonymous novel.
2   Echoing ideas already developed by Peter Kropotkin and William Morris, Bookchin (1980) imagined a future of decentralized but interdependent eco-communities, run by direct democracy.
3   Biomimicry is a concept introduced by Janine M. Benyus (1997) to describe a logic of design and innovation that mimics the problem-solving strategies observed in the spontaneous organization of ecosystems.
4   On agroecology, see Altieri (1987).

References

Altieri, M. (1987) *Agroecology: The Scientific Basis of Alternative Agriculture*, Boulder, CO: Westview Press.

Asara, V. (2019) 'The redefinition and co-production of public services by social movements: the Can Batlló social innovation in Barcelona', *Participation and Conflict*, 12(2): 539–65.

Asara, V. (2020) 'Untangling the radical imaginaries of the Indignados' movement: commons, autonomy and ecologism', *Environmental Politics* [online], available from https://www.tandfonline.com/doi/full/10.1080/09644016.2020.1773176

Beckert, J. and Aspers, P. (2011) *The Worth of Goods: Valuation and Pricing in the Economy*, Oxford and New York: Oxford University Press.

Benyus, J.M. (1997) *Biomimicry: Innovation Inspired by Nature*, New York: Morrow.

Boggs, C. (1977) 'Marxism, prefigurative communism and the problem of workers' control', *Radical America*, 11(6): 99–122.

Bookchin, M. (1980) *Toward an Ecological Society*, Montreal: Black Rose Books.

Bulle, S. (2018) 'Formes de vie, milieux de vie: la forme-occupation', *Multitudes*, 71(2): 168–75.

Callenbach, E. (1975) *Ecotopia: The Notebooks and Reports of William Weston*, New York: Bantam Books.

Centemeri, L. (2018) 'Commons and the new environmentalism of everyday life: alternative value practices and multispecies commoning in the permaculture movement', *Rassegna Italiana di Sociologia*, 64(2): 289–313.

Centemeri, L. (2019) *La permaculture ou l'art de réhabiter*, Versailles: QUAE Editions.

Coles, R. (2012) 'The promise of democratic populism in the face of contemporary power', *The Good Society*, 21(2): 177–93.

De Angelis, M. (2017) *Omnia Sunt Communia on the Commons and the Transformation to Postcapitalism*, London: Zed Books.

Escobar, A. (2018) *Designs for the Pluriverse: Radical Interdependence, Autonomy, and the Making of Worlds*, Durham, NC: Duke University Press.

Holmgren, D. (2002) *Permaculture: Principles and Pathways Beyond Sustainability*, Hepburn, Australia: Permanent Publications.

Hopkins, R. (2011) *The Transition Companion: Making Your Community More Resilient in Uncertain Times*, Totnes: Green Books.

Jordan, J. (2009) 'Think like a forest, act like a meadow', *Field*, 3(1): 23–33.

Lockyer, J. and Veteto, J.R. (eds) (2013) *Environmental Anthropology Engaging Ecotopia: Bioregionalism, Permaculture, and Ecovillages*, New York and Oxford: Berghahn.

Mol, A. (1999) 'Ontological politics: a word and some questions', *The Sociological Review*, 47(1): 74–89.

Mollison, B. (1988) *Permaculture: A Designer's Manual*, Tyalgum: Tagari Publications.

Moore, J.W. (2015) *Capitalism in the Web of Life*, London and New York: Verso.

Pellizzoni, L. (2015) *Ontological Politics in a Disposable World: The New Mastery of Nature*, Surrey: Ashgate.

Pepper, D. (1996) *Modern Environmentalism: An Introduction*, London and New York: Routledge.

Pepper, D. (2005) 'Utopianism and environmentalism', *Environmental Politics*, 14(1): 3–22.

Pepper, D. (2007) 'Tensions and dilemmas of ecotopianism', *Environmental Values*, 16(3): 289–312.

Pink, S. (2009) *Doing Sensory Ethnography*, London: Sage.

Rothe, K. (2014) 'Permaculture design: on the practice of radical imagination', *communication +1* [online], 3(1), available from: https://scholarworks.umass.edu/cpo/vol3/iss1/4

Schlosberg, D. (2019) 'From postmaterialism to sustainable materialism: the environmental politics of practice-based movements', *Environmental Politics* [online], available from: https://doi.org/10.1080/09644016.2019.1587215

Schlosberg, D. and Coles, R. (2016) 'The new environmentalism of everyday life: sustainability, material flows, and movements', *Contemporary Political Theory*, 15(2): 160–81.

10

The Paradox of the Commons: The Spatial Politics of Prefiguration in the Case of Christiania Freetown

Jilly Traganou

Introduction

Acts of political disagreement often oscillate between 'speaking truth to power' and using violence to express rage. Prefigurative politics is a repertoire of political action that presents a different form of resistance: dissenting through making. The processes of materiality in which participants in prefigurative movements are involved include developing a differentiated spatiality – one that establishes distinct values and principles from the surrounding world and engages in intensive acts of maintenance and affective labour that bring the desired society into being.

I use the term 'prefigurative politics' here to refer to the embodiment, 'within the ongoing political practice of a movement, of those forms of social relations, decision-making, culture, and human experience that are the ultimate goal' (Boggs, 1977, p 100). What distinguishes prefigurative political processes from others is the aim to not only oppose a given condition but also build a preferred one. In what follows, I examine spatial and material prefigurative politics and their paradoxes from the viewpoint of Christiania Freetown in Copenhagen. I go on to discuss Christiania's methods of establishing a distinct spatiality autonomous of the state since the early 1970s, as well as their process of commoning – the act of participation in the creation of common resources through both directly engaging with materiality and building internal institutions of infrastructural provision and maintenance.

As much as Christiania is a remarkable case of perseverance and collective ingenuity, it also presents some troubling paradoxes that might be emblematic of prefigurative politics at large. In the last 50 years, while the external conditions of Danish political life have shifted from state-managed capitalism to a neoliberal or 'competition' state (Cerny, 1997), Christiania's focus on managing its socio-spatial autonomy – coupled with a limited degree of porosity and intergenerational renewal – appears to have distanced it from broader social struggles. Indeed, despite its own success and inspirational trajectory, it might be difficult to argue that Christiania has prefigured a model that other communities can adopt today, one that could be adapted to address the current concerns of urban social movements in Denmark or elsewhere.

A brief history of Christiania Freetown

Christiania Freetown – an autonomous, self-managed district of approximately 1,000 residents, proclaimed to be the 'biggest opportunity to build up a society from scratch' (Ludvigsen, 1971, p 10) – encapsulates some of the ideals of prefigurative political movements. Christiania was established in 1971 in the former 17th-century military base of Bådsmansstræde in the Christianshavn neighbourhood of Copenhagen. The early 1970s was an era of housing crisis in Copenhagen, and Christiania's first inhabitants were a group of young people – activists in the city's strong social movements – who broke in to the premises. These youth were in dire need of housing; many of them had become homeless after the police dismantled their squatted buildings in the area.[1] Residents of the overpopulated neighbourhood who sought opportunities to create open spaces and children's playgrounds were among the first to initiate the intrusion into this military area. As an autonomous community, Christiania has since operated beyond the state through processes of self-governance. In this, it expresses important principles of the right to the city movement – a notion of community determination first suggested by Henri Lefebvre in the late 1960s. As urban theorist Mark Purcell claims, Lefebvre's idea 'reorients decision-making away from the state … fundamentally shifting control … toward urban inhabitants' (2002, pp 101–2).

Christiania occupies 84 acres (34 hectares) and is subdivided into 14 residential areas, each with its own name and assembly. While Christiania perceives itself primarily as an anarchist community, it is mostly renowned for Pusher Street – an open-air cannabis market near its main entrance – and its frequent confrontation with law enforcement. An estimated one million people visit Christiania every year; busloads of tourists attend guided tours every weekend, and it is also a popular destination for locals, who attend music concerts at its venues, participate in its membership-based workshops, use its sauna and spend time in its green open-air grounds away from the city noise, vehicular traffic and night lights.

While, to a large degree, Christiania operates beyond the purview of the state, its autonomy would not be possible without the particular agreements it has signed with the Danish state. The political acknowledgement of Christiania came in 1972 when it was given the legal status of 'social experiment'. In 1973, the Christiania Law passed, giving permission for the inhabitants to live in the area – which still technically belonged to the state – provided they paid for electricity and water. After numerous legal battles, in 2011 the Danish government made Christiania an offer based on separating the land into three categories – the city area, the suburbs and the countryside; it proposed that Christiania purchase the buildings and land within the city area, rent the land in the suburbs and rent the buildings and land in the countryside. After much deliberation, Christiania decided to accept the offer, and in 2012 the newly created Christiania Foundation bought the land for €16.8 million. Approximately one third was deducted from the price because Christiania agreed to renovate and maintain the water, sewage and electrical facilities, as well as the streets and green areas. An additional percentage will be deducted from the mortgage if, as planned, Christiania renovates listed buildings of historical importance,[2] such as the 'Air Condition' (Aircondition) and the 'Dog House' (Hundehuset).[3] For urban sociologists Alessandro Coppola and Alberto Vanolo, who have studied Christiania's transformations since its establishment, this recent change signified a shift from an era of 'insurgent' autonomy to one of 'regulated' autonomy (regulated by the state law) (2015, p 1164); here, autonomy is considered 'a temporary and situated social construct' (2015, p 1155). Within this neoliberal framework, Christiania's autonomy is no longer based on separation from the state, since Christiania's current status is determined by its contractual agreements with state-based institutions.

Theoretical framework

Henri Lefebvre (1991) provides us with a conceptual framework for understanding space as both the condition and the product of social action. His trialectical understanding of space – space perceived, conceived and lived – addresses both the realm of spatial production (physical and conceptual space) and the interconnected realms of use, appropriation and agency (lived space). Although space and everyday life in the capitalist world are highly commodified and controlled, for Lefebvre, space 'holds the promise of liberation: ... from the tyranny of time, ... from social repression and exploitation, from self-imprisoning categories' (Smith, 2003, p xiii). Lefebvre uses the term 'differential spaces' (or 'counter-spaces') to describe spaces that operate 'against the Eye and the Gaze' (1991, p 382), restoring 'unity to what abstract space breaks up ... put[ting] an end to those localizations which shatter the integrity of the individual body, the social body, the corpus of human needs, and the corpus of knowledge'

(1991, p 52). This, according to Łukasz Stanek (2011, p 170), means that the everyday has the potential to become political by restituting the 'unity of understanding and action' (although, to clarify, Stanek adds that the politicization of the everyday does not assume 'its absorption into the political life, as in Stalinism').

Prefigurative political formations often acquire the character of place-bound, microcosmic experimental societies. Unlike the temporary framework of recent emblematic prefigurative efforts such as Occupy or Standing Rock, which functioned as protest camps, Christiania has a permanence. Yet, they are all characterized by the delineation of differentiated spatialities and the establishment of do-it-yourself (DIY) infrastructures (Feigenbaum et al, 2013) based on values – equality, horizontality and participation – that are distinct from those of the outside world. The space of prefigurative politics is different from public space in that it emerges beyond and in tension with the jurisdiction of the state or other authorities, through direct participation (of protestors, social movement activists, residents) in both its material making and its governance.

The microsociety that emerges in these territories is based on methods akin to commoning, collective egalitarian processes that guarantee the reproduction of life (Caffentzis and Federici, 2014, pp i101). According to Federici (2003), commons are the opposite of enclosures. Spaces of capitalism par excellence, enclosures originate from the privatized agricultural estates where waged labour was introduced at the fall of European feudalism. The term 'enclosure' is associated with the 'expropriation of workers from their common wealth' (Federici, 2003, p 69). Enclosures continue to proliferate today, and can be seen in a variety of typologies characteristic of late capitalism, such as gated communities and Silicon Valley-style campuses. Commons have recently emerged either as a means to 'reclaim' historically enclosed resources (claiming citizens' rights to use land, water and so on) or as emerging practices of creating new common provisions (such as community gardens in reclaimed vacant spaces, and open-access software). The act of participation is the basis of commoning and what creates the social bonding and collective governance of a commons. As Caffentzis and Federici emphasize, 'commons entail obligations as much as entitlements' (2014, p i102). But 'historically commons have not been prime examples of egalitarian relations' (2014, pp i102–i103). There is a delicate balance between the porosity of the commons – in other words, their openness to new community members – and the delineation of a commons territory, which often distinguishes between an outside and an inside. In addition, there is an eminent antagonism from external forces that threaten to repossess or appropriate the space of the commons, since capitalist conditions always render the land a contested category.

Christiania Freetown as a differential space

> Originally we were some people who grew tired of talking. … Instead
> of talking about how life could be, we said let's do it – here were
> the possibilities.
>
> (Interviewee in Nils Vest's film, *Christiania,*
> *You Have My Heart,* 1991)

The 'let's do it' attitude in this quote (from a Christianite) is characteristic of
protestors involved in prefigurative politics. Christianites began inhabiting
the abandoned military area through makeshift arrangements in the existing
barracks, as well as by constructing temporary sheds and bringing in portable
shelters, such as train wagons and trucks, which were gradually integrated
into more permanent structures. Christiania's status as a free town was
enacted with the gradual installation of an elaborate network of interlinked
DIY infrastructures and self-governing institutions for supporting shelter,
energy supply, learning and sanitation.[4] On the other hand, Christiania's
self-government has been undertaken mainly by the assemblies. There is an
assembly for each of the 14 local areas inside Christiania, a general assembly
for the whole of Christiania and financial assemblies that make decisions
about expenditure. This dual process of DIY materialization of space and
infrastructure, on the one hand, and participation in governing structures,
on the other, has nurtured the collective identity of Christianites as subjects
of an autonomous collectivity who take in their hands both the making of
their spatio-material environment and their governance structure (issues of
policing, financing, public works and so on).

The spatio-material production of Christiania has been substantially
different from that of the outside world. Within Christiania's defined
territory, we see the emergence of 'differential space' away from the spatial
practices and conceptions that characterize their surrounding city and
where the agency and imaginary of the inhabitants play a constitutive role.
According to architectural theorist Maria Hellström (2006), Christiania's
distinct conception of spatial development emerged through the 'paradigm
of *performativity*' (pp 17–20), while Christiania's space is characterized by
a counter-version of aestheticization (p 299). Indeed, Christiania's visual,
spatial and material languages are distinct from those prevalent in its direct
neighbourhood of Christianshavn – or in the rest of Copenhagen – while
also being far from unified; they vary from the visual languages typical of
squats (such as graffiti and bricolage) to include elements that for Ahnfeldt-
Mollerup (2004, p 59) are rooted in 18th-century bourgeois romanticism
and its critique of modernity. The different experiments found in Christiania
'have one decisive thing in common and that is the limitation that they must
be realized within a scavenger economy' (Ahnfeldt-Mollerup, 2004, p 61).

148

For Ahnfeldt-Mollerup, this aesthetic seems to be a commodity promoted in various parts of Denmark, such as small towns in the countryside, as an alternative Danish chic. Nevertheless, Christiania's spatial and material production derives from a socio-economic organization that is different from or even oppositional to the competitive economy that dominates the rest of the national territory.

Christiania's political economy is interlinked with the group's communitarian spirit and has a direct effect on spatial production and use. Christiania's 'purse' is a collective monetary fund that collects fees from residents, as well as a form of rent based on square-metre usage. This pays for all public consumption expenses and property tax. Christiania's funds are used to make and renovate homes (which do not belong to their inhabitant and cannot be inherited by family members), rendering its spatial production as one of use value rather than exchange value. Christiania also carries its own currency, which is used within its own grounds on a voluntary basis.

The principal method of spatial production in Christiania is spatial appropriation or spatial reclamation, which, to use Lefebvre's words, is what gives inhabitants the right to 'full and complete usage' of urban space in the course of everyday life (Lefebvre, 1996, cited in Purcell, 2002, p 103). For Purcell, 'appropriation reworks control over urban space, resisting the current hegemony of property rights and stressing the primacy of the use-rights of inhabitants. … When coupled with a central role for inhabitants in decision-making, appropriation poses a direct challenge to … the accumulation of capital in the modern era' (2002, p 103). Given this ideological distinction, it is not surprising that the state's offer to the Christianites – to buy Christiania's land – was initially repudiated by many of its members and found to be incompatible with their anarchist ideology.

The main access to Christiania from the side of the Christianshavn neighbourhood is defined largely by an external wall that separates it from the rest of the neighbourhood.[5] The wall – the hard border of barracks of the military precinct on Prinsessegade Street – lent itself to the delineation of the free town (Figure 10.1). The sign one sees at the main gate when about to exit Christiania, which reads 'You are now entering the EU', points to this sharp separation of a differentiated interiority, which is governed by a system that is self-defined as neatly distinct from that of Denmark and the European Union (Figure 10.2). Looked at from the outside, the wall encloses Christiania. Looked at from the inside, the wall leaves Christiania outside, free (a description inspired by Ursula K. Le Guin's [1974] *The Dispossessed: An Ambiguous Utopia*). Things are different outside the wall, and much of what Christianites need is available inside Christiania's borders. 'I hardly get outside of the fence because everything is here', declares a young mother, a Christiania-born woman interviewed in Vest's (1991) film. But this does not mean life in Christiania is easy: 'Sometimes I wanted to leave

Figure 10.1: External wall of former military building on Prinsessegade Street, Christiania, September 2018

Source: Jilly Traganou

Figure 10.2: You are now entering the EU. Gate of Christiania from the inside, September 2018

Source: Jilly Traganou

because life is different in Denmark and the outer world. The rules of the game are much simpler out there', says another Christianite, after 18 years of living in the community (in Vest, 1991).

It is an oxymoron that a fortified former military territory defines the spatiality of a community that envisioned itself as performing an exodus from the state. The dominance of the external wall becomes emblematic of numerous types of separation that Christiania reinstalls – perhaps inadvertently – by appropriating this piece of land. According to Christiania's archivist, Ole Lykke, in the 1970s, when Christiania was still publicly owned land, this closure was also convenient from the state's perspective:

'The thing about Christiania is that it belonged to the state – while whenever you squat a private house, you get thrown out. Immediately. But this belonged to the state. It was so big and there was no idea how to use it. Actually, when Christiania was created, there were quite a lot of squat houses, but two years after Christiania started, all the squatted houses had been raided and everyone went to Christiania. So I think they thought, let's get all those fucking squatters in one place.' (Interview with the author, September 2018)

As such, the spatial distinction of Christiania served both insiders – who were left free to develop their own distinct community in the spatially defined territory – and the state – which freed the rest of the city from squats by pushing all the squatters into Christiania, as Lykke stated above (a view which is not shared however by all Christianites who witnessed the Danish government's attempts to evacuate Christiania on April 1, 1976).

Within this demarcated territory, a strong materialist ethos emerged, as seen in the numerous new houses (Figure 10.3) and renovations of existing buildings. However, in the transition to regulated autonomy, this ethos has been severely compromised. The state's restrictions on new constructions infringes on the community's capacity to self-realize its material – and, by extension, social – environment. For Ole Kristensen, interviewed in Jackman and Lawson's 2014 film *Christiania: 40 Years of Occupation*, the very act of DIY building, which is at the core of appropriation, has a revolutionary capacity: 'After the government imposed the moratorium on the construction, everyone keeps their construction material ready. ... It becomes a small surrender if you let go of ... the building materials ... I call them weapons of mass construction.'

Christiania Freetown as a space of commons

Christiania's open areas (see Figure 10.4) are open to all citizens and visitors for a stroll, consumption or congregation, thus functioning as a form of

Figure 10.3: A house in Christiania, September 2018

Source: Jilly Traganou

Figure 10.4: Christiania's Main Street, September 2018

Source: Jilly Traganou

public space. But most importantly they comprise the communal space of Christiania, and are cared for and governed by its members. Numerous authors, including architects Steen Eiler Rasmussen (1976) and Maria Hellström Reimer (2011), have discussed the territory of Christiania as a space of commons. Commons have a specific social purpose. According to Hellström, they allow for 'deviations from the norm; at the same time providing protection for those who deviate' (Hellström Reimer, 2011, p 125). 'The connectedness offered by the commons is … impregnated with a socially conditioned desire for vagrancy, for the exploration of "escape routes"' (Hellström Reimer, 2011, p 127, quoting Papadopoulos et al, 2008).

The spatial and material agency of Christiania's actors – who vary from people with no or little monetary power to 'pushers' who gain high untaxed revenues through their involvement in the cannabis market – has shaped a particular political imaginary, and vice versa. It is important to note that Christiania's differential space is open to not only individuals who aspire to principles of anarchism or autonomy but also to people experiencing hardship, such as homelessness, who might have different ideology, or, as Christiania's own leaflets put it, to society's 'black sheep'[6] – which is how Christianites saw themselves in the early 1970s. If Christiania's exterior – the formal space of the city and the state – has no space for these subjects, the Freetown offers them an opportunity to both belong to a community and have a safety net. This has meant that certain groups at the fringes of society have been welcomed in Christiania and found it to be a refuge, while others – such as motorbike gang members and individuals who deal hard drugs – have been expelled by Christianites when their presence or activities were deemed incompatible with the community's wellbeing or other shared principles. Copenhagen planner Kai Lemberg saw Christiania as a place that had taken upon itself the task of 'resocialising' individuals who, for different reasons, had given up on traditional society (Lemberg, 1978, quoted in in Thörn et al, 2011, p 17), while criminologist Flemming Balvig and colleagues indicated that Christiania's crime rate between 1972 and 1975 showed a downward trend compared to the rest of Copenhagen (Balvig et al, 1978, cited in Thörn et al, 2011, p 15). Thus, the handling of crime by Christianites themselves – today assisted by the text-message group 'Christiania Accute SMS Chain' (Christiania Akut Sms-kæde) – and their sheltering of certain subjectivities that would be unwelcomed in the outside world, has been considered effective.

Embodied infrastructures and communal knowledge

Nobody comes and fixes things like in the city. So you start digging. You must do it all yourself with the help of those who know.

(Interviewee in Vest, 1991)

With their collective engagements in the spatial and material making of their territory, Christianites' commoning comes into life. As in other spaces of prefigurative politics (protest camps, occupied spaces, municipal cities), the work of spatial and material maintenance and the labour of social reproduction are emphatically recognized, valorized, redistributed between genders and brought to the fore as core aspects of what it means to be a community member. Christiania's spatial development was, until recently, undertaken directly by the inhabitants, either through building new constructions or by renovating existing ones. Christianites learned about building construction by virtue of living in the community. As one resident claims: 'I have been living here for 18 years and I have been building a lot and partly that is what [it] is all about. This is about building houses and how to organise a society' (in Jackman and Lawson, 2014). Through processes of participatory governance in the early years, Christianites had to obtain the approval of their neighbours and the building assembly before making physical changes to their houses, and were asked to leave Christiania if they left their homes empty for an extended period of time, as was the case of long-term resident, Irma Clausen (interview with the author, September 2018).

In the era of insurgence autonomy, Christianites faced everyday difficulties due to the lack of infrastructure; amenities like toilets, running water and sewage could not simply be taken for granted. To manage and maintain these necessities, people had to learn from others and eventually become able to install and fix things themselves. These processes are examples of 'embodied infrastructures' (Traganou, 2016, 2019) that emerge from participants' collective action and direct engagement with things, as opposed to the passive use of products and services provided by the market or state. The acceptance of vulnerability – of both bodies and machines – and an understanding of their interdependence are at the core of embodied infrastructures.

When infrastructure began to be installed to support the houses – initially directly by the women of Christiania, who dug trenches in the streets and laid pipes for water – the community recognized that something was lost (Irma Clausen, interview with the author, September 2018). The social transformations wrought by eliminating collective and affective practices of labour in the use of resources were also felt in the subsequent decline in collective cooking and daily support for each other's lives and sustainment. This is further accentuated by the invisibility of the infrastructural provision and its technical apparatus. Inherent in modernity, and taken for granted in capitalist society, infrastructural changes – often framed as improvements – affected Christiania's everyday living modalities and, subsequently, social relationships. Infrastructure rendered 'naturalized' and consumed by individual units has, in some ways, become a norm in Christiania, especially in its nuclear-family households, minimizing the differences between their everyday lives and life outside Christiania.

Creating and self-managing infrastructure, however, was essential to Christiania's autonomy from the state, and an internal communal knowledge of technical issues became indispensable to the community's survival and radicalization in the early years. From early on, Christianites engaged in garbage collection and recycling – a profitable undertaking that has now developed into the fully comprehensive service of the Machine Hall (*Maskinhallen*), where the garbage trucks and tools are kept. Christianites also installed their own water treatment systems, while Nabovarme – a sophisticated self-managed heating system based on wood pellets[7] – is gradually replacing older, polluting technologies such as wood-burning stoves.[8] As well as being a means of reducing dependence on both the state and the market, these changes reflect the community's environmental goals.

While individual engagement with infrastructure is not standard among Christiania's residents, the notion of communal knowledge, which is still carefully safeguarded, differentiates Christiania's infrastructural approach from the conventional attitudes of the modern capitalist system. The line between communal knowledge and communal institutionalization, however, is blurry. The further away the community moves from the practices of embodied infrastructures, the more it risks falling into the paradigm of mediation, abstraction, hierarchical division of labour and passive consumption of resources, which is antithetical to ecological consciousness and practice as well as incompatible with the principles of self-governance and horizontality. One strategy that Christiania is using as a way to mitigate this is by not fully avoiding internal hierarchy, which they find necessary at times, but by constantly dismantling it. 'Hierarchies are created all the time', and destroyed all the times', Emmerik Warburg, Christiania's caretaker said in an interview.

> 'Hierarchy is a good thing, a very good thing. But it is not good to have a stable hierarchy. So don't organize it too well. Because then you just have it on your back. It's like fire. It's a very good servant but it's a bad ruler.' (Emmerik Warburg, interview with the author, September 2018)

A similar transformation is noted in the realm of spatial production, which, in the era of regulated autonomy, has become normalized due to being fully regulated by municipal law. Permissions for all new construction and renovations are mandatory, and there are restrictions on new construction,[8] which is only allowed for replacement of severely compromised buildings. For this reason, Christiania has hired non-resident professional architects and administrators to help out in the Construction Office (*Byggekontoret*) – an important section of Christiania's governance structure. These experts are in charge of general liaison with municipal offices, designing or drafting the drawings for renovations or new constructions, compiling and submitting the required paperwork to the municipal office, managing the permissions process and undertaking or supervising, in close collaboration with Christianites, the construction processes. In this way, spatial action and knowledge are being gradually removed from individual community members; these practices become institutionalized and professionalized internally in accordance with the state or municipal law, unlike the communal self-determination that characterized the earlier era. Notwithstanding these changes, construction methods developed by the community over the decades of its existence – such as breathable buildings and participatory processes of designing, renovating and constructing – are still incorporated in current practices. At the same time, these practices keep budgets significantly lower and timelines faster compared to the approaches taken outside Christiania, and this is important for Christiania's – now regulated – autonomy.

The paradox of enclosed commons

The illegitimate marriage between a fenced territory and the anarchist imagination that gave birth to Christiania seems, today, to have been turned on its head. The congruence of residency and membership in Christiania has created a sometimes rigid division between insiders and outsiders. This observation is not to minimize the degrees of differentiation among insiders, who make up a far from monolithic community. Nevertheless, through the socio-spatial differentiation of Christiania into an outside and an inside – criticized by Marta Llobet Estany (2005), a sociologist and friend of Christiania – a number of conflicts and contradictions have emerged.[9] The realm of Christiania's outside is constituted by the state and its institutions, as well as by individuals or groups of non-residents with or without ties to the community, whose actions and affiliation are scrutinized by the insiders. These non-residents include friends, employees, visitors, tourists, candidate residents and undesirables.

While the ethos of hospitality is present in today's Christiania as far as the use of the open space is concerned, and members' support to people who face homelessness, outside members' use of open space alone does not provide rights of membership. The community's selection of new residents follows restrictive processes (also due to the Anders Fogh Rasmussen government's restrictions of new people settling in Christiania from 2004 to 2011), and outsiders criticize it for being based on non-transparent criteria. Estany (2005) notes that a noted hesitancy of adding new members has led to a lack of intergenerational renewal in Christiania. She sees this as a major hindrance to Christiania's future, because much of the energy the community needs could come from young people. Christiania's inflexible regulations have also made it difficult for members' children to regain their residence status in Christiania after being away.

This lack of porosity is a major compromise to Christiania as commons. A commons, by definition, should challenge the private or exclusive status of any enclosures. While Christiania opposes the ideas of capitalist enclosures and (arguably) still provides a sanctuary to its own members and people in need, today it faces the danger that Mark Purcell detected in the very concept of the right to the city movement, which – unlike other advocates of the concept – he doesn't consider inherently emancipatory. Rather, Purcell (2002, p 105) calls for a broader definition of political participation, suggesting the term 'transurban inhabitants' – an identification that defeats insularity and transcends narrowly defined understandings of place-bound identity and local governance. For Purcell, the right to the city needs to introduce an entirely different arrangement for overcoming the distinction between the '"us" [as] those who inhabit the city … [and] "them" [as] those who inhabit other places' (2002, p 105).

While Christiania operates under conditions of self-determination, it is often perceived as exclusive, insular, and indifferent to struggles in its surrounding territory. Non-Christianites complain that Christianites are absorbed in their own legal battles and are unresponsive to problems faced by young people, migrants and those with low income today – which are analogous to those the Christianites faced in the early 1970s. Today's Christiania seems to contradict its own origins and the type of future it endeavoured to prefigure for all those self-identified as the 'black sheep' of Danish society. As a result, Christiania's credibility as a political undertaking is called into doubt due to its limited social porosity with the outside world.

Conclusion

As an egalitarian community that aspired to forge an alternative society in 1970s Copenhagen, Christiania Freetown has resonated with the dreams of young people and social movements across the globe. Christiania today is one of the few enduring examples of socio-spatial autonomy in which a fairly large group of people practice 'right to the city' principles in an environment that operates beyond state control. Five decades since its inception, Christiania continues to operate in a differentiated spatial territory, self-managed and self-governed by its members.

Tracing Christiania Freetown's trajectory allows us to see the permutations of a community that began by prefiguring an alternative society for all marginalized people and slowly transformed into a self-referential, place-bound community. Christiania still offers important insights as a laboratory of self-governance, but its connection with the struggles of its surrounding society has become less visible. While Danish society is affected by a broader crisis of care – as seen in today's welfare deficits and commercialization of public goods – Christiania has been intensely preoccupied with its self-preservation in response to the numerous waves of attacks from the Danish government in the 50 years of its history. This has weakened the 'diffusion and the contamination of its ideas, messages and goals among wider networks and constituencies' (Yates, 2015, p 1), which, for Yates, is one of the conditions for prefigurative politics.[10] Christiania's case, therefore, requires us to contend with the challenges and paradoxes inherent in the notions of differential spatialities and the commons, which are imminent in place-bound prefigurative political formations – and are only further accentuated when a community's political horizon loses its capaciousness and attends mainly to localized needs. A trans-urban Christiania beyond its spatial, social and political limits is yet to emerge.

Acknowledgments

I conducted this research as a Christiania Researcher in Residence during my sabbatical in fall 2018. I am grateful to Emmerik Warburg, Ole Lykke, Irma Clausen, Britta Lillesøe and Kristoffer Ek for sharing with me their work in and on Christiania, as well as Kristine Samson and Michael Haldrup Pedersen of Roskilde University for hosting me as a visiting professor (research appointment) during my residency in Christiania, and to Parsons School of Design, The New School, for financial and intellectual support.

Notes

[1] Such was the Sofiegården squat – part of the Slumstormer movement – in the same area.

[2] The overall sale price was kr 125 million (equivalent to approximately €16.8 million). From this, kr 40 million (€5.4 million, or 32 per cent) was deducted for the infrastructural work, and kr 30 million (€4.0 million, or 24 per cent) was to be deducted on the basis of renovation work (Christiania, nd).

[3] In addition, Christiania is currently renovating the Ark of Peace (*Fredens Ark*) built in 1837, 'the largest half-timbered house in Northern Europe' (Christianites, 2004, p 21). According to Emmerik Warburg, this building 'is not historically listed, but in a very poor condition. Before the 2011 agreement, the government claimed that prior to making any agreement or sale, the Foundation had to promise to buy the house for kr 1.00 (€0.13) which Christiania agreed to do. Based on a partnership agreement with the City of Copenhagen, the Christiania Foundation will pay 2/3 of the renovation costs and the city will pay the remaining 1/3' (email communication with Emmerik Warburg, July 2020).

[4] These categories are analogous to those found in protest camps, as analysed by Feigenbaum et al (2013).

[5] The wall does not fully enclose Christiania's territory, only the side that borders with the Christianshavn neighbourhood.

[6] One of Christiania's early mottoes was 'Black sheep from all classes unite!'

[7] Nabovarme, meaning 'neighbour heating', is an independent pellet heating system with open-source software and hardware, and the goal of optimizing usage for economic and climate reasons. It is built on ideas of social empowerment and is transforming passive heat consumers into active users, causing community members to take ownership of the infrastructure (Valbjorn and Warburg, 2017).

[8] The replacement of old constructions with new ones must not exceed the existing footprint. However, the current conservative administration passed a bill that mandates the construction of 15,000 square metres of subsidized housing in Christiania, which is currently contested by Christianites.

9   A well-known example of a conflict that led to Christianites' enforcement of a ban against a specific group is the restriction of the biker gang Bullshit from Christiania in the 1980s. A recent example of a self-imposed enclosure was the COVID-19 lockdown in spring 2020, when the community closed its doors to the outside world and barricaded its exits (email communication with Emmerik Warburg, June 2020).

10 According to Yates (2015, p 1), 'prefigurative politics combines five processes: collective experimentation, the imagining, production and circulation of political meanings, the creating of new and future-orientated social norms or "conduct", their consolidation in movement infrastructure, and the diffusion and contamination of ideas, messages and goals to wider networks and constituencies'.

References

Ahnfeldt-Mollerup, M. (2004) 'Christiania's aesthetics: you can't kill us/we are part of you', in K. Dirckink-Holmfeld and M. Keiding (eds) *Learning from Christiania/Christianias lære*, Copenhagen: Arkitektens förlag, pp 56–7.

Balvig, F., Koch, H. and Vestergaard, J. (1976) *Politiets virksomhed på Christiania* (Police Operation on Christiania), Kriminalistisk institut: Københavns universitet.

Boggs, C. (1977) 'Marxism, prefigurative communism and the problem of workers' control', *Radical America*, 11(6): 99–122.

Caffentzis, G. and Federici, S. (2014) 'Commons against and beyond capitalism', *Community Development Journal*, 49(1): i92–i105.

Cerny, P. (1997) 'Paradoxes of the competition state: the dynamics of political globalization', *Government and Opposition*, 32(2), 251–74.

Christiania (nd) 'Christiania 2013' [online], available from: https://www.christiania.org/info/christiania-2013/

Christianites (2004) *Christianias Guide* (4th edn) [online], available from: https://www.diggers.org/christiania/ChristianiaGuide2004.pdf

Coppola, A. and Vanolo, A. (2015) 'Normalising autonomous spaces: ongoing transformations in Christiania, Copenhagen', *Urban Studies*, 52(6): 1152–68.

Estany, M.L. (2005) In conversation with Itziar González Virós, *Diálogo a dos voces sobre Christiania* (private correspondence with Marta Llobet Estany and Irma Clause).

Federici, S. (2003) *Caliban and the Witch: Women, the Body and Primitive Accumulation*, New York and London: Autonomedia, Pluto.

Feigenbaum, A., Frenzel, F. and McCurdy, P. (2013) *Protest Camps*, London and New York: Zed Books.

Hellström, M. (2006) *Steal this Place: The Aesthetics of Tactical Formlessness and 'The Free Town of Christiania'*, PhD dissertation, Swedish University of Agricultural Sciences [online], available from: https://pub.epsilon.slu.se/1319/1/reimer_hellstrom_m_201119.pdf

Hellström Reimer, M. (2011) 'Christiania Copenhagen: a common out of the ordinary', in A. Jorgensen and R. Keenan (eds) *Urban Wildscapes*, London: Routledge, pp 120–30.

Jackman, R. and Lawson, R. (2014) *Christiania: 40 Years of Occupation* [film], NTSC, Dreamscape.

Le Guin, U.K. (1974) *The Dispossessed: An Ambiguous Utopia*, New York, NY: Harper Prism.

Lefebvre, H. (1991) *The Production of Space*, trans D. Nicholson Smith, Oxford: Blackwell.

Lefebvre, H. (1996) *Writings on Cities*, Cambridge, MA: Blackwell.

Lemberg, K. (1978) 'A squatter settlement in Copenhagen: slum, ghetto or social experiment?' International Review, 1, US Department of Housing and Development.

Ludvigsen, J. (1971) 'Emigrer med linie 8', *Hovedbladet*, 39(1): 10–11.

Purcell, M. (2002) 'Excavating Lefebvre: the right to the city and its urban politics of the inhabitant', *GeoJournal*, 58: 99–108.

Rasmussen, S.E. (1976) *Omkring Christiania* [*Around Christiania*], København: Gyldendals.

Smith, N. (2003) 'Foreword', in H. Lefebvre (ed) *Urban Revolution*, London and Minneapolis: University of Minnesota Press, pp vii–xxiii.

Stanek, Ł. (2011) *Henri Lefebvre on Space: Architecture, Urban Research, and the Production of Theory*, Minneapolis, MN: University of Minnesota Press.

Thörn, H., Wasshede, C. and Nilson, T. (2011) 'Introduction: from "social experiment" to "urban alternative" – 40 years of research on the Freetown', in H. Thörn, C. Wasshede and T. Nilson (eds) *Space for Urban Alternatives?* Goteborg: Gidlunds förlag, pp 7–37.

Traganou, J. (2016) *Designing the Olympics: Representation, Participation, Contestation*, London: Routledge.

Traganou, J. (2019) 'Learning from the Standing Rock as a site for transformative intercultural pedagogy', in R. Halter and C. Walthard (eds) *Cultural Spaces and Design: Prospects of Design Education*, Basel: Librum Publishers & Editors, pp 77–91.

Valbjorn, J. and Warburg, E. (2017) '"Nabovarme" opensource heating infrastructure in Christiania' [online], available from: https://media.ccc.de/v/34c3-8989-nabovarme_opensource_heating_infrastructure_in_christiania

Vest, N. (1991) *Christiania You Have My Heart* [film], Copenhagen: Nils Vest Film.

Yates, L. (2015) 'Rethinking prefiguration: alternatives, micropolitics and goals in social movements', *Social Movement Studies*, 14(1): 1–21.

11

Prefiguring Post-Patriarchal Futures: Jineolojî's Matristic Praxis in the Context of Rojava's Revolution

Eleonora Gea Piccardi

Introduction

Prefigurative politics are practised by social movements that embody, in the here and now, the future society they desire. These movements do not represent 'pure' utopias, free from the contradictions of our times (see du Plessis and Husted, this volume), but by engaging in 'radical' forms of politics (Dinerstein and Deneulin, 2012), they pursue the daily collective effort of fostering a post-capitalist and post-development society in the midst of a systemic crisis. Among them, the Zapatista uprising and Rojava revolution are recognized as prominent examples of prefiguration (Monticelli, 2018, 2021) or 'pluriversal prefiguration' (Dinerstein, this volume; Escobar, this volume); they are 'concrete utopias' (Dinerstein, 2017) based on indigenous stateless democracy, autonomous self-government, ecological and communal economy, and women's leadership.

Democratic Confederalism, a new paradigm of sociopolitical organization installed by the Kurdish Freedom Movement in North and East Syria since 2012, has the original characteristic of grounding its revolutionary project on: (a) the subversion of patriarchy as the root of modern/colonial capitalism and nation states and (b) the liberation of women as the first step towards socioecological freedom. As a consequence, either decolonization or the transition to a post-capitalist society are assumed to be part of a larger process of de-patriarchization. The latter is based on the recovering and renewing of the Kurdish and Rojava's matristic culture, towards what I call a 'matristic perspective', or the emancipatory horizon of a post-patriarchal society.

Indeed, the idea of a matristic culture as both an ancestral past and a possible emancipatory future is at the centre of Jineolojî – the science of women and life – an epistemology and methodology of women's liberation created by the Kurdish women's movement over the last decade, and the main guiding knowledge of Democratic Confederalism (Piccardi and Barca, 2022).

In this chapter, I aim to analyse both the theoretical discourse and concrete application of the matristic perspective developed by Jineolojî in the context of the Rojava revolution. In particular, I highlight the leading role of Jineolojî's pedagogical activities, which I argue are the crucial terrain of a matristic prefigurative praxis that – paraphrasing Monticelli (2018) – works towards a post-patriarchal society by embodying that society in the present. As such, Jineolojî represents not just a science but also a militant pedagogy or a knowledge practice able to further the process of de-patriarchization endorsed by Democratic Confederalism in North and East Syria.

New matriarchies and the Kurdish matristic perspective

Spurred by the growing relevance of women's, indigenous and peasant movements and struggles across the world, the ideas of 'matriarchy', 'matristic culture' and 'new matriarchy' have recently been rediscovered as highly relevant to alternative worldmaking. In a recent work on the pluriverse, Arturo Escobar argues that overcoming patriarchy and recovering 'matristic cultures' can lay the foundations for civilizational alternatives (Escobar, 2018, p 13; see also Escobar, this volume). In *Pluriverse: A Post-Development Dictionary*, Kothari et al list matriarchy as a global vision and practice 'grounded in women's struggles for survival' (Kothari et al, 2019, p 31) that links political emancipation with environmental justice and counters the Western model of development.

This emancipatory perspective is rooted in materialist and postcolonial (eco)feminisms, which have contributed to critical approaches on growth and development by arguing that capitalism and colonialism are the latest stage of patriarchy (Salleh, 2017; Gregoratti and Raphael, 2019). In particular, these scholars have defined patriarchy as a world-scale system that, by exploiting and devaluing women's work, colonized people and the natural world, has allowed the accumulation of capital and the exhaustion of the Earth's resources (Mies and Shiva, 1993; Merchant, 1996; Federici, 2012). In other words, women's unpaid labour and the labour of the 'forces of reproduction' (Barca, 2020) are 'systematically backgrounded' (Plumwood, 1993, p 21), representing the material and historical conditions in which productive forces, technological innovation and 'modernization' projects in postcolonial contexts are developed.

The idea of matriarchal cultures and societies emerges from this line of thought. In particular, it emerges from the need to search for materialistic origins of the sexual division of labour and of the subordination of reproduction to the production of goods under capitalism (Mies, 1986). Engaging in this search, authors like Maria Mies and Claudia von Werlhof describe patriarchy as a 'predatory' (Mies, 1986) or 'alchemical' system (von Werlhof, 2019, p 255), one that has progressively robbed and destroyed pre-patriarchal/matriarchal ways of organizing and (re)producing life, replacing societies based on the Earth, life and subsistence with societies aiming to accumulate profit and power.

In a recent writing, von Werlhof (2019, p 254) speaks of 'matriarchy today as a "second culture" within patriarchy'; she argues that matriarchy is the only possible solution to capitalism and to prevent post-development movements from 'evolving into post-capitalist neo-patriarchies' (2019, p 255). She argues that remnants of matriarchal culture have survived and that new ones have emerged, particularly among indigenous societies, suggesting that the Zapatista movement and Rojava revolution are examples of 'new matriarchy' and 'alternatives to modernity' in their attempts to move 'beyond destructive and violent relationships with nature, women, children, and society in general' (Werlhof, 2019, p 255).

Theoretically elaborated by Abdullah Öcalan – leader of the Kurdistan Workers' Party (Partiya Karkerên Kurdistanê, PKK) – both Democratic Confederalism and Jineolojî (its guiding knowledge) ground their emancipatory proposal in arguments similar to those of ecofeminism (Piccardi, 2022). The main idea at the basis of Öcalan's writings on the subject is that women are the 'oldest colonised people' and that their oppression is a matrix of both human–nature alienation and social hierarchies between classes, ethnicities, religions and genders (Öcalan, 2013). Beginning 5,000 years ago, when the communal and 'matricentric' Neolithic society transitioned to the first patriarchal, class and statist societies, Öcalan writes that the degradation of women's role reached its greatest expression in capitalist modernity (Öcalan, 2013, p 13). Building on Maria Mies' concept of 'housewifization' (the relegation of women to the role of housewife), Öcalan argues that capitalism led to women's household domestication and, through the institution of the family, to the exploitation and devaluation of their 'life-producing work' (as Mies defined it) – work that was at the centre of 'Neolithic Mother–Goddess' societies (Öcalan, 2020). As such, his proposal of a 'sociology of freedom'[1] for the Middle East is based on women's need to free themselves from housewifization, restore their pivotal role in society and recover the matristic forms of communality that were attacked by modernization, environmental devastation and cultural assimilation in the Kurdish territory (Öcalan, 2017).

However, I am not sure we can comprehend either Democratic Confederalism or the Rojava revolution as 'new matriarchies', as von Werlhof does. As she admits, the majority of the movements or indigenous societies she refers to 'do not call themselves matriarchies' (2019, p 255). On the contrary: the idea of matriarchal societies is highly contested within both ecofeminist movements, since it risks reproducing essentialist visions of women as naturally closest to Mother Earth and nature (see Gaard, 2011), and indigenous and decolonial feminisms, since it risks romanticizing supposedly pre-modern traditional cultures as bearers of non-patriarchal values. Indeed, referring to Latin America history, Rita Segato and Julieta Paredes point out that patriarchal relations were not absent in African American or indigenous communities; rather, the modernity/coloniality process produced a 'junction of patriarchies' (Paredes, 2012, p 71, translation by the author), with colonial patriarchies co-opting, transforming and strengthening 'low-intensity' indigenous and tribal patriarchies (Segato, 2014, p 77, translation by the author).

Decolonial and indigenous feminists thus emphasize that the de-patriarchization of their movements and communities is a necessary process, one inextricably linked with decolonization (Galindo, 2015) and collective memory reconstruction (Cabnal, 2010). For this reason, I prefer to talk about 'processes of "matriarchalization"' (Escobar, 2018, p 16) or matristic perspectives to describe not what a society *is* but the emancipatory horizon that informs daily prefigurative praxis towards a post-patriarchal world.

It is through these lenses that I approach the revolutionary process occurring in North and East Syria today. The development of a matristic perspective has characterized the Kurdish movement's praxis since the declaration of Democratic Confederalism in 2005;[2] encompassed in the Kurdish slogan *jin, jiyan, azadi* (woman, life, freedom), this outlook is currently at the core of women's mobilization in Rojava. I deepen this argument in the following sections, presenting women's leading role within Rojava's confederalist system and identifying Jineolojî as the main pedagogical praxis that has turned the matristic perspective into a concrete utopia – a decolonial, de-patriarchal strategy for socioecological emancipation, led by women but addressing society as a whole.

Rojava's women's revolution: towards a matristic future

After the outbreak of civil war in Syria in 2011 and the liberation of the major cities of Kobane, Afrin and Qamislo from Syrian state troops, the Kurdish Freedom Movement promoted the implementation of an autonomous administration in Rojava (in the north and later also the east of Syria). This administration was based on the three pillars of Democratic

Confederalism: radical democracy, ecology and women's liberation (Saed, 2015; Leezenberg, 2016). From this moment, a system of grassroots communes and councils in every city neighbourhood, village and canton[3] became the main instrument of people's self-organization, as ratified by the Social Contract of the Democratic Federation of Northern Syria.[4] This reorganization subverted the state and replaced liberal representative democracy with the direct participation of citizens in every decision about their life – from justice to education, self-defence and economic management (Knapp and Jongerden, 2016).

This radical revolution attracted the attention of scholars and activists, particularly for the emphasis Democratic Confederalism places on women's liberation, not as a marginal or secondary aim – a 'women's affair' to be postponed until after decolonization – but as a key strategy towards an ecological and stateless socialism. Since the beginning of the revolution, a huge process of women's self-determination and self-defence has taken place – not only at the military level, with the constitution of the autonomous female guerrilla Women's Protection Units (Yekîneyên Parastina Jin) (Tank, 2017; Ferreira and Santiago, 2018), but also through the construction of a women's autonomous administration, called Kongra Star (Star Congress). The latter, which parallels the mixed-sex self-government structure of Tev-Dem (Movement for a Democratic Society), has the power to establish rights and laws on gender issues, and even to veto the decisions of the mixed-sex structure (Dirik, 2018a). Thanks to this autonomous structure, women have created their own grassroots assemblies (*Mala Jin*, Houses of Women), economic cooperatives, justice committees, Asayish (Women's Guard) and many other institutions, giving them autonomous political agency, the ability to meet their own needs and the conditions to express their will – all free from the control of men (Pavičić-Ivelja, 2017; Şimşek and Jongerden, 2018).

Comparing Rojava's experience with the Marxist–Leninist and anarchist experiences, Rasit and Kolokotronis argue that Rojava's innovative shift relies on the representation of women as 'a revolutionary middle stratum' – that is, 'a distinct revolutionary group with autonomous power that can push forward the revolutionary process while dispersing the authority of the vanguard movement' (Rasit and Kolokotronis, 2020, p 2). The authors identify three spheres in which the women's movement's capacity to lead appears. The first is the ideological sphere; women are seen 'as a primary historical revolutionary agent that will contribute to emancipation of all' (Rasit and Kolokotronis, 2020, p 7) – this reflects Abdullah Öcalan's and the Kurdish women's movement's theoretical elaboration of Democratic Confederalism's matristic perspective. The second is the organizational sphere, in which women's autonomous structures are considered 'the most central tenet of revolutionary struggle' (Rasit and Kolokotronis, 2020, p 8), corresponding to the afore-mentioned self-organizing process. The third sphere is characterized as what enables these organizational achievements, and coincides with 'recruitment', 'education' or 'mobilization' practices led by women. Though this last sphere is empirically underexplored (with the exception of Biehl, 2015, and Dirik, 2018b), women's political education in North and East Syria is a crucial field of the women's movement's praxis; it not only serves to articulate the other two spheres but is also the junction between the movement's matristic perspective and its organizational efforts. This is evident if we look at the revolutionary pedagogical process led by Jineolojî's committees in Rojava.

Until now, Jineolojî has been framed as an original Kurdish epistemology closed relatedly to intersectional (Shahvisi, 2018) or decolonial/transnational feminisms (Al-Ali and Käser, 2020). It is seen as 'a framework of radical feminist analysis' (Neven and Shäfers, 2017), one that condenses the philosophical developments of the Kurdish women's struggle within the PKK, and that informs each institution in Rojava. However, in addition to this framing, I consider Jineolojî to be a prefigurative praxis of de-patriarchization/matriarchalization, due to its practical commitment to women's education and emancipatory pedagogy. Indeed, it is a common ground in the literature to consider (adult self-)education and militant pedagogy as fundamental practice of prefiguration (see Raekstad, this volume; De Vita and Vittori, this volume) and, vice versa, to conceive prefigurative praxis as able to form new/revolutionary subjectivities. As Motta (2016, p 42) argues, 'prefigurative epistemologies are inherently pedagogical, in that they involve the development of practices of (un)learning that enable decolonizing [and, I would add, de-patriarchizing] practices of transformation'.

I develop this argument in the subsequent sections, looking at the pedagogical strategies the Jineolojî committees carry out at grassroots level. In particular, I outline some characteristics of this process that, during my militant ethnography in Rojava and Europe (2018–20), emerged as crucial: the promotion of women's *xwebûn* (being/becoming oneself), the attempt at building communal forms of life between women and the efforts to subvert dominant masculinities.

Perwerde: sharing women's experiences, elaborating collective solutions

Starting from 2011, when Jineolojî's work began within the Free Women's Party of Kurdistan (Partiya Azadîya Jinên Kurdistan), Jineolojî committees have been organized in the four regions of Kurdistan, in the Middle East, as well as in Europe. In Rojava, Jineolojî is an interrelated part of the Kongra Star, the women's autonomous system of government. Its members organize themselves under the umbrella name Jineolojî Academy, which consists of different autonomous projects: six centres in the cities of Derik, Kobane, Haseke, Manbij and Tabqa, and the Shehba refugee camps, where people who fled the Turkish occupation of Afrin now live; schools, where Jineolojî classes have been included in the curriculum since 2017, and the University of Rojava, which has a Jineolojî department; the Andrea Wolf Institute, an internationalist structure that includes women from all over the world in Jineolojî work; and Jinwar, a women's autonomous ecovillage. Beyond these structures, Jineolojî training activities have been carried out in grassroots communes, economic cooperatives, councils and every academy (mixed-sex and women-only) in Rojava – from the popular academies to those for the armed self-defence units.

Educational practices (*perwerde* in Kurdish) are the main tool through which Jineolojî updates matristic theoretical research with women's experiential knowledge and collective memory, shares this knowledge and memory with others and uses it to elaborate collective solutions. Even if these activities are not restricted to women only, women are considered the main subjects of Jineolojî and are the ones who should create 'their own disciplines, build up their meanings and share them with the society' (Deniz, 2018, p 53). Some of the most important features of Jineoliojî *perwerde* are analysed in the following subsections.

Building women's *xwebûn*

Training activities – which can range in length from one day to ten days to three months – are usually organized to answer a community demand, and women of that community are involved in planning the training programme. The programmes may consist of general topics – such as women's history and struggles; the rise of patriarchy, the nation state and capitalism; and the role of the family in social life – or practical issues linked to the organization of life within the confederalist system. As emerged from my 'observant participation' (Pons Rabasa, 2018) of Jineolojî *perwerde* in Rojava and Europe, the educational activities are not top-down pedagogies but rather sharing moments, and they are ridden with discussions, questions, critique and self-critique. Instructors are not 'experts'; they are either Jineolojî members who shift between the roles of 'student' and 'teacher' or women with responsibilities in different areas of the movement.

Opening questions – such as: What is it to be a woman for you? When did you meet patriarchy in your life? What is the history of your people, of your family? – help to stimulate a 'self-reflexive collective practice' (Mohanty, 2003, p 8) in which each woman's class, ethnicity, religion and age become central to both personal and collective liberation. bell hooks describes a similar process in her discussion of 'becoming subjects', which occurs when 'one comes to understand how structures of domination work in one's own life'; it is characterized by the development of critical thinking and consciousness, as well as creating 'alternative habits of being' (hooks, 1990, p 15). This is what Jineolojî members call *xwebûn* – a practice of self-definition and self-consciousness that strengthens self-determination and autonomy as the bases of women's collective agency. Indeed, it is through women's *xwebûn* that the matristic perspective can be activated:

> 'We must reflect on matriarchal society, without the state and without the mentality of power and patriarchy. It is difficult, but it can be done. We have lost a lot, but a lot still survives and if you know how to recover it, you can create Democratic Confederalism. What is still alive? The resistance of women, their *xwebûn*.' (Zilan, Jineolojî committee member, interviewed January 2019)

The "matriarchal society" Jineolojî activists refer to suggests neither the desire to return to a pre-modern era nor the existence of an already given alternative: "Of course we don't speak about ideal and pure matriarchal societies, but there are still some elements that show their influence" (Necibe, Jineolojî committee member, interviewed February 2019). There are traces embedded in 'the most unblemished and unpretentious of knowledge' contained in 'the experiences of a woman troubadour, a woman healer, the diary of a woman guerrilla, the biography of a woman resister' (Diyar, 2018). However, these 'ancestral practices' (see Dinerstein, this volume), only assume a revolutionary meaning when women creatively recover them and include them in the reconstruction of their memories and identities.

Jineolojî's *xwebûn* thus promotes the possibility of prefiguring a matristic culture via collective efforts of remembering, renaming and rebuilding women's resistant past as the source of their present and future emancipation. Through this practice, the distinction between postfigurative and prefigurative cultures (Mead, 1973) seems to partially melt away. Ancestors are evoked, but their lessons are decided by present needs and future desires – a process that strongly resonates with Motta's storytelling practice 'in which through each thread of our weaving we remember and honour our histories and rework novel structures, conceptions of self and social relationships' (2016, p 45).

Communalizing life

From my participation in the training practices and discussions with other women attendees, it emerged that they found the long training sessions to be the most impactful. During a ten-day or month-long *perwerde*, seminars are integrated with the practice of sharing and 'commoning' life (Federici, 2012), or what the Kurdish Freedom Movement calls 'democratic communality' (Öcalan, 2020, p 243).

As Amara explains in reference to the first Jineolojî *perwerde* with Arab women from Raqqa, it is the collective care of reproductive activities that makes the pedagogy of these long training sessions anti-patriarchal:

'We were sleeping together, preparing food in the academy, cleaning, and we had daily discussion about what is needed for a daily life. And *there* is the education. This is one of the most important things, that women come to live together and create a collective way of living. They come from so different backgrounds, so they have the feeling of freedom, there is no man telling you to bring the *chay* [tea], so you do yourself, you do it for your friends. What the women told me is that was one of the most impressive things and they didn't want to go back home.' (Amara, Jineolojî committee member, interviewed January 2019)

For most of the women, this experience "is the first thing they do for themselves, and not on behalf of the husband or the father" (Ronahi, member of the diplomacy of the Kurdish women's movement, interviewed December 2018). This is a first step to break women's housewifization and domestic isolation, and to free their care work from patriarchal exploitation and transform it into collective self-care.

This approach reflects a specific emancipatory praxis promoted by Jineolojî in each women's project of the Kongra Star. One of its aims is to revalue women's invisible reproductive labour – considered pivotal for socioecological life, and originally at the heart of matriarchal societies – and to put it "back at the centre of social organization" (Avrin, Jineolojî committee member, interviewed January 2019). As such, Jineolojî does not believe women's emancipation can be reached by entering the capitalist labour market or accessing public subsidies, but neither does it romanticize women's care work in the household; rather, it strives to build autonomous communal spaces in which women can collectivize life-orientated/reproductive work, producing new economic rules and values:

'Being forced as a young woman to bake bread in the *tenur* [oven] every morning for a big family cannot be romanticized as ecological and self-sufficient but must be defined as one shape of women's oppression. Jineolojî takes the role to show the strength, richness, importance and beauty of communal and ecological forms of living and working, separating them from the narrow forms of organising life that have been developed through rigid religious moral, state, patriarchy and capitalism. Its approach would be to underline the importance of economical self-organisation, but in communal ways.' (Collective answer by members of the Andrea Wolf Institute, September 2020)

Within this perspective, under the umbrella of the Jineolojî Academy, a women's ecovillage, called Jinwar, was built in Rojava and inaugurated on 25 November 2018. Around 70 women and children live there and are self-organizing the production and reproduction of their lives in a sustainable and communal way (Aguilar Silva, 2019). Similarly, the *Aborya Jin* (women's economy) has been created as a field for discussion and action, and many women's autonomous economic cooperatives have been established in North and East Syria, mostly in the agricultural field and in food production, shops and markets (Azeez, 2017).

Killing or transforming the man

Organizing educational sessions with men has also become an important aspect of Jineolojî, because "Jineolojî is not the science just of women, but of communal society. Today, the only way to rebuild a balance is through women's *xwebûn* and the transformation of men" (Zozan, Jineolojî committee member, July 2019).

The problem of changing men, or 'killing the dominant male' (Öcalan, 2013, p 49), is not new in the history of the Kurdish Freedom Movement. Since the end of the 1990s, PKK militants (encouraged by Öcalan) have started to work on 'the problem of man', with the belief that while women organize their autonomous structures and communal life, men should also work on dismantling the mentality of domination, possession and power that the patriarchal system imposed on them (Öcalan, 2013, p 50).

In Rojava, this perspective has led to the organization of many Jineolojî training programmes for men. These often take place during mixed-sex *perwerde*, but there are also training activities exclusively for men. The latter correspond to a recent project (2019–20) that, under the name *kuştina* or *veguhartina zilam* (killing or transforming the man), included a series of men-only training activities organized by the women's movement – mainly by Jineolojî committees.

I had the chance to visit the first of these activities, which was held at the Kobane Women's Academy in July 2019. Thirty men participated for a few weeks. The first impressive feature of the training, suggesting the clear intention of subverting gender roles, was that men were taught only by women, which is a basic rule for these *perwerde*. Men were taking classes and organizing their communal lives as guests in a women's space – a place normally closed to men. Jineolojî members explained to us that the method is quite similar to that of *xwebûn*; it begins with questions about what it is to be a woman, then what it is to be a man, stimulating analysis of the power system operating in their lived experiences in the family, household and political life. So far, they have only organized a few long *perwerde* with men, and these have solely involved men working in the self-government system.

Training activities for men are an original aspect of the movement's matristic perspective. They are proof of the Jineolojî aim to subvert dominant masculinities, sharing with men the duties and responsibility for realizing the *hev jiyan azad* (free life together) in both the family and politics. On the one hand, they serve to familiarize men with the new women's rights promoted by the law, which prohibits polygamy, forced marriage and child marriage and condemns 'honour'-based killings, domestic violence and gender-based discrimination (Dirik, 2018a; Shahvisi, 2018). On the other hand, as Dîrok, a Jineolojî member, affirms, they answer women's need to overcome 'some problems that were happening in the co-chair system' (in Andrea Wolf Institute, 2021, p 52) – that is, they carry out the strategic task of providing the basis for, and facing the obstacles and conflicts generated by, the institutionalized co-leadership system (see Tank, 2017) and the parallel autonomous women's system. These systems are radical forms of organization that require a shared anti-patriarchal mentality and a broad popular understanding and consensus.

Conclusion

Like a recent branch of decolonial and ecofeminist thought, the Kurdish Freedom Movement grounds its revolutionary proposal of Democratic Confederalism on renewing and recovering indigenous forms of matristic society, which it positions as pivotal to overcome the present socioecological and political crisis – both in the Middle East and around the world. In particular, Abdullah Öcalan stresses the importance of women's struggle against housewifization and considers gender liberation and women's self-determination – in every field of life – as vital to achieving decolonization and stateless socialism.

This matristic perspective, which rejects any essentialist or romanticized vision of 'pre-modern' or 'new' matriarchies, has emerged in the past decade as an emancipatory horizon of a post-patriarchal society, and it informs all the structures of the confederal system in Rojava. Women's self-organizational efforts – and, mostly, the educational activities led by Jineolojî in the region – are the main terrain of this praxis, since they articulate women's daily emancipatory strategies at the grassroots level with the desire for a matristic future.

By promoting a pedagogy based on collective self-reflection (*xwebûn*), Jineolojî training activities enable women of different classes, ethnicities and religions to recover and revalue their invisibilized history, knowledge and life-sustaining work as sources of agency and social transformation. Jineolojî *perwerde* subvert and de-patriarchize the gender roles imposed by housewifization for two main reasons: first because during the training weeks, women build a new sense of community by self-managing their daily life together, socializing their needs and care work beyond male power; and, second, because educating men allows the deconstruction of dominant masculinity by intervening directly in men's behaviour, starting with those who have social and political responsibilities within the movement. In other words, Jineolojî activities strengthen women's autonomy and material self-defence by promoting communal subsistence practices, such as economic cooperatives or the women's ecovillage, Jinwar. At the same time, they contribute to democratizing both the movement's political structures and the family, which Kurdish women see as the key unit of social organization, as well as the main device of capitalist–patriarchal power.

Largely due to the war situation, Jineolojî training activities, which are still too episodic, have only reached a small number of the five million people in North and East Syria. As activists testify, this process is far from complete and nor is it free from limits and contradictions, and its larger-scale effects might only become apparent in the long term. However, the importance of these activities cannot be neglected; they have been pivotal for keeping the process of de-patriarchization alive in North and East Syria and for pushing forward the constant unlearning and relearning practices that inform women's – and people's – self-organization and (re)production of life.

Notes

[1] 'In attempting to define social sciences, I stressed that the ultimate goal must be to develop the option of freedom ... then I see no difficulties in calling the social sciences the "sociology of freedom"' (Öcalan, 2020, p 372).

[2] See https://web.archive.org/web/20160929163726/http://www.freemedialibrary.com/index.php/Declaration_of_Democratic_Confederalism_in_Kurdistan

[3] A canton is a self-governing autonomous region confederated with others.

[4] See the full text here: https://internationalistcommune.com/social-contract/

References

Aguilar Silva, E. (2019) 'Mujer-vida-linertad. Participación de las mujeres en el proyecto económico/ecológico de la Federación Democrática del norte de Siria-Rojava', *Revista de Estudios Internacionales Mediterráneos*, 27: 150–69.

Al-Ali, N. and Käser, I. (2020) 'Beyond feminism? Jineolojî and the Kurdish women's freedom movement', *Politics and Gender*, 16(2): 1–32.

Andrea Wolf Institute (2021) 'Killing and transforming the dominant man', *Jineolojî* [online], 5 February, available from: http://jineoloji.org/en/2021/01/20/booklet-killing-and-transforming-the-dominant-man/

Azeez, H. (2017) 'Women's cooperatives: a glimpse into Rojava's economic model', *Green Left* [online], 27 February, available from: https://www.greenleft.org.au/content/women%E2%80%99s-cooperatives-glimpse-rojava%E2%80%99s-economic-model

Barca, S. (2020) *Forces of Reproduction: Notes for a Counter-Hegemonic Anthropocene*, Cambridge: Cambridge University Press.

Biehl, J. (2015) 'Revolutionary education: two academies in Rojava', in R. in der Maur and J. Staal (eds) *Stateless Democracy*, Utrecht: Bak, pp 57–72.

Cabnal, L. (2010) 'Acercamiento a la construcción de la propuesta de pensamiento epistémico de las mujeres indígenas feministas comunitarias de Abya Yala', *Feminista Siempre*, Madrid: ACSUR – Las Segovias, pp 11–25.

Deniz, Y. (2018) 'Jineoljî. La ciencia de la Modernidad Democrática. Una vida libre y comunal', in European Committee of Jineoljî (eds) *Jineolojî: Campamento del Mediterráneo*, Neuss: Mesopotamien Verlag e Vertriebs GmbH, pp 43–56.

Dinerstein, A.C. (2017) 'Concrete utopia: (re)producing life in, against and beyond the open veins of capital', *Public Seminar* [online], 7 December, available from: www.publicseminar.org/2017/12/concrete-utopia/

Dinerstein, A.C. and Deneulin, S. (2012) 'Hope movements: naming mobilization in a post-development world', *Development and Change*, 43(2): 585–602.

Dirik, D. (2018a) 'Self-defense means political autonomy! The women's movement of Kurdistan envisioning and pursuing new paths for radical democratic autonomy', *Development*, 60(1): 74–9.

Dirik, D. (2018b) 'The revolution of smiling women: stateless democracy and power in Rojava', in O.U. Rutazibwa and R. Shilliam (eds) *Routledge Handbook of Postcolonial Politics*, New York: Routledge, pp 222–38.

Diyar, Z. (2018) 'What is Jineoljî?', *Jineoljî* [online], 2 January, available from: http://jineoloji.org/en/2018/12/14/what-is-jineoloji/

Escobar, A. (2018) *Designs for the Pluriverse: Radical Interdependence, Autonomy, and the Making of Worlds*, Durham, NC: Duke University Press.

Federici, S. (2012) *Revolution at Point Zero: Housework, Reproduction, and Feminist Struggle*, New York: PM Press.

Ferreira, B. and Santiago, V. (2018) 'The core of resistance: recognising intersectional struggle in the Kurdish women's movement', *Contexto Internacional*, 40(3): 479–500.

Gaard, G. (2011) 'Ecofeminism revisited: rejecting essentialism and re-placing species in a material feminist environmentalism', *Feminist Formations*, 23(2): 26–53.

Galindo, M. (2015) 'La revolución feminista se llama despatriarchalización', *Feminista Siempre*, Madrid: ACSUR – Las Segovias, pp 27–50.

Gregoratti, C. and Raphael, R. (2019) 'The historical roots of a feminist "degrowth": Maria Mies and Marilyn Waring's critiques of growth', in E. Chertkovskaya, A. Paulsson and S. Barca (eds) *Towards a Political Economy of Degrowth*, London: Rowman and Littlefield International, pp 83–98.

hooks, b. (1990) *Yearning: Race, Gender and Cultural Politics*, Cambridge, MA: South End Press.

Knapp, M. and Jongerden, J. (2016) 'Communal democracy: the social contract and confederalism in Rojava', *Comparative Islamic Studies*, 10(1): 87–107.

Kothari, A., Salleh, A., Escobar, A., Demaria, F. and Acosta, A. (eds) (2019) *Pluriverse: A Post-Development Dictionary*, New Delhi: Tulik.

Leezenberg, M. (2016) 'The ambiguities of democratic autonomy: the Kurdish movement in Turkey and Rojava', *Southeast European and Black Sea Studies*, 16(4): 671–90.

Mead, M. (1973) 'Prefigurative cultures and unknown children', in P.K. Manning (ed) *Youth: Divergent Perspectives*, New York: John Wiley and Sons, pp 193–206.

Merchant, C. (1996) *Earthcare: Women and the Environment*, London: Routledge.

Mies, M. (1986) *Patriarchy and Accumulation on a World Scale: Women in the International Division of Labour*, London: Zed Books.

Mies, M. and Shiva, V. (1993) *Ecofeminism*, London: Zed Books.

Mohanty, C.T. (2003) *Feminism without Borders: Decolonizing Theory, Practicing Solidarity*, Durham, NC: Duke University Press.

Monticelli, L. (2018) 'Embodying alternatives to capitalism in the 21st century', *TripleC: Communication, Capitalism & Critique*, 16(2): 501–17.

Monticelli, L. (2021) 'On the necessity of prefigurative politics', *Thesis Eleven*, 167(1): 99–118.

Motta, S.C. (2016) 'Decolonising critique: from prophetic negation to prefigurative affirmation', in A.C. Dinerstein (ed) *Social Sciences for an Other Politics: Women Theorizing without Parachutes*, Cham: Palgrave McMillan, pp 33–48.

Neven, B. and Schäfers, M. (2017) 'Jineology: from women's struggles to social liberation', *ROAR* [online], 25 November, available from: https://roarmag.org/essays/jineology-kurdish-women-movement/

Öcalan, A. (2013) *Liberating Life: Woman's Revolution*, London: Mesopotamia Publishers and International Initiative Edition.

Öcalan, A. (2017) *Capitalism: The Age of Unmasked Gods and Naked Kings: Manifesto for a Democratic Civilization: Volume II*, London: New Compass Press and International Initiative Edition.

Öcalan, A. (2020) *The Sociology of Freedom: Manifesto of the Democratic Civilization, Volume III*, London: PM Press and International Initiative.

Paredes, J. (2012) *Hilando fino desde el feminismo comunitario*, La Paz: ded (Deutscher Entwicklungsdienst).

Pavičić-Ivelja, K. (2017) 'The Rojava revolution: women's liberation as an answer to the Kurdish question', *West Croatian History Journal*, 6(11): 131–49.

Piccardi, E.G. (2022) 'The challenges of a Kurdish ecofeminist perspective: Maria Mies, Abdullah Öcalan, and the praxis of Jineolojî', *Capitalism Nature Socialism*, 33(1): 46–65.

Piccardi, E.G. and Barca, S. (2022) 'Jin-jiyan-azadi. Matristic culture and Democratic Confederalism in Rojava', *Sustainability Science* [online], https://doi.org/10.1007/s11625-022-01099-x

Plumwood, V. (1993) *Feminism and the Mastery of Nature*, London: Routledge.

Pons Rabasa, A. (2018) 'Vulnerabilidad analítica, interseccionalidad y ensamblajes: hacia una etnografía afectiva', in A. Pons Rabasa and S.G. McManus (eds) *Afecto, Cuerpo e Identidad. Reflexiones encarnadas en la investigación feminista*, Ciudad de México: Universidad Nacional Autónoma de México, pp 23–52.

Rasit, H. and Kolokotronis, A. (2020) 'Decentralist vanguards: women's autonomous power and left convergence in Rojava', *Globalizations* [online], https://doi.org/10.1080/14747731.2020.1722498

Saed (2015) 'Rojava', *Capitalism Nature Socialism*, 26(1): 1–15.

Salleh, A. (2017) *Ecofeminism as Politics: Nature, Marx and the Postmodern* (2nd edn), London: Zed Books.

Segato, R. (2014) 'Colonialidad y patriarcado moderno: expansión del frente estatal, modernización, y la vida de las mujeres', in Y. Espinosa, D. Gómez and K. Ochoa (eds) *Tejiendo de otro modo: Feminismo, epistemología y apuestas descoloniales en Abya Yala*, Popayán: Editorial Universidad del Cauca, pp 75–90.

Shahvisi, A. (2018) 'Beyond orientalism: exploring the distinctive feminism of Democratic Confederalism in Rojava', *Geopolitics*, 26(4): 998–1022.

Şimşek, B. and Jongerden, J. (2018) 'Gender revolution in Rojava: the voices beyond tabloid geopolitics', *Geopolitics*, 26(4): 1023–45.

Tank, P. (2017) 'Kurdish women in Rojava: from resistance to reconstruction', *Die Welt des Islams*, 57(3): 404–28.

von Werlhof, C. (2019) 'New matriarchies', in A. Kothari, A. Salleh, A. Escobar, F. Demaria and A. Acosta (eds) *Pluriverse: A Post-Development Dictionary*, New Delhi: Tulika, pp 253–6.

PART III

Doing Research
on Prefigurative Politics

12

The Concept of Prefigurative Politics in Studies of Social Movements: Progress and Caveats

Luke Yates and Joost de Moor

Introduction

As the contents of this book attest, prefigurative politics plays an interesting role in a diverse constellation of themes relevant to contemporary political activity. This chapter focuses on and problematizes this diversity in the application of prefiguration with respect to studies of social movements. Debates about prefiguration began in the discussion of social movements and political strategy within and outside academia in the late 1960s and 1970s. Since then, its meaning has evolved and its use has diversified. Over time, it has been associated with a range of collectives, political themes and orientations to activism, perhaps most prominently feminism, anarchism, environmentalism, direct action, alter-globalization, anti-austerity and new democracy mobilizations.

In this chapter, we review the term's trajectory: first, its origins in discussions of Left political strategy, in which the social movement is understood more expansively to include political parties and projects (1968–89); second, its increasing use in labelling new social movements (1990–2004); and third, its increasingly diffuse attribution as an orientation to a variety of different political activities in predominantly Left-wing social movements (2005–20). Across these periods, the concept has been used to qualify or distinguish activities, actors and spaces in diffuse ways, which have shifted considerably. The aim of the first part of this chapter is therefore to provide clarity about the *explicit* use of the concept across these periods. In the second part of the paper, we shift our focus to the *implicit* use of the term. Specifically, we observe that prefiguration is at risk of being overused to describe non-hierarchical Left-wing movements and underused to describe Right-wing movements, suggesting an implicit association with particular political positions that the concept's definition does not warrant. Hence, it remains to be seen whether prefigurative politics are actually much rarer, or simply overlooked, in Right-wing movements. We conclude the chapter by discussing implications for future research.

A genealogy of prefigurative politics: 1968–2020

There has recently been an explosion in academic use of the concept 'prefigurative politics' – from around 30 citations between 1975 and 1995 to almost 2,000 between 1995 and 2015 – a trend that appears to be accelerating (see Table 12.1, for a more detailed discussion see Yates, 2020). This increased use of the term is disproportionate to the expansion of social science research, the digitization of research and the development of social movement studies as a sub-discipline. Sampling work for the period shows this massive expansion has been accompanied by shifts in the work the concept does. This section is based on reading of all texts featuring the term 'prefigurative politics' from its first use in 1975 up to 2020, and analysis of a random selection of one in five of these texts to identify what empirical phenomena the term was applied to, the theoretical provenance of the arguments and where the study was carried out. We looked for thematic and theoretical drift in the concept, and distinguished three main phases: 1975–89, 1990–2004 and 2005–20 (see Yates, 2020).

Carl Boggs' two articles in 1977 (1977a, 1977b) are widely credited for coining the term 'prefigurative politics', yet Boggs was simply the first to formally define this particular variant of a term that several authors had been using for at least nine years. These authors interchanged 'prefiguration' with 'prefigurative socialism', and used 'prefigurative' as an adjective and 'to prefigure' as a verb to qualify political activity (for example, Gorz, 1968; Magri, 1970). Between 1968 and 1989, these terms were used in three related senses. The first was to describe counter-hegemonic projects of 'prefigurative socialism' – which, for Gorz (1968) and Magri (1970), referred to a way of immediately socializing political power and was part of revolutionary strategy that included the participation of actors often classified today as being outside social movements, including political parties and unions. The second way it was used was in reference to how local councils, workplaces, worker cooperatives and other institutions might be run on socialist principles. Here, it merges with the notions of 'local socialism' and 'municipal socialism', which referred to the UK Labour Party's radical councils in Sheffield, Manchester and London, undertaken in the context of the party's alternative economic strategy (see the discussion in Cooper, 2017). Third, writers working on social movements began to use the term

Table 12.1: Keywords in academic texts, 1975–2019

Years	Keyword 'prefigurative politics'	Keyword 'prefigurative socialist' or 'prefigurative socialism'	Total returns for time period (no keywords) (000s)	Keyword 'social movement'
1975–84	8	12	492	6,140
1985–94	37	9	492	12,730
1995–2004	152	3	1,609	37,900
2005–14	927	6	2,488	83,600
2015–19★	1,760	4	777	38,700

Note: ★ five-year period

Source: Google Scholar, 8 January 2020

directly, most notably Sheila Rowbotham and co-authors (1979) in their writing on the women's movement and Wini Breines (for example, 1989) on the American New Left. Subsequent developments in the use of the term drew only selectively on these early formulations.

Between 1990 and 2004, the term 'prefigurative politics' was no longer used to describe an overall Left strategy that included parties, movements, states and local government institutions. Instead, it was mainly used to describe new social movements, particularly feminism but also the peace movement (for example, Epstein, 1991), the New Left and movements for racial justice (such as the 1960s civil rights movement). Most authors used the concept in this way and cited Breines without much debate. For the last five years of this period (2000–04) and the first five years of the next (2005–09), the concept continued to be used to label movements, but its focus expanded to different movements – from feminism and the anti-war movement to antiglobalization (for example, Juris, 2008), direct action or anarchist mobilizations (Graeber, 2002) and alternative media. During this period, we observe a shift towards prefiguration describing protest events and mobilizations rather than movements per se, particularly the prefiguration of anarchist principles, such as horizontalism, in movement strategies and organization. Likewise, the concept is applied to discussions of space, mainly in relation to occupations and territorially bounded 'free spaces' or activist projects (for example, Polletta, 1999; Leach and Haunss, 2009).

In the period 2005–20, there was an explosion in the use of the term 'prefigurative politics', including explicit theoretical development and appearances in major books on social movements. The movements it is most often attached to are anti-austerity and new democracy (for example, Razsa and Kurnik, 2012) and alter-globalization (for example, Maeckelbergh,

2009, this volume). Also, anarchist studies continues to reclaim the term (for example, Swain, 2017; Gordon, 2018). We note, as well, continued references to environmental protest, everyday environmentalism and ecologically orientated grassroots initiatives (for example, Schlosberg and Craven, 2019). This proliferation takes the concept far beyond social movement studies into themes and fields including the politics of art, theatrical practice, community work, community psychology, consumption, philosophy, critical theory, translation studies and computer game studies. The term is also prevalent in debates around political consumerism and lifestyle politics, part of the motivation for which is to demonstrate to wider society that certain lifestyles and ways of consuming are more sustainable (de Moor, 2017; Lorenzini, 2019). Generally, across all of this literature, the term is used as a label or a qualifier for political orientations, mobilizations or movements, which has allowed prefiguration to retain a set of different meanings that have only recently begun to be considered directly.

Most recently, a set of contributions have treated prefigurative politics more analytically. The first of these explores the *theoretical contexts* of prefiguration in a way that complements this chapter, noting that the Left's intellectual history has important resonances with one or more key meanings of the term (for example, van de Sande, 2013; Swain, 2017; Gordon, 2018). The intellectual debt of anarchism is widely noted, but others usefully compare the anarchist tradition to Marxist influences, including the work of Antonio Negri (Raekstad and Gradin, 2020; see also Raekstad, this volume).

A second set of recent analytical literature examines different *modalities* of prefiguration, cataloguing the political phenomena the term refers to and differences in movements' application of prefigurative politics. Some work delves into the question of time in relation to prefiguration (for example, Jeffrey and Dyson, 2016; Wagner-Pacifici and Ruggero, 2018) in an attempt to clarify the relationship it suggests between present and future, and considers the implications for movement goals (Van de Sande, 2013, p 232; Yates, 2015b; Swain, 2017; see also Maeckelbergh, this volume). Wagner-Pacifici and Ruggero (2018, p 19), for example, persuasively argue that 'to talk of prefiguration is to necessarily talk of temporality. ... In the case of Occupy Philadelphia, multiple versions of prefigurative approaches to time and history vied for control across multiple levels of action, interaction, and organizing'.

Third, a theoretically sophisticated understanding of prefiguration has increasingly been operationalized in *diverse empirical applications* – for example, applying the concept to local states (Cooper, 2017) and, increasingly, contexts outside of the Global North (Bonilla, 2010; Baker, 2016). These applications continue to expand the relationship between prefigurative politics and social movements.

Across this work, multiple definitions have been proposed. The shifting history of the concept's use means that any definition introduces potentially contentious distinctions and qualifications, and we can see the value of a broad approach (see Raekstad and Gradin, 2020) for the purposes of this collection. Other recent work shows that prefigurative politics refers to several distinct but overlapping logics of activism, which usually combine utopianism and political imagination ('prolepsis') with either practical projects, infrastructures, counterpower and examples ('building alternatives'), or orientations of protest where the political processes themselves are considered politically significant ('means–ends equivalence') (Yates, 2015b). Following Yates (2015b, p 19), we would consider an activity to be most convincingly a case of prefigurative politics when it combines the imaginative and experimental construction of 'alternative' modes of conduct – within either mobilization or everyday activities – with some attempt to ensure these alternatives' future political relevance, either through material consolidation or diffusion of new ideas or practices (see also de Moor et al, 2017).

In summary, during the period 2005–19, there was a massive increase in the use of prefiguration. The term has proliferated beyond social movements and the disciplines of sociology and politics. It is increasingly used to describe a political orientation towards action rather than to label particular types of movements (as in the 1990s) or to describe an overall Left strategy (as in the 1970s and 1980s). The term is now being used analytically, and several promising avenues of work can be observed.

Research gaps, contradictions and opportunities

The most recent period of rapid expansion has both increased the need for conceptual clarity and made some important steps towards achieving this. However, in this section we argue that the notion of prefigurative politics is implicitly associated with Left-wing political activity and movements – particularly non-hierarchical movements – as well as a number of dynamics therein that are not necessarily either 'political' or 'prefigurative'. To increase conceptual clarity, we need to interrogate these patterns and critically reflect on their relation to the explicit definitions being used. Doing so offers an opportunity to reflect on some research gaps, contradictions and opportunities for future research.

Like Jaster (2018), we observe that 'prefigurative politics' is primarily used to depict progressive, horizontal, green and emancipatory activities in Left-wing movements, and rarely to depict activities by more conservative, authoritarian or reactionary Right-wing movements. It is also disproportionately used to describe informally organized and 'anti-authoritarian' movements and mobilizations. For example, prefiguration is not generally applied to single-issue campaign organizations, nor to Trotskyist or Marxist–Leninist groups. Due to the shifting history of the concept and its very expansive applications, it is hard to know whether these lacunae are due to an actual lack of prefiguration in such movements or simply reflect the concept's long-standing associations with, and origins in, Left theory and especially anarchism. The way in which the concept of prefigurative politics is applied in social movement scholarship reveals blind spots and ambiguities that will be useful to explore further.

The argument we want to develop here is that the way in which the concept of prefigurative politics is applied may result in it doing both too much and too little. It does too much when prefiguration comes to stand in for certain kinds of activity even when the typical criteria of the concept are not fulfilled. It does too little when prefiguration is applied very selectively, suggesting an implicit shared understanding that prefigurative politics is intrinsically progressive and non-hierarchical. We finish by highlighting the implications of our argument for how prefiguration, as a concept, might be deployed most fruitfully.

Prefigurative politics may be overused in relation to progressive movements in at least three ways. First, some attempts to reflect values or politics in strategies may be more accurately depicted as cases of moral behaviour or identity construction than as prefigurative politics (de Moor et al, 2017). That is, attempts to reflect political goals or values in social movement processes may be explained by participants as an effort to simply do the 'right' things, rather than as a strategy for social change. For instance, Laura Portwood-Stacer (2012) demonstrates that North American anarchists' alternative consumption practices are not necessarily (only) about prefigurative activist strategy. They may also be about constructing and communicating personal identity (one interviewee describes their vegetarianism as 'just part of the lifestyle'; another suggests not watching television is 'more symbolic than anything else') or moral commitments (other interviewees discuss wearing used clothing to avoid contributing money to companies that employ sweatshop labour) (Portwood-Stacer, 2012, p 96). In a recent article, Deflorian (2021) argues that the development of a morally consistent identity and practice should be seen as a central feature of prefigurative politics. However, although there are analytical and theoretical reasons to not ascribe too much significance to stated motivations when exploring political activity, most claims about prefigurative politics do suggest its underpinning logic is an attempt to affect social change. When research participants do not discuss any political motivations in explanations of their actions, scholars may want to be hesitant to depict these actions as prefigurative *politics*.

Second, prefigurative politics is sometimes used interchangeably with the idea of 'alternatives' (projects, practices, counter-institutions and so on) without specifying whether a utopian or proleptic approach – acting as though the change you are wishing to see in society is already achieved – is important for participants. Put differently, political activity is often qualified as prefigurative because it presents practical alternatives to the current order, but without considering whether it is part of a collective attempt to realize alternatives here and now as a step towards achieving broad social change in the future (Young and Schwartz, 2012; see also du Plessis and Husted, this volume).

Finally, we observe accounts in which politics are qualified as prefigurative because actions ('means') are found to reflect some goals ('ends') that activists see as desirable. However, it is not always clear whether this overlap is intended to establish a causal link between means and ends, nor whether the ends the researcher considers important are similarly important to the participant. Scholars of democratic innovation may, for instance, depict instances in which movements are organized to prefigure a more democratic society (such as horizontalism), without clarifying whether the activists share those aims (to a similar degree) or are simply organizing themselves according to what they consider just or effective (for example, della Porta, 2012). As authors often do not have the space to provide all evidence, the point is not that such use of the term 'prefigurative' is necessarily inaccurate; rather, the problem is that it often remains unclear to the reader *why* something is labelled prefigurative. We therefore think it is good practice for researchers to be up front about what the term is meant to qualify: an empirically verified, strategic intent on behalf of the movement (ideally mentioning potential disagreement within the movement), or a sign of the materialization of a social change the researcher ascribes to the movement or would themselves want to see materialize in the future.

We also believe prefigurative politics may be *under*used to the extent that the term is hardly applied in the context of conservative or reactionary movements, or to hierarchically organized progressive movements. Focusing on the former, Futrell and Simi (2004) show that within the American white power movement, prefigurative spaces are developed in which to practice and promote 'Aryan dominance' – which, the activists hope, will contribute towards advancing a society of white domination. So-called 'indigenous-prefigurative' spaces are local milieux protected from social control where members can prefigure 'Aryan dominance', whereas 'transmovement-prefigurative' spaces – broader, more open movement scenes around white power culture or identity – are used to attract new members to the cause. These spaces could thus be said to relate to the development and diffusion of alternatives. Yet apart from Futrell and Simi's seminal work, Creasap (2012) concludes, we know very little about prefigurative politics in Right-wing movements. This is not necessarily because they do not engage in diffusing alternatives or attempting to reflect political principles in their strategies; it may simply be because prefigurative politics is generally considered intrinsically progressive (Jaster, 2018) or because Right-wing movements lack distinctive activist logics around horizontalism (see Sitrin, 2006; Maeckelbergh, 2009).

It is worth pointing out, however, that the classic prefigurative 'practices' described in Maeckelbergh's (2009) work on horizontality and diversity are organizational principles advocated in some way by a range of organizations, such as corporations and government ministries, that are obviously not Left-wing anti-authoritarian movement networks. Furthermore, Blee and Creasap (2010) point to the New Right's strategic emphasis on involving women centrally and in leadership positions in anti-feminist campaigning; this illustrates that, while their political ends may be entirely at odds with those of progressive groups, the means may be similar – it is possible to organize a fascist grouping using horizontal organizing methods, and to 'prefigure' 'Aryan dominance'. Hence, not all progressive practices necessarily prefigure a progressive future, and while some practices may represent means–ends equivalence, others may be at odds with this. Finally, Blee and Creasap (2010) also point out the American New Right's attempt to 'build alternatives', including in music, computer games, amusement parks, publishing houses, radio and bookstores.

All of these examples highlight that, based on common definitions of prefigurative politics, there is no convincing reason why the term is used almost exclusively for anti-authoritarian and informally organized Left-wing movement groups. Not all progressive practices are intended to prefigure progressive futures, and Right-wing groups are not unlikely to practice means–ends equivalence or alternatives with the intent of promoting wider social change.

Conclusion

This chapter has reviewed how concepts relating to prefiguration are used in social movement literature, how this has changed over time and some of the questions this raises for prefiguration's further conceptual development and application. The first part of the chapter showed how and in what ways the term 'prefigurative politics' has become an intellectually generative concept, while the second half suggested the rise in the casual use of the concept reveals blind spots in which the term appears to do too much or too little work. One conclusion, if we continue to use such open-ended definitions of the term, would be that nearly all movements (and many other collective actors) are prefigurative, rendering the qualification meaningless. For example, nearly every movement thinks (to some degree) that how they organize is itself a question of some political interest, and most movements use political alternatives as well as protest. We think the answer to this challenge lies in carefully defining how we use the term 'prefigurative politics' or in clarifying what we are arguing. Are we making a claim about how activists understand their participation in protest? Or are we suggesting that the logic of political transformation is, could be, or is hoped to be prefigurative in some way? It may also be useful for researchers to suggest how central prefiguration is to the activity described, and the exceptions, limitations and degree to which the combination of practices we understand as prefigurative are traded off by other organizational and political logics around, for example, leadership, discipline, efficiency, roles and divisions of labour.

A related issue, based not on activists' motivations but on the assumption (or desire) that observed behaviour prefigures future social change, is that work on the consequences of social movements (for example, Bosi et al, 2016) has paid scant attention to the *outcomes* of prefigurative politics. Establishing such outcomes can be difficult; the causal mechanisms and time frames around prefiguration and success are rarely specified, making such assumptions hard to substantiate (on this, see Maeckelbergh, this volume). This certainly presents an interesting research gap, and addressing it can potentially draw from research in affiliated fields, such as on the diffusion of grassroots alternatives and transformative innovations (for example, Seyfang and Longhurst, 2016). Yet there is evidence to suggest that establishing alternative institutions, practices and perspectives can be part of the process of political transformation, and theoretical explanations of how this might work should therefore go beyond the notion of 'diffusion' (for example, Wright, 2010; see also Monticelli's introduction to this volume). Where the size or proliferation of prefigurative projects can be assessed over time, there is clearly another opportunity to assess the impacts of social movements.

We think a more self-conscious and qualified application of the concept would also allow prefigurative politics to continue to inspire and inform the investigation of new areas related to movements (some are alluded to in other chapters in this volume). We have noted that several of these are particularly promising, including recent generative focuses on movement temporalities (Maeckelbergh, this volume) and the application of the concept to study movements outside of the Global North (see Dinerstein on decolonizing prefiguration, this volume). As mentioned, we also consider there to be interesting potential in exploring how Right-wing social movements may be considered prefigurative. We also advocate a return to the term's origins to consider how other types of actors relevant to movements, like institutions of the state or political parties, might practise prefigurative politics. Moreover, we anticipate that analysis of environmental protest and prefigurative politics remains important given that environmental crises foreground the need to reinvent the economy and social relations at scale and that social movements are widely recognized as privileged zones for experimentation, innovation and imagination (Eyerman and Jamison, 1991; Schulz, 2016; Schlosberg and Craven, 2019). For instance, sustainable food and energy movements develop alternative practices not only to directly benefit a community but also to show viable alternatives that could be used for larger-scale social change (de Moor, 2017; Lorenzini, 2019; Forno and Wahlen, this volume).

Finally, we also consider the concept useful for making sense of the often ambiguous and much-contested boundaries between activism and everyday life (Yates, 2015a; de Moor, 2017; Forno and Wahlen, this volume). In a context of increasingly fragmented forms of collective political action and the rise of lifestyle and consumer politics, we need conceptual resources to help make sense of political activity that is only partially collective and is political in very specific – and sometimes very limited – senses. Consumer movements, dispersed forms of resistance and the potential for new collective actors, based on shared practices or experiences (see Welch and Yates, 2018), could be explored using a refined understanding of prefigurative politics. Prefigurative politics also has the potential to improve understandings of the relationship between the habits and routines of daily life and participation in, and solidarity with, social movements. Overall, however, a more careful application of the term is needed to realize these potentials.

References

Baker, M. (2016) 'The prefigurative politics of translation in place-based movements of protest: subtitling in the Egyptian Revolution', *The Translator*, 22(1): 1–21.

Blee, K.M. and Creasap, K.A. (2010) 'Conservative and Right-wing movements', *Annual Review of Sociology*, 36: 269–86.

Boggs, C. (1977a) 'Marxism, prefigurative communism and the problem of workers' control', *Radical America*, 11(6): 99–122.

Boggs, C. (1977b) 'Revolutionary process, political strategy, and the dilemma of power', *Theory and Society*, 4(3): 359–93.

Bonilla, Y. (2010) 'Guadeloupe is ours: the prefigurative politics of the mass strike in the French Antilles', *Interventions*, 12(1): 125–37.

Bosi, L., Giugni, M. and Uba, K. (eds) (2016) *The Consequences of Social Movements*, Cambridge: Cambridge University Press.

Breines, W. (1989) *Community and Organization in the New Left 1962–68: The Great Refusal*, New Brunswick, NJ: Rutgers University Press.

Cooper, D. (2017) 'Prefiguring the state', *Antipode*, 49(2): 335–56.

Creasap, K. (2012) 'Social movement scenes: place-based politics and everyday resistance', *Sociology Compass*, 6(2): 182–91.

de Moor, J. (2017) 'Lifestyle politics and the concept of political participation', *Acta Politica*, 52(2): 179–97.

de Moor, J., Catney, P. and Doherty, B. (2017) 'Conceptualizing the politics of everyday life: prefiguration and its relatives', paper presented at the Alternative Futures conference, Manchester, 10–12 April.

Deflorian, M. (2021) 'Refigurative politics: understanding the volatile participation of critical creatives in community gardens, repair cafés and clothing swaps', *Social Movement Studies*, 20(3): 1–18.

della Porta, D. (2012) 'Mobilizing against the crisis, mobilizing for "another democracy": comparing two global waves of protest', *Interface*, 4(1): 274–7.

Epstein, B. (1991) *Political Protest and Cultural Revolution*, Berkeley: University of California Press.

Eyerman, R. and Jamison, A. (1991) *Social Movements: A Cognitive Approach*, University Park, PA: Penn State University Press.

Futrell, R. and Simi, P. (2004) 'Free spaces: collective identity, and the persistence of US white power activism', *Social Problems*, 51(1), 16–42.

Gordon, U. (2018) 'Prefigurative politics between ethical practice and absent promise', *Political Studies*, 66(2): 521–37.

Gorz, A. (1968) 'The way forward', *New Left Review*, 52(Nov/Dec): 47–66.

Graeber, D. (2002) 'The new anarchists', *New Left Review*, 13(Jan/Feb): 61–73.

Jaster, D. (2018) 'Figurative politics: how activists lead by example to create change', *Mobilization: An International Quarterly*, 23(1): 65–81.

Jeffrey, C. and Dyson, J. (2016) 'Now: prefigurative politics through a north Indian lens', *Economy and Society*, 45(1): 77–100.

Juris, J.S. (2008) *Networking Futures: The Movements against Corporate Globalisation*, Durham, NC: Duke University Press.

Leach, D.K. and Haunss, S. (2009) 'Scenes and social movements', in H. Johnston (ed) *Culture, Social Movements, and Protest*, Aldershot: Ashgate, pp 255–76.

Lorenzini, J. (2019) 'Food activism and citizens' democratic engagements: what can we learn from market-based political participation?', *Politics and Governance*, 7(4): 131–41.

Maeckelbergh, M. (2009) *The Will of the Many*, London: Pluto Press.

Magri, L. (1970) 'Problems of the Marxist theory of the revolutionary party', *New Left Review*, 60(Mar/Apr): 97–128.

Polletta, F. (1999) '"Free spaces" in collective action', *Theory and Society*, 28(1): 1–38.

Portwood-Stacer, L. (2012) 'Anti-consumption as tactical resistance', *Journal of Consumer Culture*, 12(1): 87–105.

Raekstad, P. and Gradin, S.S. (2020) *Prefigurative Politics: Building Tomorrow Today*, Cambridge: Polity Press.

Razsa, M. and Kurnik, A. (2012) 'The Occupy movement in Žižek's hometown: direct democracy and a politics of becoming', *American Ethnologist*, 39(2): 238–58.

Rowbotham, S., Segal, L. and Wainwright, H. (1979) *Beyond the Fragments*, London: Merlin Press.

Schlosberg, D. and Craven, L. (2019) *Sustainable Materialism: Environmental Movements and the Politics of Everyday Life*, Oxford: Oxford University Press.

Schulz, M.S. (2016) 'Social movements and futures research', *World Futures Review*, 8(2): 98–107.

Seyfang, G. and Longhurst, N. (2016) 'What influences the diffusion of grassroots innovations for sustainability? Investigating community currency niches', *Technology Analysis & Strategic Management*, 28(1): 1–23.

Sitrin, M. (ed) (2006) *Horizontalism*, Oakland, CA: AK Press.

Swain, D. (2017) 'Not not but not yet: present and future in prefigurative politics', *Political Studies*, 67(1): 47–62.

van de Sande, M. (2013) 'The prefigurative politics of Tahrir Square', *Res Publica*, 19(3): 223–39.

Wagner-Pacifici, R. and Ruggero, E.C. (2018) 'Temporal blindspots in Occupy Philadelphia', https://doi.org/10.1080/14742837.2018.1474096

Welch, D. and Yates, L. (2018) 'The practices of collective action: practice theory, sustainability transitions and social change', *Journal for the Theory of Social Behaviour*, 48(3): 288–305.

Wright, E.O. (2010) *Envisioning Real Utopias*, London: Verso.

Yates, L. (2015a) 'Everyday politics, social practices and movement networks: daily life in Barcelona's social centres', *The British Journal of Sociology*, 66(2): 236–58.

Yates, L. (2015b) 'Rethinking prefiguration: alternatives, micropolitics and goals in social movements', *Social Movement Studies*, 14(1): 1–21.

Yates, L. (2020) 'Prefigurative politics and social movement strategy: the roles of prefiguration in the reproduction, mobilisation and coordination of movements', *Political Studies*, 69(4): 1033–52.

Young, K. and Schwartz, M. (2012) 'Can prefigurative politics prevail? The implications for movement strategy in John Holloway's *Crack Capitalism*', *Journal of Classical Sociology*, 12(2): 220–39.

13

Organizing Prefiguration

Mikko Laamanen

Introduction

Prefiguration as a specific idea signposts a strategy towards an empowered, humanized sociality. Prefigurative organizing has come to stand in contrast to traditional, formalized modalities of organization. How participants (should) engage with one another, how their communities discuss and decide on important matters and, ultimately, how they reproduce their community is guided by horizontal, structureless, leaderless (yet leaderful), participatory, solidaristic and diversity-orientated principles. By eschewing formality, bureaucracy and oligarchy as models for forming groups, keeping them together and getting things done, prefiguration emphasizes the strategic practice of experimentation in the present towards a politically relevant future. Prefiguration is typically understood as the alignment of means and ends (Leach, 2013); in practice, however, the expressive politics (means) and strategic politics (ends) exist in dynamic, shifting tension (Yates, 2015; Reinecke, 2018). These tensions are highlighted in attempts to organize prefiguration.

In this chapter, I consider how prefiguration can be organized. Ontologically, prefigurative organizing is paradoxical in that prefigurative action leans on (some) organization but, in practice, is characteristically anti-organizational (Polletta, 2002). Throughout, I use prefiguration in its original Leftist sense: as a future-orientated progressive politics attempting to secure a just society through (more or less) consistent strategic action in the present (Boggs, 1978). I acknowledge, however, that conceptually prefiguration could indicate any attempt to move society from a foreboding idea to a preferred future reality (Jaster, 2018). Indeed, religious utopias, transnational capitalist institutions (such as the World Economic Forum) or political countermovements (such as the white power movement) mobilize in such future-shaping manners (see, for example, Graz, 2003; Futrell and

Simi, 2004; for a discussion on this, see also Yates and de Moor, this volume; du Plessis and Husted, this volume). We should be cautious about the kind of polyvocal ambiguity created when various 'future-makers' mix fantasy and fiction to herald alternative futures within unsettled political milieus (Wenzel et al, 2020). The ensuing post-truth politics affect not only the meaning but also the very nature of social reality and justice. Consequently, the use of prefiguration as an organizing principle cannot come with limited moral evaluation. At the root of prefigurative politics are the four anti-positions of anti-authoritarianism, anti-capitalism, anti-oppression and anti-imperialism (Dixon, 2014). Organizing that follows these ideals rejects the types of modality that carry regressive revolutionary politics, which instead should be called 'figurative ideal types' (Jaster, 2018, p 66).

In what follows, I first review literature at the intersection of organization studies and social movement studies, in which organization oscillates between formalized, regime-specific *structures* and emergent, society-wide *processes* (McAdam and Scott, 2005). Prefiguration occupies a specific niche status in this literature, and studies have discussed how collective action aligns with the appropriate modality of organization (for example, Reinecke, 2018; Zanoni, 2020). Organization, as a formal entity, sits uneasily with the ideals of prefigurative politics. To develop this point, I evaluate the paradox of prefigurative organizing through the conceptual lens of partial organization theory (Ahrne and Brunsson, 2011). Emphasizing the acts of organizing, recent studies drawing on partial organization as a framework have demonstrated the incompleteness of organization and the dynamics of organizing in collective action settings (for example, den Hond et al, 2015; de Bakker et al, 2017; Simsa and Totter, 2017; Laamanen et al, 2019; Laamanen et al, 2020). For illustration, I draw on a first-hand action research account of experimentation with prefigurative organizing practices in an alternative economy community. Contradictory individual and collective responsibilities and implications regarding the future become apparent in community practice. The community deals with these through a process of blending various elements of formal and emergent (or informal) order. In conclusion, this focus on the dynamics between the elements of organizing contributes to understanding how inclusive futures are enacted and exercised in present organizing practice.

The paradox of prefigurative organizing

Organization may not only influence but also define social actors' ideologies, relations and goals, both among themselves and with others. The question of how to build a democratic organizational culture veers between reliance on 'pre-existing identities and familiar ways of interacting – and whether one can afford the time that it takes to craft new ones' (Polletta, 2002, p 29). The promise of prefiguration materializes in the active, reflexive reconstruction of social relationships and spaces towards equity. It is essential to grasp that 'power relations, whether in activist groups or broader society, don't change through good intentions or wishful thinking; they change through agitating and organizing' (Dixon, 2014, p 95). In the field of organization studies, organization is typically ontologically fixed as universal, formal, technical–managerialist instruments for administering workflows and implementing strategic plans (Böhm, 2006). In social movement studies, organization remains controversial inasmuch as it either trumps equality in constraining direct participation or represents an invaluable resource for effective movement coordination and maintenance.

Prefigurative initiatives contain much of both of these foci (and debates), in that they politicize formal modalities of organizing. Context and practices for organizing prefiguration are those that challenge the prevailing status quo of the political, cultural and economic order. Prefigurative initiatives position themselves against repressive, unequal institutions by creating alternatives through inclusive, reflexive practice aiming to radically restructure the social order, rather than attempting to reform it. Their political acts connect to countercultural lifestyles within purpose-built counter-institutions that organize with a horizontal orientation and practice egalitarian modes of interacting (Dixon, 2014). Democratic work organizations represent alternative institutions in which internal interactions restrict administration through inclusive decision-making practices (Kokkinidis, 2015; Jaumier, 2016). Countercultural lifestyles foster solidarity by localizing resources and relations in collaborative production and consumption (Forno and Graziano, 2014; Laamanen et al, 2018; Laamanen and Wahlen, 2019; Forno and Wahlen, this volume). Lifestyle movements as counter-institutions are diffuse in their organizational practices, and their shared values and moral vision(s) connect everyday acts of personal and social transformation. Thus, while organization may have become less visibly manifested, organizing has not disappeared. Melucci (1996) observes how (new) social movements wane in visibility during moments of movement latency and visibility. During latency, a movement engages in the strategic construction of future utopian realities; in contrast, when it is directly confronted by the dominant ideology and institutions, it is rendered visible. Prefiguration connects intimately with such internal and external dynamics of organizing, moving our focus from the entity (*organization*) to the acts of *organizing* (de Bakker et al, 2017). Looking for organizations, or those formal entities that prefigurative organizing aims to avoid, leads to the probable conclusion that formalization and oligarchization are unavoidable and that prefigurative organizing will fail (Breines, 1980). Instead, in prefigurative organizing, organization as an entity becomes reimagined and transformed in experimentation with the kind of social order that is locally preferred.

This represents a dilemma for prefigurative organizing and leads to the question: how can/do/will participants navigate between the impossibility of structure and the impracticality of openness? Practically, even the most anti-authoritarian initiative may exercise some authority over participants or decision-making so as to coordinate activities, manage scale and sustain action. Organizing prefiguration entails how participants navigate the tension between structure and openness within their initiative, over time, by blending elements constituting a formal organization and those present in non-organizations (Laamanen et al, 2020).

Blending social order in prefigurative organizing

Maintaining social order and attempting to change it are fundamentally questions of organizing. Ahrne and Brunsson (2011) developed a typology of elements that represent a decided (social) order. Decisions made on membership, hierarchy, rules, monitoring and sanctions constitute the formality in an organization. In formal organizations, decisions on these elements are made by (qualified) decision-makers, in whom other organizational members vest such power. The ensuing hierarchy entails an organization of power that obliges compliance. Membership outlines who can legitimately participate – and, consequently, who is excluded. Rules are pronounced commands that members are to follow. Obedience is monitored and sanctions (and rewards) awarded based on the monitored behaviours. In this framework, organization is partial (not fully formal) when decisions are made on some (but not all) of the elements; nevertheless, even in partially organized settings, decisions are made.

An emergent order counterpoints the decided order. Participation maintains a form of social order while remaining anti-organizational (Polletta, 2002; de Bakker et al, 2017). Participation respects the autonomy of individuals to act towards social change, in a self-governed and self-organized manner, within their everyday contexts (Laamanen et al, 2018; Forno and Wahlen, this volume). At the same time, shared beliefs and values, acknowledging one another and recognizing correct practice ensures social (and moral) control (Wilhoit and Kisselburgh, 2015; Daskalaki et al, 2018; Laamanen et al, 2018). Effectively, in an emergent order, participants tend to come to accept things as they are practised, without formal rules and decisions: by contrast, cohesion relies on routine, habit and adaptation (Laamanen et al, 2019). Emergence in prefigurative, lifestyle counter-institutions contours action in two ways. First, the internal 'structures' of prefigurative organizing spaces are 'characterized by a minimal division of labour, decentralized authority, and an egalitarian ethos and … decision-making is direct and consensus oriented' (Polletta, 2002, p 6). Second, the configurations of authority are 'managed' through

Table 13.1: Decided and emergent elements of organizing

Decided		Emergent
Official registered membership	←→	Informal affiliation with mutual recognition
Authoritative power furnished by hierarchy	←→	Inclusive participation in direct democratic practice
Explicit, written rules with an expectation of obedience	←→	Autonomy to act guided by shared norms and values
Monitoring performance and compliance with rules	←→	Social control through mutual observation
Behaviour sanctioned with rewards and punishments	←→	Intrinsic motivation based on (active) participation

Source: Based on Ahrne and Brunsson (2011), de Bakker et al (2017) and Laamanen et al (2020)

rotating responsibilities and inclusive governance structures, such as spokes councils (Sutherland et al, 2014; Kinna et al, 2019).

Affiliation, horizontal participation, norms and values, social control through mutual observation and intrinsic motivation are sources of emergent social order and functional equivalents to decided order elements (see Table 13.1) (Laamanen et al, 2020). In the following illustration, I draw on participatory research engagement in an alternative currency community – the Stadin Aikapankki (STAP, Helsinki Timebank) – to demonstrate how these elements and their blending are empirically observable in prefigurative organizing.

Practising prefigurative organizing at Stadin Aikapankki

Alternative economy organizations represent a theoretically and empirically pertinent playground of experimentation in prefigurative organizing. Time banks, as part of the alternative currency movement (North, 2007), embody the ideals of localized autonomy, communal work, equal distribution and multilateral reciprocity. Based on documents, exchange records, participant observation and activist interviews, I recount the community's attempts to match its prefigurative ideals with the everyday realities in which participants attend to individual needs and common goals. Based on this engagement, I have, with colleagues, theorized the blending of various decided and emergent organizational elements (Laamanen et al, 2019; Laamanen et al, 2020) that highlight the internal dynamics in communities, as well as their relations with outsides (for example, Zanoni, 2020).

Table 13.2: Blending of organizational elements in Stadin Aikapankki

Decided	Blended	Emergent
Registered membership		'Anonymous' affiliation
No formalized hierarchy	*Core group*	Inclusive participation
Decision-making authority with the membership meeting	*Coordinator*	Practical experience
No strict rules	*ABC*	Community values
No formal monitoring mechanisms	*Exchange platform*	Mutual observation
No formal sanctioning mechanisms		Motivation through participation

Source: Adapted from Laamanen et al (2020)

STAP is a Finnish alternative exchange network that has operated since 2009 in the Helsinki metropolitan area. It is the largest time bank in the country, with some 4,000 members and over 38,300 hours of exchanges overall (Stadin Aikapankki, 2009). STAP relies on multilateral reciprocity, whereby one member can help another member and, in return, receive help from a further member. STAP does this by registering and maintaining an electronic ledger of the hours members work. With its activities, STAP aims to prefigure an inclusive community where economic value, work and consumption remain within the community boundaries. Constructing inclusive, transparent and non-coercive social relationships is, in the prefigurative sense, supposed to empower the participants and be formative of a new social order.

Nevertheless, organizing STAP has been challenging. Throughout its existence, STAP has emphasized inclusive, open participation and decision-making. The community has endeavoured to rely mostly on elements of emergent order in its organizing (see Table 13.2). A prominent decision is the formalized nature of membership; registering as a member is required to operate on the exchange platform. However, with little control over the correctness and completeness of the personal details members submit, any single member can, in effect, be 'anonymously' affiliated. There is little the community can (or will) do to counteract this anonymity. Although this practice is discussed at regular intervals in the membership meetings, no monitoring or sanctioning is established. Anonymity is a predicament for the community because it decreases trust and the willingness to interact. In practice, members refuse to trade with anonymous members. Similarly, although fictional, idea-supporting, non-practising members add to the overall numbers of the group, active participation – not idea patronage – is considered imperative for prefiguring alternative economies.

Authority is vested in the collective (Laamanen et al, 2020). The membership meeting, in which every member is invited to participate, decides on matters based on the consensus of those present. Power is transitory because in any subsequent membership meeting members can decide to reverse any or all previous decisions. Still, there have been voices calling for a more decided order. Recently, such demands resulted from interventions by dominant social institutions. When the Finnish tax authority declared time-banking as tax evasion and a formal response from the community was necessary, the effectiveness of the prevailing decision-making and representational structures became contested (for a detailed discussion of this intervention, see Laamanen et al, 2019). Subsequently, there were calls for a clearer formal structure, as this would benefit interactions with public institutions – such as the City of Helsinki – that could also provide legitimacy to time-banking. A formal structure would also remove any hidden structures, allow the collective to oust toxic individuals and clarify positions of privilege (for example, related to gender). Yet, the fear that a formalized authority would centralize power and increase inequality between participants hindered a decision on a formal structure. Eventually, the only decision made was to appoint a 'coordinator', whose role is to communicate on and manage activities – but not make decisions. STAP remained unregistered and politically and religiously unaffiliated (Laamanen et al, 2019).

The community appears structureless, leaderless and reliant on inclusive participation. This logic of direct democracy requires active participation and socialization, as prefigurative processes cannot be built by force. Problematically, the membership's engagement in decision-making tends to be minimal. When the active membership, who take on the workload of organizing, is effectively composed only of the few individuals in the so-called 'core group', these members become deeply entrenched in advancing issues and agendas and 'orchestrating' decisions. Beyond this, they gain expertise and ownership. Some core members consider such benevolent oligarchy acceptable (Laamanen and den Hond, 2015), but the opaque manner in which power becomes wielded is frequently questioned. Debates emerged when informal power structures 'materialized' during the discussion related to responding to the tax authority. With no formal sanctioning of non-participation in place, tensions kept mounting due to expectations that active members set – for themselves and others – regarding the levels of participation and responsibility in governing the collective. Even with discursive interventions to this emergent order, central roles remained occupied by a few individuals – typically, those who had joined in the early days and/or founder of the community. At the same time, any protest against this centralization in the larger membership of this time-banking community is difficult to find.

It would appear that the rank-and-file members' activities in STAP focus on lifestyle and institution-building rather than organizing. In the social construction of the time bank, alongside the political project of organizing, there is a quotidian project of localized service exchange. Members trade with each other by using the community exchange platform. Exchanges occur according to the community values, set out in quasi-rules called the 'ABC'. These values have been agreed on to guide good interactions. The ABC is necessary for two purposes: first, to familiarize new members with community practice and, second, to allow the community to exclude those who do not align with these values. As an example of the latter, in the early years, businesses had joined the community to capitalize on the network's sales and marketing potential. As a set of values, the ABC is nevertheless rather flexible (compared to rules that have to be observed) and, on occasion, members do not conform (for example, when using the national currency for partial payment of exchange). Mutual observation is allowed, as all exchange data on the exchange platform is transparently accessible to the entire membership. For instance, account balances are reviewed to see how reciprocity is working (or if value is being hoarded). Interventions are rare; on occasion, the membership meeting discusses large surpluses and deficits, but usually takes no decision or action.

Over time, due to internal tensions and external interventions, decisions on formal elements have been thoroughly discussed in the membership meetings. Still, organizational elements have mostly not been decided on; indeed, indecision and the blending of order seem to have sustained the prefigurative essence of the community.

Lessons learned on prefigurative organizing

The STAP case holds insights for how an anti-structural group with non-coercive participation can, to some extent, be managed over time. A prefigurative community can be severely challenged by the wavering between more or less structure and openness. In prefigurative initiatives, political uniformity of the dominant social order is mistrusted and dismissed (Maeckelbergh, 2011; de Bakker et al, 2017). Bureaucracies are rejected because they impose hierarchies of authority (Laamanen et al, 2019). Reliance on a vanguard leadership is similarly refused (Boggs, 1978). Representative structures are thought to lead to political and economic domination, and the imposition of an elite agenda on all others involved (Teivainen, 2016). Organizing *done for others* is not considered appropriate, as individual participation in the processes of organizing holds central significance (Piven and Cloward, 1979). As such, authority from beyond the participants and the locality is deemed illegitimate.

The emergence of divisions among the participants and anti-inclusionary power structures require constant vigilance and calling out of incongruous practices (Blee, 2012; Breton et al, 2012; Reinecke, 2018). Consequently, decision-making must be organized to counteract any position of privilege. Inclusion is performed in STAP and other prefigurative initiatives through Occupy-style working groups and open task division among participants. Authority is further contained through the moral obligation to participate. Yet, notably, Maeckelbergh's (2009) account of the European Social Forum (ESF), as well as Reinecke's (2018) and Kinna et al's (2019) retelling of the processual challenges managed by Occupy Wall Street camps, illustrate how communities without restrictions on participation (including formal membership) are confronted with some need for boundaries on inclusion when strains on consensus and community resources intensify. Relatedly, although formal leadership is decidedly rejected, participants' perceptions of their ownership of a cause may lead to the formation of a leadership that is officially eschewed but nevertheless maintained by the passive/ tangential participation of the majority (Blee, 2012; Laamanen et al, 2019). Prefigurative organizing turns oligarchical when informal, self-interested authority is purposefully veiled and used to dominate without contestation (Leach, 2013). For the core group of STAP activists, the major concern of prefigurative organizing is staying true to the ideals of the initiative, as well as managing taking responsibility for advancing change. In practice, core activists struggle to keep the process of decision-making open and participatory while also having to take charge of moving things forward (by holding meetings, recording discussions and advancing collaborations). In effect, by virtue of being active, a few individuals influence (or orchestrate) decisions or non-decisions, such as those relating to the form of organizing.

Inclusive participation further invites the question of how to motivate participants without resorting to coercion. Collective action can be a multiplication of actions of individuals with ambivalent relationships to communities (Lichterman, 1996; Micheletti, 2003; Haenfler et al, 2012). The caveat is that individualized action in a plurality of (non-aligned) practices leads to disconnectedness. Diverse groups of participants, with their individual goals and understandings, may favour different (and potentially contradictory or repressive) methods in which alternative futures are set in motion and ultimately brought about. In the time bank, alternative valuation of every participant's work has not been fully embraced, and exchanges in national currency are sometimes observed. This finding coincides with the suggestions of some recent work that without a common ideological foundation, lifestyle-based collective action merely cumulates without any *intentionality* of political change, and individualized participation can thus undo prefigurative organizing in the long run (Deflorian, 2020). If group-level institutions – beliefs, norms and values – are weak, the consequent organizing action would be more formal – through rules, monitoring and sanctions. In the case of STAP, these elements are currently not used. Instead, the recurring discussion on community norms and motivations to participate is considered to provide a collective, morally coherent and meaningful reference point for personal and collective identification. A strong collective moral reference point may also be missing. This is suggested by the absence of active participation in organising by the majority, the ensuing vesting of authority in a few well-networked activists, the bending of normative expectations of exchange by some and, ultimately, the possibility of remaining a supportive, non-trading member.

Conclusion

This chapter has considered how organizing prefiguration signifies navigating between the requirements of practical structure and a utopian openness (Kinna, 2016). Prefigurative organizing appears permanently open in its rejection of all formal organization and any hierarchy and method of representation. Communities still need to somehow structure and coordinate relations and interactions while also ideologically rejecting authoritarianism, oppression and capitalism as the status quo. Rather than an abstract political philosophy or fully fleshed out ideology, prefiguration creates order that is constantly shifting and discontinuous, existing between decided and emergent dimensions of order. This is what I put forward as the paradox of organizing prefiguration. Establishing organizing in perpetual openness carries a moral imperative of participation through which forms of inequality, such as emergent covert power structures in lieu of formally decided ones, are regulated. Internal politics and participant (in)actions can effectively pervert – or, at least, run opposite to – such ideals, as I have attempted to demonstrate with the case of STAP (see also Leach, 2013). The political project of prefigurative organizing may collide with participants' diverging everyday practices and subjectivities. Thus, finding a pure, ideal form of prefigurative (anti-)organizing is a difficult quest, inasmuch as many organized settings are effectively blended forms of formal and emergent partaking, intervening, reacting and structuring. The continuous blending of organizing in the present moves us towards a future that is similarly ever ephemerally organizable.

References

Ahrne, G. and Brunsson, N. (2011) 'Organization outside organizations: the significance of partial organization', *Organization*, 18(1): 83–104.

Blee, K.M. (2012) *Democracy in the Making: How Activist Groups Form*, Oxford: Oxford University Press.

Boggs, C. (1978) 'Marxism, prefigurative communism, and the problem of workers' control', *Radical America*, 11/12(1): 99–122.

Böhm, S. (2006) *Repositioning Organization Theory*, Basingstoke: Palgrave Macmillan.

Breines, W. (1980) 'Community and organization: the New Left and Michels' "iron law"', *Social Problems*, 27(4): 419–29.

Breton, E., Jeppesen, S., Kruzynski, A. and Sarrasin, R. (2012) 'Prefigurative self-governance and self-organization: the influence of antiauthoritarian (pro)feminist, radical queer, and antiracist networks in Quebec', in A. Choudry, J. Hanley and E. Shragge (eds) *Organize! Building from the Local for Global Justice*, Oakland, CA: PM Press, pp 156–73.

Daskalaki, M., Fotaki, M. and Sotiropoulou, I. (2018) 'Performing values practices and grassroots organizing: the case of solidarity economy initiatives in Greece', *Organization Studies*, 40(11): 1741–65.

de Bakker, F., den Hond, F. and Laamanen, M. (2017) 'Social movements: organizations and organizing', in C. Roggeband and B. Klandermans (eds) *Handbook of Social Movements across Disciplines*, Cham: Springer, pp 203–31.

Deflorian, M. (2020) 'Refigurative politics: understanding the volatile participation of critical creatives in community gardens, repair cafés and clothing swaps', *Social Movement Studies* [online], 20(3), available from: https://www.tandfonline.com/doi/full/10.1080/14742 837.2020.1773250

den Hond, F., de Bakker, F.G.A. and Smith, N. (2015) 'Social movements and organizational analysis', in D. della Porta and M. Diani (eds) *The Oxford Handbook of Social Movements*, Oxford: Oxford University Press, pp 291–305.

Dixon, C. (2014) *Another Politics: Talking across Today's Transformative Movements*, Oakland, CA: University of California Press.

Forno, F. and Graziano, P.R. (2014) 'Sustainable community movement organisations', *Journal of Consumer Culture*, 14(2): 139–57.

Futrell, R. and Simi, P. (2004) 'Free spaces: collective identity, and the persistence of US white power activism', *Social Problems*, 51(1): 16–42.

Graz, J. (2003) 'How powerful are transnational elite clubs? The social myth of the World Economic Forum', *New Political Economy*, 8(3): 321–40.

Haenfler, R., Johnson, B. and Jones, E. (2012) 'Lifestyle movements: exploring the intersection of lifestyle and social movements', *Social Movement Studies*, 11(1): 1–20.

Jaster, D. (2018) 'Figurative politics: how activists lead by example to create change', *Mobilization: An International Quarterly*, 23(1): 65–81.

Jaumier, S. (2016) 'Preventing chiefs from being chiefs: an ethnography of a co-operative sheet-metal factory', *Organization*, 24(2): 218–39.

Kinna, R. (2016) 'Utopianism and prefiguration', in S.D. Christowska and J.D. Ingram (eds) *Political Uses of Utopia*, New York, NY: Columbia University Press, pp 198–215.

Kinna, R., Prichard, A. and Swann, T. (2019) 'Occupy and the constitution of anarchy', *Global Constitutionalism*, 8(2): 357–90.

Kokkinidis, G. (2015) 'Spaces of possibilities: workers' self-management in Greece', *Organization*, 22(6): 847–71.

Laamanen, M. and den Hond, F. (2015) 'Prefigurative partial organization in local social movements: examining decided and emergent order in a time bank', paper presented at the 31st European Group of Organizational Studies Colloquium, Athens, Greece.

Laamanen, M. and Wahlen, S. (2019) 'Sharing economy and lifestyle movements', in R. Belk, G.M. Eckhardt and F. Bardhi (eds) *Handbook of the Sharing Economy*, London: Edward Elgar, pp 49–60.

Laamanen, M., Bor, S. and den Hond, F. (2019) 'The dilemma of organization in social movement initiatives', in G. Ahrne and N. Brunsson (eds) *Organization Outside Organizations: The Abundance of Partial Organization in Social Life*, Cambridge: Cambridge University Press, pp 293–317.

Laamanen, M., Wahlen, S. and Lorek, S. (2018) 'A moral householding perspective to the sharing economy', *Journal of Cleaner Production*, 202: 1220–7.

Laamanen, M., Moser, C., Bor, S. and den Hond, F. (2020) 'A partial organization approach to the dynamics of social order in social movement organizing', *Current Sociology*, 68(4): 520–45.

Leach, D.K. (2013) 'Prefigurative politics', in D.A. Snow, D. della Porta, B. Klandermans and D. McAdam (eds) *The Wiley–Blackwell Encyclopedia of Social and Political Movements*, Oxford: Blackwell, pp 1004–5.

Lichterman, P. (1996) *The Search for Political Community: American Activists Reinventing Commitment*, Cambridge: Cambridge University Press.

Maeckelbergh, M. (2009) *The Will of the Many: How the Alterglobalisation Movement Is Changing the Face of Democracy*, London: Pluto Books.

Maeckelbergh, M. (2011) 'Doing is believing: prefiguration as strategic practice in the alterglobalization movement', *Social Movement Studies*, 10(1): 1–20.

McAdam, D. and Scott, W.R. (2005) 'Organizations and movements', in G.F. Davies, D. McAdam, W.R. Scott and M.N. Zald (eds) *Social Movements and Organization Theory*, New York, NY: Cambridge University Press, pp 4–40.

Melucci, A. (1996) *Challenging Codes: Collective Action in the Information Age*, Cambridge: Cambridge University Press.

Micheletti, M. (2003) *Political Virtue and Shopping: Individuals, Consumerism, and Collective Action*, Basingstoke: Palgrave Macmillan.

North, P. (2007) *Money and Liberation: The Micropolitics of Alternative Currency Movements*, Minneapolis, MN: University of Minnesota Press.

Piven, F.F. and Cloward, R.A. (1979) *Poor People's Movements: Why They Succeed, How They Fail*, New York, NY: Vintage Books.

Polletta, F. (2002) *Freedom is an Endless Meeting*, Chicago, IL: University of Chicago Press.

Reinecke, J. (2018) 'Social movements and prefigurative organizing: confronting entrenched inequalities in Occupy London', *Organization Studies*, 39(9): 1299–321.

Simsa, R. and Totter, M. (2017) 'Social movement organizations in Spain: being partial as the prefigurative enactment of social change', *Qualitative Research in Organizations and Management*, 12(4): 280–96.

Stadin Aikapankki (2009) *Stadin Aikapankki exchange platform* [online], available from: https://stadinaikapankki.wordpress.com/

Sutherland, N., Land, C. and Böhm, S. (2014) 'Anti-leaders(hip) in social movement organizations: the case of autonomous grassroots groups', *Organization*, 21(6): 759–81.

Teivainen, T. (2016) 'Occupy representation and democratise prefiguration: speaking for others in global justice movements', *Capital and Class*, 40(1): 19–36.

Wenzel, M., Krämer, H., Koch, J. and Reckwitz, A. (2020) 'Future and organization studies: on the rediscovery of a problematic temporal category in organizations', *Organization Studies*, 41(10): 1441–55.

Wilhoit, E.D. and Kisselburgh, L.G. (2015) 'Collective action without organization: the material constitution of bike commuters as collective', *Organization Studies*, 36(5): 573–92.

Yates, L. (2015) 'Rethinking prefiguration: alternatives, micropolitics and goals in social movements', *Social Movement Studies*, 14(1): 1–21.

Zanoni, P. (2020) 'Prefiguring alternatives through the articulation of post- and anti-capitalistic politics: an introduction to three additional papers and a reflection', *Organization*, 27(1): 3–16.

14

Process–Time and Event–Time: The Multiple Temporalities of Prefiguration

Marianne Maeckelbergh

Introduction

More and more social movement scholars are turning their attention to the concept of prefigurative politics. These scholars trace the practice back into history along multiple trajectories, but the historical narratives most often identify the movements of the 1960s, Latin American movements such as the Zapatistas and/or anarchist movements. While these movements certainly embodied forms of politics we could consider prefigurative (among other forms), and while today's prefigurative movement practices certainly find their roots in these movements, the term 'prefiguration' only proliferated in scholarly analysis of social movements post 2000, and especially post 2010 (see Yates and de Moor, this volume; du Plessis and Husted, this volume). This shift had to do with the growth of social movements that more explicitly embodied a politics of prefiguration and, eventually, movements that used this term to refer to their own political practices – practices that may already have been prefigurative, but that were not always referred to as such.

The term 'prefigurative' can be applied to any movement practices that involve some element of trying to embody, in the present moment, a more ideal society or social relationship. Prefiguration is based on unmediated action – that is, actions that do not address others (especially politicians) in the hope they will act on your behalf in the future. Instead, the emphasis is on taking action yourself, to some degree, in the present moment, thereby conflating future aspirations and present actions.

In this chapter, I explore two periods of political mobilization: the alter-globalization movement in the 2000s and the occupation- and assembly-based movements that swept across the world in the early 2010s, including the Arab Spring (van de Sande, 2015; Abdalla, 2016; Baker, 2016; Rizk, 2016), the Indignados in Spain (Maeckelbergh, 2012; Estalella and Corsín Jiménez, 2013, 2017; Flesher Fominaya, 2015), the movement of the squares in Greece and elsewhere in Europe (Dalakoglou, 2013; Howard and Pratt-Boyden, 2013; Simiti, 2016), the Occupy movement internationally (Juris, 2012; Razsa and Kurnik, 2012; Maharawal, 2013; Szolucha, 2013; Sitrin and Azzellini, 2014; Wagner-Pacifici and Ruggero, 2018) and the Gezi uprising in Turkey (Inceoglu, 2015; Koç, 2015).

These two periods of political mobilization embodied a specific type of prefiguration – they prefigured forms of *horizontal* politics. The term 'horizontal' emerged during the years of the alter-globalization movement to refer specifically to groups of people who, despite having a diverse set of political beliefs, all agreed that the movement's main goal was to reinvent global democracy in a new and radically egalitarian form, and that this egalitarianism needed to be reflected in the everyday organizing practices of the movement itself (Graeber, 2002, 2009; Juris, 2008; Maeckelbergh, 2009, 2011; Razsa, 2015). Movement actors began referring to each other as either 'horizontals' or 'verticals' – a dividing line drawn depending on how much hierarchy they felt was acceptable within the movement's daily organizing practices (see also Laamanen, this volume). The horizontals felt strongly that movement spaces needed to be open to all and that the movement's decision-making practices should include everyone, foster diversity by ensuring outcomes acceptable to all and actively confront any form of hierarchy that emerged (Maeckelbergh, 2009). This politics, referred to as 'horizontality', resulted in elaborate organizing structures and practices, which flowed into – and, indeed, became central to – the occupation- and assembly-based movements of the 2010s (see Juris, 2008, 2012; Maeckelbergh, 2012; Razsa and Kurnik, 2012; Sitrin, 2012). In both the alter-globalization movement and the occupation- and assembly-based movements post 2011, horizontal politics meant a substantial degree of anti-capitalist sentiment, anti-state or non-state emphasis and some form of consensus decision-making – or, at the very least, open assembly-based decision-making procedures. These movements consisted of a wide variety of actors with various aims, so this claim should not be taken to imply that all those involved were anti-capitalist or anti-state; indeed, quite the opposite is true. Nevertheless, in all these movements, there was (either predominantly or alongside other forms of politics) a strong ethos of horizontal prefiguration.

Despite a shared emphasis on horizontal prefiguration, there were many differences between these two periods of political mobilization. In this chapter, I focus on one such difference: how movement actors conceptualized the relationship between the temporality of movement *processes* and the temporality of movement *events* – what I am calling 'process-time' and 'event-time'. Process-time refers to how movement actors view the temporality of the ongoing organizing work – the everyday organizing practices needed to sustain a social movement over time. Event-time refers to moments of action and public mobilization. How movement actors conceptualize the relationship between these two temporalities (implicitly or explicitly) influences how they assess their own success or failure as a movement, as well as when a movement is determined to be 'over'. I argue that the alter-globalization movement articulated process-time with event-time through the punctuated time of the anti-summit mobilization, whereas the occupation- and assembly-based movements integrated process-time and event-time through the continuous time of occupation. I further argue that these different ways of articulating process-time and event-time impacted on the assessment of the 'success' or 'failure' of these historic moments of political mobilization. The dominance of a process-orientated approach within the alter-globalization movement allowed the movement to organize from one event to the next, across time and space, without losing a conception of a singular political process that expands infinitely into the future. In the occupation- and assembly-based movements, however, the conflation of process and event made it difficult to continue the process of political organizing after the event of occupation came to an end.

Articulating process–time with event–time
The alter-globalization movement

International media first recognized the alter-globalization movement as a coherent phenomenon in November 1999, when movement actors staged a massive protest (attracting tens of thousands of people) during the third ministerial conference of the World Trade Organization (WTO) in Seattle. The anti-WTO summit protests were not the first anti-summit mobilization; they were, however, the start of activists perceiving anti-summit mobilizations as part of a continuum of a movement that moved from city to city around the world to protest – and, indeed, blockade – the meetings of the world's most powerful multilateral organizations. As summit meetings of the Group of Eight (G8) and the WTO, or the World Bank and International Monetary Fund, moved around the world, so too did the anti-summit protest events. An organizational structure emerged: there would be a protest event once or twice a year, which would last for a predetermined amount of time – usually about a week – to coincide with the timing of the world leaders' summit. To make this event happen, a very long process of organization was necessary. Activists sometimes planned years ahead, with increased intensity as the week of protests neared. The event of the protests, however, always had a clear start and end date. Before an event began, it was always already known when it would end – an anti-summit mobilization would usually involve a convergence of people for only one or two weeks of protests and gatherings. As such, if the events stopped and the convergence dissolved at the end of those two weeks, this had no bearing on perceptions of the success or failure of the movement. In other words, the *duration* of the event was not an indicator of success.

The alter-globalization movement placed a great deal of emphasis on the notion of 'process', by which they meant the political process that went into planning the annual anti-summit mobilizations – as well as the other local, regional and global gatherings, such as the European Social Forum (ESF) and World Social Forum (WSF). Many of the conflicts that occurred between movement actors of different political strands centred on the question of what was the right organizational process. Although not everyone was a fan of consensus decision-making, consensus was nevertheless the main decision-making method used in all of the movement's collective meeting spaces. While staff hired to organize an ESF or a WSF were able to make daily decisions without the consensus of all involved, the larger political matters were decided in open meetings with the goal of consensus (though, in practice, this was not always achievable). As I have argued elsewhere (Maeckelbergh, 2009), this process was more important to movement actors than the events themselves; indeed, it was the glue that tied these politically diverse actors together:

> There is no single 'vision'/'goal', no single 'adversary', and no single 'identity' (cf. Touraine 1985; Castells 1997) shared by all movement actors. There is, however, enough overlap between the various goals, adversaries and identities to tie all the movement actors together and to ensure that these actors with various goals, adversaries and identities often find themselves partaking in the same processes. (Maeckelbergh, 2009, p 7)

The 'process' was not only the main physical and temporal space (spaces of meetings, spaces of housing) that tied the various movement actors together but it was also viewed, by many of the horizontals, as politically more important than the anti-summit protest events. One participant in an anti-G8 planning meeting in London describes the importance of building an 'ecovillage' that can both provide housing for activists travelling from all over the world to the United Kingdom for the protests and act as an example of how to better organize society:

> 'For me, it's not so important what happens at the summit, but more what we create, how we organise. The ecovillage will become a model of how we want to organise our world ourselves, a new way of working together. … This network was about anti-capitalism, antistate and about

taking control of our own lives and creating alternatives.' (Participant at South East Assembly Meeting, London, 28 May 2005)

While shutting down the G8 meeting was certainly a very highly valued goal, the ultimate aim was to transform how democracy functions at the global level. For this goal to be achieved, the G8 (and similar sources of centralized power) certainly had to be stopped; but the movement also needed an alternative form of democratic practice that would be able to take the place of these global institutions. For the horizontals, this needed to be a system of decision-making that was global, decentralized and far less hierarchical.

The fact that the alter-globalization movement spent far more time in preparation processes than in the actual anti-summit mobilization events created a specific temporal dynamic of prefiguration, one in which the process is viewed to be more important politically – more defining of the movement – than the event being planned through that process. Perhaps the most clearly articulated statement to this effect is the charter of principles for the WSF – one of the most important events (if not *the* most important event) the alter-globalization movement organized:

> The World Social Forum at Porto Alegre (in 2001) was an event localized in time and place. From now on, in the certainty proclaimed at Porto Alegre that 'another world is possible', it becomes a *permanent* process of seeking and building alternatives, which cannot be reduced to the events supporting it. (WSF, 2001, emphasis added)

At one of the planning meetings for the 2004 ESF, this point was made even more clearly when a key organizer from the Italian contingent argued: "The ESF is a process, not event. ... If we look to this as a process, methodology is the most important thing. Our experience in Florence, we had no model, we had no experience" (13 December 2003). In this quote, the event of the ESF is quite literally viewed primarily as a 'process'. By linking the 2004 ESF in London to the first ESF two years earlier in Florence, the speaker is framing these multiple ESF events as a continuous learning process in which the ESF is one entity that simply moves from country to country, year to year. Even though the Florence ESF has ended, the ESF process continues, and lessons learned are carried forward so that each ESF can be better than the last.

The process was the overarching framework through which movement actors saw the connections between the multiple events the alter-globalization movement organized, even as the events moved from country to country and year to year. This punctuated event-time (protests, meetings, gatherings) consisted of a series of relatively short events tied together by a continuous process-time of daily organizing, which was perceived to be extremely long – so long, indeed, that it was assumed to be permanent, forever, an ongoing process of prefiguring better political structures.

Importantly, this articulation between event-time and process-time was enacted through the shifting of place. Each event (protest, meeting, mobilization) was held in a different location (with some exceptions), and the shifting of location opened up the longer-term process by exposing it to new people, places, assumptions, ideas, intentions and histories. In the alter-globalization movement, therefore, prefiguration could emerge and dissipate again without ever being gone – and without undermining the long-term 'success' or importance of the process. If a meeting went badly or a mobilization failed to disrupt a summit meeting, there was always next year, next time, another setting, which provided hope that improvements were just over the horizon.

The occupation- and assembly-based movements

From 2011 to 2014, massive protests swept around the world, the most iconic act for many of these being the occupation of central squares in major cities. The Arab Spring was followed by the 15 May movement in Spain, the movement of the squares in Greece, Occupy in the United States and an international 'Day of Rage', in which nearly a thousand actions took place in more than 80 countries. By June 2013, when many commentators were declaring the era of revolt over, people all across Turkey and Brazil took to the streets, inciting the next phase of massive revolts. In February 2014, people in Bosnia-Herzegovina stormed government buildings, set them on fire and overthrew four cantonal governments. And in autumn 2014, the streets of Hong Kong were flooded with Occupy Central protests, known as the Umbrella Movement.

Not all of these occupation- and assembly-based movements focused equally on the question of horizontal prefiguration, and where this was a core theme, it was always just one political aim among many. Nevertheless, the public assembly was a key organizing form; these assemblies became spaces of political experimentation with more horizontal forms of democracy, and the occupations became sites for creating alternative infrastructures, such as kitchens, medical care, education, media production and so on. The main assemblies were held in the occupied squares, which meant the event of occupation and the political process of movement organizing were conflated from day one. In other words, the occupation itself became both the event and the process of the movement.

This conflation of event and process had the advantage of creating a longer and more inclusive event-time – in some cases, the event of occupation lasted months. But the occupations were always on a precarious timeline. Most came to an end in one of two ways: either the police violently evicted the square or the occupiers decided to leave voluntarily before such an eviction could occur. In both cases, the stay/leave discussions emphasized continuation of the movement. In Barcelona, the assembly of the occupied Plaça de Catalunya held heated discussions about whether to leave the square voluntarily (which they eventually did). The argument for leaving the square was that it would allow the political *process* initiated there to continue and grow, at the neighbourhood level, across Barcelona – in other words, beyond the act of occupation (see Wagner-Pacifici and Ruggero, 2018, pp 10–12, for an account of a similar discussion in Occupy Philadelphia).

In the case of the United States, most of the Occupy movements were evicted on 15 November 2011 due to a coordinated nationwide police operation, just under two months after the start of the first occupation in Zuccotti Park, near Wall Street, New York City. Here again, though, the main point activists wanted to emphasize after the eviction was that the Occupy movement would continue in a new form. In New York, one year after the start of Occupy Wall Street, activists emphasized the creation of the Strike Debt campaign to cancel student debt, which launched the Rolling Jubilee project 'that buys debt for pennies on the dollar, but instead of collecting it, abolishes it'.[1] They also emphasized the launch of the Occupy Homes campaign, as well as the anti-stop-and-frisk organizing (against racial profiling by the police) that grew stronger after Occupy. A year later, this continuity was the main message they wanted to get across (see Jourdan and Maeckelbergh, 2012). And when Hurricane Sandy devastated New York City, it was the infrastructure Occupy created that swept in and provided fast relief to those who needed it. But despite the obvious continuation of Occupy in many initiatives after 15 November 2011 (with the same logos, props and people), activists still needed to repeatedly emphasize that Occupy did actually continue after the eviction – because this wasn't obvious, even to themselves. The relationship between the Strike Debt campaign and the occupation of Zuccotti Park needed to be both demonstrated and explained. Indeed, the conflation between the political process and the physical occupation of space was such a dominant framing that, despite the many initiatives that came out of Occupy, the movement's history is written with a clear end date:

> The Occupy movement splintered after NYC [New York City] Mayor Bloomberg had police raid the encampment in Zuccotti Park on November 15, 2011. The timeline here is limited to this particular protest during this approximate timeframe (ie., September 17 to November 15, 2011). However, the chronology does encompass subsequent events if they are specific to both [Occupy Wall Street] and Zuccotti Park. After November 2011, various events and protests have continued at Zuccotti Park that claim to be associated with [Occupy Wall Street]. (Wikipedia, nd)

Here, in the language such as 'events … that claim to be associated with [Occupy Wall Street]' (rather than events that simply are a manifestation of this movement), we see that these links need to be justified, defended and explained – as connections between two separate entities – which has the indirect effect of reinforcing, rather than countering, the idea that the movement ended when the occupation ended. As a result, many people quickly declared Occupy and similar movements a failure after the camps were evicted, even as the lasting impacts could be seen all around. Although the event-time of these movements was longer than that of the alter-globalization movement, allowing for a more sustained and expansive movement, the emphasis on occupation meant the movement's process-time came to be defined by the event of occupation. Ultimately, this meant the movement's process-time was far shorter, because it was merged with the presence in the physical space, which was tenuous and finite.

Waiting for success

At first sight, prefiguration is the strategic pursuit of what we might call long-term goals (fundamental social and political transformation). Horizontal prefiguration aims to create a non-capitalist and non-hierarchical society through a gradual process of learning rather than a radical break with the past; as such, it tends to view social change in a temporal frame that is long term. In the 1990s, the Zapatistas put it like this: 'We walk, not run, because we are going very far' (quoted in Sitrin, 2005). Or as one alter-globalization activist in the United Kingdom put it in 2005: 'What is the hurry here? Capitalism is not going to fuck off immediately' (Maeckelbergh, 2009, p 224). Or, indeed, as a Spanish Indignada put it in 2014:

> We want to change the economic, social and political structures that are organising our lives. This is not going to happen in two years, or five years or maybe even ten years. We are talking about that we are in a system that is based on exploitation of all of the resources, all the time, everywhere in the world. (Quoted in Jourdan and Maeckelbergh, 2014)

Such fundamental societal transformation cannot be fully accomplished in the lifespan of a single movement – much less a single occupation – leading many participants and observers to declare movements a failure.

And yet the appeal of prefiguration for many is precisely that waiting is not required. Even though the goals are revolutionary and far reaching, the privileged temporality of action is the present moment. Prefiguration is a form of unmediated political action. The emphasis is not on asking politicians to enact change but on embodying political goals yourself, in the present moment, as a way to bring them into being – on both a preliminary small scale (immediately) and a larger, more permanent scale (in the long run). As one participant in the 2013 Gezi uprising in Turkey (Occupy Gezi) put it:

'Every individual gained confidence. People saw that when they do something, it will have an effect and they can change things and protect things in their country. The masses that these individuals compose realised that when they act together, fight together and depend on their own strength, they can win or at least they can have an effect. They do not wait for a saviour anymore. They see that they can earn their lives by fighting for themselves, they can claim their lives, they can claim their health, water resources, common areas and their labour. I think this is the biggest accomplishment. The fact that they do not wait for a saviour and realise that they have to fight for themselves.' (Interview with the author and B. Jourdan, Istanbul, June 2014)

In this quote, we see the tension mentioned earlier: at first, the past tense is used, indicating that the period of uprising is clearly understood as over; yet the individual continues in the present tense, emphasizing the lasting effect – that which continues into the present and future. We see prefigurative politics being presented here as a way to avoid having to wait – to view oneself and the movement as the key actor capable of bringing about the change desired, rather than expecting political representatives to respond. This shifts the temporal sense of when change can happen. If you can do it yourself, you can get started right away. You do not have to wait until a politician takes note. One of the reasons prefiguration appeals is because people are tired of waiting, but of course a complete transformation of capitalist society takes a long time. This creates an inherent tension in prefigurative politics. While the immediate impact can often be easily seen (creating new decision-making structures and new ways of distributing food, resources, medical care, knowledge and so on), the long-term impacts are often viewed as lost once the process of movement organizing is perceived to be over. However, while it may be easy to see when an event has ended, it is much less clear to identify when a political process has ended. Since prefiguration lies primarily in the process and not the event, the temporal frame through which the process-time of the movement is understood plays an important role in determining how (and when) success and/or failure is perceived.

Conclusion

This chapter has shown that in relation to prefigurative politics, the time frame we choose for assessing our successes and failures wields significant power. In most cases, when a shorter time frame is used, we see more failures than successes – especially when movements enact a prefigurative politics with the long-term goal of transforming how power operates.[2] Prefigurative politics is a process that cannot be measured through short-term perspectives. Have the alter-globalization and Occupy movements failed because they did not successfully end capitalism in just a few years? How long should we wait before we say prefiguration has failed? Or can we see both of these movements as part of a single – much longer – movement-organizing process, one of continuous learning from movements past, in a way that transcends the separation into different 'movements'? What would be lost or gained in our analysis if we shifted the analytical lens in this way?

Prefiguration involves the creation of a model of social organization that in the long run is meant to replace the existing political and economic order. Measuring whether the existing order is successfully being replaced (slowly or quickly) is not a simple matter. While the temporal structure of the alter-globalization movement is more fragmented and each event is much shorter than the duration of the occupations enacted by most Occupy movements, the ties between events are more explicitly articulated. This articulation – the viewing of each meeting, summit and mobilization as part of one long process – made it possible to maintain a sense of continuation into an indefinite future. In the occupation-based movements, in contrast, the spatial centrality of occupation merged the event and process of prefiguration within specific locations. The result was a perception (among both participants and spectators) that the movement as a whole ended when the occupation of the square ended. The alter-globalization movement could maintain the idea that the movement could simply shift place/location and continue the same process in another place, but the tactic of occupation made this open and fluid framing of movement boundaries less convincing.[3]

To understand how success and failure are perceived within prefigurative movements, we need to think of movement praxis as an articulation of process-time and event-time, where the process-time is a continuous temporality that consists of the everyday, ongoing, non-spectacular organizational practices of a movement and the event-time is a punctuated temporality of actions and gatherings. How movements create and envision (intentionally or accidentally) different ways of articulating process-time and event-time – and, consequently, different ways of imagining the connections, continuities and discontinuities between various movements and events – shapes how they view their own successes or failures. Understanding the dynamic between process-time and event-time would lead to analyses that do not declare movements over, but rather allow movements to continue into the future, as a political process, long after event(s) have ended – even if this view leaves us with an uncomfortably unbounded subject.

Notes

1. See https://wiki.p2pfoundation.net/Rolling_Jubilee
2. As I have argued elsewhere (Maeckelbergh, 2009), one of the ways in which learning is embodied in horizontal prefigurative politics is through conflict; movement actors challenge each other to be less hierarchical and, as a result, conflicts arise. Therefore, in the short run, prefiguration results primarily in a series of conflicts that arise when we fail to embody our principles fully – or when we succeed in embodying them only partially. While these conflicts often feel like failure in the moment itself, they are how movements learn, over time, to enact and continuously improve the new political structures required to transform how power operates. However, the result is that if we measure success only in the short term, we mainly see conflict and failure – not learning.
3. An important caveat to this perception is that the emergence of new movements – with similar principles, in other countries, at later times – was perceived to be the continuation of previous movements. When the Gezi protests began in Turkey, people in other countries who had been involved in the 15 May movement or in Occupy saw these protests as the next stage in their own struggle. But this was a more abstract connection between struggles across space than the literal movement of people around the world that formed the basis of the alter-globalization movement.

Funding acknowledgement

The ideas at the heart of this chapter were born from my participation in the research project 'The Future is Elsewhere', funded by the Dutch National Research Foundation in its Cultural Dynamics programme, led by Professor Peter Pels (file number: 312-99-105). The fieldwork was funded by an Aspasia Grant from the Dutch Research Foundation and The Democracy and Media Foundation. The writing time for this chapter was funded by the European Research Council under the European Union's Horizon 2020 research and innovation programme (grant agreement number: 771795).

References

Abdalla, K. (2016) 'Changing frames & fault lines: notes towards a map of a revolution's shifting narratives', in M. Baker (ed) *Translating Dissent: Voices from and with the Egyptian Revolution*, London: Routledge, pp 33–44.

Baker, M. (2016) 'The prefigurative politics of translation in place-based movements of protest: subtitling in the Egyptian revolution', *The Translator*, 22(1): 1–21.

Dalakoglou, D. (2013) 'The movement and the "movement" of Syntagma Square', *Fieldsights, Society for Cultural Anthropology* [online], 14 February, available from: https://culanth.org/fieldsights/the-movement-and-the-movement-of-syntagma-square

Estalella, A. and Corsín Jiménez, A. (2013) 'Asambleas al aire: La arquitectura ambulatoria de una política en suspensión', *Revista de Antropología Experimental*, 13(4): 73–88.

Estalella, A. and Corsín Jiménez, A. (2017) 'Political exhaustion and the experiment of street: Boyle meets Hobbes in Occupy Madrid', *Journal of the Royal Anthropological Institute*, 23(1): 110–23.

Flesher Fominaya, C. (2015) 'Debunking spontaneity: Spain's 15-M/ Indignados as autonomous movement', *Social Movement Studies*, 14(2): 142–63.

Graeber, D. (2002) 'The New Anarchists', *New Left Review*, 13(Jan/ Feb): 61–73.

Graeber, D. (2009) *Direct Action: An Ethnography*, Oakland, CA: AK Press.

Howard, N. and Pratt-Boyden, K. (2013) 'Occupy London as pre-figurative political action', *Development in Practice*, 23(5–6): 729–41.

Inceoglu, I. (2015) 'Encountering difference and radical democratic trajectory', *City*, 19(4): 534–44.

Jourdan, B. and Maeckelbergh, M. (2012) 'Occupy Wall Street: one year later', *Global Uprisings* [online], 17 September, available from: www.glob aluprisings.org/occupy-wall-street-one-year-later/

Jourdan, B. and Maeckelbergh, M. (2014) 'Pieces of Madrid', *Global Uprisings* [online], 21 April, available from: http://www.globaluprisings.org/new-documentary-pieces-of-madrid/

Juris, J. (2008) *Networking Futures: The Movements against Corporate Globalization*, Durham, NC: Duke University Press.

Juris, J. (2012) 'Reflections on #Occupy Everywhere: social media, public space, and emerging logics of aggregation', *American Ethnologist*, 39(2): 259–79.

Koç, G. (2015) 'A radical-democratic reading of the Gezi resistance and the Occupy Gezi movement', in G. Koç and H. Aksu (eds) *Another Brick in the Barricade: The Gezi Resistance and Its Aftermath*, Bremen: Wiener Verlag für Sozialforschung, pp 163–87.

Maeckelbergh, M. (2009) *The Will of the Many: How the Alterglobalisation Movement Is Changing the Face of Democracy*, London: Pluto Press.

Maeckelbergh, M. (2011) 'Doing is believing: prefiguration as strategic practice in the alterglobalization movement', *Social Movement Studies*, 10(1): 1–20.

Maeckelbergh, M. (2012) 'Horizontal democracy now: from alterglobalization to occupation', *Interface: A Journal for and about Social Movements*, 4(1): 207–34.

Maharawal, M.M. (2013) 'Occupy Wall Street and a radical politics of inclusion', *The Sociological Quarterly*, 54(2): 177–81.

Razsa, M. (2015) *Bastards of Utopia*, Indianapolis: Indiana University Press.

Razsa, M. and Kurnik, A. (2012) 'The Occupy Movement in Žižek's hometown: direct democracy and a politics of becoming', *American Ethnologist*, 39(2): 238–58.

Rizk, P. (2016) 'Solidarity, translation and the politics of the margin', in M. Baker (ed) *Translating Dissent: Voices From and with the Egyptian Revolution*, London: Routledge, pp 225–38.

Simiti, M. (2016) 'Rage and protest: the case of the Greek Indignant movement', *Contention: The Multidisciplinary Journal of Social Protest*, 3(2): 33–50.

Sitrin, M.A. (2005) '"Walking we ask questions": an interview with John Holloway', *Left Turn* [online], 1 February, available from: http://www.leftt urn.org/"walking-we-ask-questions"-interview-john-holloway

Sitrin, M. (2012) 'Horizontalism and the Occupy movements', *Dissent Magazine* [online], available from: https://www.dissentmagazine.org/arti cle/horizontalism-and-the-occupy-movements

Sitrin, M. and Azzellini, D. (2014) *They Can't Represent Us! Reinventing Democracy from Greece to Occupy*, London and New York: Verso Press.

Szolucha, A. (2013) 'No stable ground: living real democracy in Occupy', *Interface: A Journal for and about Social Movements*, 5(2): 18–38.

van de Sande, M. (2015) 'Fighting with tools: prefiguration and radical politics in the twenty-first century', *Rethinking Marxism*, 27(2): 177–94.

Wagner-Pacifici, R. and Ruggero, E.C. (2018) 'Temporal blindspots in Occupy Philadelphia', *Social Movement Studies* [online], available from: https://doi.org/10.1080/14742837.2018.1474096

Wikipedia (nd) 'Timeline of Occupy Wall Street' [online], available from: https://en.wikipedia.org/wiki/Timeline_of_Occupy_Wall_Street

WSF (World Social Forum) (2001) *Charter of Principles* [online], available from: https://wsm2016.org/en/sinformer/a-propos-du-forum-social-mondial/

15

Five Challenges for Prefiguration Research: A Sympathetic Polemic

Erik Mygind du Plessis and Emil Husted

Introduction

Initially defined by Carl Boggs (1977a, p 100) as 'the embodiment, within the ongoing political practice of a movement, of those forms of social relations, decision-making, culture, and human experience that are the ultimate goal', the concept of prefiguration has played an important role in social movement studies for almost half a century (for example, Breines, 1980; Epstein, 1991; Polletta, 1999). However, with the rise of the alter-globalization movement in 1999 and the invention of novel procedures for ensuring what Luke Yates (2015) calls 'means–ends equivalence', the term has now also acquired a central position in activist communities around the world (Maeckelbergh, 2009). Perhaps the most illustrative contemporary example of prefigurative politics is the Occupy movement, which emerged in New York City in 2011 and proliferated globally the following year. Due to its persistent focus on consensus, participation, inclusion and deliberation, the movement has been the subject of a plethora of studies, many of which celebrate Occupy's aversion to conventional politics and ambition of changing the world without taking power (for example, Pickerill and Krinsky, 2012; Brissette, 2013; Hammond, 2015; van de Sande, 2015). As Occupy co-initiator David Graeber (2013, p 233) puts it:

> The original inspiration of Occupy Wall Street was the tradition not just of direct democracy, but of direct action ... the idea that the form of our action should itself offer a model, or at least a glimpse of how free people might organize themselves, and therefore what a free society could look like. In the early twentieth century it was called 'building the new society in the shell of the old', in the 1980s and 1990s it came to be known as 'prefigurative politics'.

Figure 15.1: Number of published articles containing the word 'prefiguration' in the title, abstract and/or keywords, 2000–20

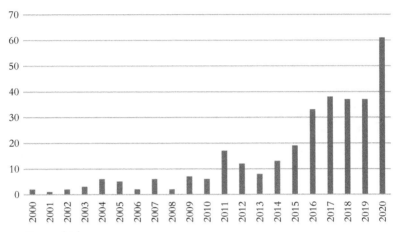

Source: Scopus database

The increased importance of prefiguration for activists and scholars is also reflected in the literature. As shown in Figure 15.1, the number of articles published each year that contain the word 'prefiguration' has increased dramatically since the turn of the century. Debates about prefigurative politics were once confined to political theory journals with Left-leaning sympathies (for example, *Rethinking Marxism* or the *New Left Review*); in recent years, however, more mainstream academic fields – such as organization studies and psychology – have embraced the concept (see Laamanen, this volume). This has not only expanded the stock of cases analysed through the lens of prefiguration – from worker cooperatives (Kokkinidis, 2015) and community gardens (Guerlain and Campbell, 2016) to alternative organizations (Reedy et al, 2016) and political parties (Husted, 2018) – but also spawned a number of new analytical strategies and methodologies that reconfigure the concept's explanatory utility.

Although we certainly applaud this proliferation (and have contributed to it ourselves), we also see a number of issues with how the concept of prefiguration is currently deployed across academic disciplines. First, the literature often fails to account for the effectiveness of prefiguration as a political strategy. Second, it frequently subscribes to puritan ideals, which render the studied movements prone to failure. Third, it almost completely neglects to study examples of Right-wing activism. Fourth, it sometimes commits the fallacy of circular reasoning, whereby the premise and the conclusion of the argument overlap. Finally, it tends to portray prefigurative practices as particularly performative, vis-à-vis more strategic actions, without properly substantiating this claim. This chapter unfolds these five challenges in the form of a 'sympathetic polemic'. Our ultimate aim is to advance the study of prefigurative politics beyond its current limitations through a constructive but forthright – and, at times, slightly generalizing – critique (for a smiliar analysis of prefiguration in theory and practice, see Parker, 2021).

First challenge: effectiveness assumed

Who has succeeded most in improving living conditions for the 99 per cent – Occupy Wall Street or Democratic senators like Elizabeth Warren? If impact and effectiveness are measured in terms of legislation and policy initiatives, the answer is obvious. For instance, whereas Warren has sponsored a number of progressive bills and achieved oversized influence in the Senate (Mimms, 2015), Occupy Wall Street has had little assessable impact on electoral politics, aside from a few co-optations by Left-leaning politicians (Malone and Fredericks, 2013). To be sure, there are many other ways of assessing effectiveness, and most movements based on prefigurative practices deliberately circumvent conventional politics (Taylor, 2013; see also Monticelli, introduction to this volume). The problem, however, is that the literature on prefiguration often fails to account for these alternative assessments of effectiveness. Instead of spelling out how and why prefigurative practices are effective vis-à-vis more 'strategic' practices, such as lobbying and media messaging, they too frequently assume this is self-evident (for notable exceptions, see Breines, 1980; Polletta, 2002).

One example is Richard Day's (2005) post-anarchist examination of the 'newest' social movements, published in his widely read monograph, *Gramsci is Dead*. The basic premise in Day's book is that the logic of hegemony, as proposed by Antonio Gramsci, cannot adequately explain the modus operandi of movements based on prefigurative practices. Since these communities do not articulate counter-hegemonic projects in an effort to forge what Gramsci (1971, p 132) called a 'national-popular collective will' – that is, since they do not aspire to gain control of the state apparatus – they must be conceptualized in different terms. As such, Day refers to them as 'non-branded strategies and tactics' to highlight their non-hegemonic character, and as 'coming communities' to emphasize their presumed ability to create 'new possibilities for radical social change that cannot be imagined within existing paradigms' (Day, 2005, p 18). However, according to Day, non-hegemonic communities are not only useful for expanding the limits of our imagination but also more effective – in terms of building 'sustainable alternatives to the neoliberal order' – than hegemonic communities, such as political parties and trade unions (2005, p 186). Precisely how and why that is the case is, unfortunately, left almost entirely to the reader's imagination.

The need for answers to such questions is accentuated by a wave of literature that questions the effectiveness of prefigurative communities as means of instigating social change. For instance, followers of Gramsci argue that a commitment to what Chantal Mouffe (2009) calls 'critique as withdrawal' – that is, refusal to engage with existing institutions – risks leaving the door wide open for authoritarian groups to assume control of the state (Rohgalf, 2013; Smucker, 2014; Mouffe, 2018). Others go so far as to claim that non-hegemonic movements are non-political, in the sense that they merely represent an *opportunity* for politics, rather than a political project as such (Roberts, 2012; Dean, 2016). Finally, a more recent branch of literature questions whether we have time for prefigurative politics given the urgency of the escalating climate and biodiversity crises (Gordon, 2018). Such critiques are, however, not exclusive to academic circles; activists have also criticized the current infatuation with prefiguration. One example is Micah White, another co-initiator of Occupy Wall Street, who argues that the movement was a failure due to its inability to articulate political demands. As he puts it,

> an adherence to the ideology of prefigurative anarchism, the notion that the people must build the world we want to live in rather than make demands of the existing reality, blinded many founding Occupiers in New York City. The refusal, and inability, to reach consensus on 'our one demand' and develop complex decision-making meant that the movement could never move toward legitimate sovereignty, political negotiation, and a transfer of power – a naïve mistake. (White, 2016, p 38)

While we do not share these critics' dismissive views of prefigurative *practices*, we strongly believe prefiguration *research* must come up with better ways of accounting for the effectiveness of prefiguration as a political strategy (see Bosi et al, 2016). It is not good enough to simply assume prefiguration is 'perhaps the only viable strategy' for building alternatives (Maeckelbergh, 2011, p 15), nor that what can be achieved through the state 'can in fact be done, and done more efficiently, without passing through these mediating institutions' (Day, 2005, p 18). Hence, our first challenge to prefiguration research is to develop new – and more convincing – ways of answering the question: what does it mean for prefigurative activism to be effective?

Second challenge: puritan ideals

Like any other group of people, prefigurative movements consist of heterogeneous individuals with unique motivations, backgrounds and political beliefs. They furthermore exist and operate in a world that implicates most of us and our way of life (particularly in the Western world) in the causing of immense injustice, pollution and the suffering of others, often in ways that are too complex and massively distributed in time and space to completely understand. In spite of this, research on prefigurative activism often seems to imply a certain purity, understood as an ability (or, at least, an ambition) to create a space untouched by the maladies of the world – a space that allows for the realization of radical utopias in harmonious uniformity with, and tolerance of, each other's differences. Is embarking on such an endeavour not (at best) gruelling hard work and (at worst) setting up the movement for inevitable failure and disappointment? This is the question we raise in relation to the second challenge.

Alexis Shotwell (2016) notes how 'purity politics' seems to be an increasingly prevalent response to the messy complexity and impurity of the world. To meet and control complex situations that are fundamentally out of our control, we seek purity –bodily purity, through the intake of kombucha and organic chia seeds; racial or national purity, as in some strands of Right-wing populism; moral purity, through using the correct words; and so on. The question is: can we also understand prefiguration as a form of purity politics, in the sense of ignoring our messy entanglements with complex webs of suffering and injustice in order to live out a 'pure' utopia in the present? If prefigurative politics involves 'the unwillingness to compromise one's values', 'a determined attempt to avoid co-optation' and an adamant distaste for reformist goals (Breines, 1980, p 427), we might understand prefiguration as an attempt to remain pure and untainted by the institutional logics and concomitant injustices of the society in which these movements operate. As it turns out, however, this is quite a difficult feat.

One example of this is Juliane Reinecke's (2018, p 1312) account of Occupy London's ultimate 'failure of organizing in line with prefigurative politics', which resulted from the egalitarian attempt to include homeless people in the encampment (see Maeckelbergh, this volume, for a counterargument). While initially an empowering and community-building experience, this commitment eventually drained the activists, who felt it made the movement deviate from its political goals and focus too much on 'welfare needs' in the camp, such as providing food and shelter for everyone (Reinecke, 2018, p 1310). Along with a series of incidents regarding alcohol and drug abuse, night-time noise and aggressive behaviour (which left many female residents feeling unsafe), this gradually led the activists to abandon the project.

If we understand prefiguration as enacting change in one's own everyday interactions, it also involves the ability of activists to 'escape from being conditioned by the institutions that they wish to change' (Reinecke, 2018, p 1302). But, as this case shows, one cannot forever maintain a 'pure' state of equality and prefigure away 'the real structural divisions of society that become embodied in the body of an alcoholic or drug addict or a person without a home' (Reinecke, 2018, p 1315). And if that is the case, the question becomes: how do we conceptualize a prefigurative politics that starts from an acceptance of this impure complexity – of our inevitable entanglement in, and contribution to, harmful structures – yet still envisions better futures? This would be a prefigurative politics that does not aspire to a single pure future, but rather sets itself against the world as it is – perhaps as a kind of 'creative, dialogic, agonistic and contestatory' distortion of it (Shotwell, 2016, p 187). The second challenge we propose is to further investigate what this conception might look like.

Third challenge: allies only

From Trump to Brexit, and from Bolsonaro to Orbán, the Right currently seems to be outmanoeuvring the Left. Indeed, one could argue that this has been the case for the past three decades, during which time there has been no shortage of academic analyses of the Left's problems and how to revitalize the lost radicalism of Left-wing movements. However, as of yet, none of these analyses seem to have found the winning formula – the Right continues to dominate the political landscape and shape the world in its image of market deregulation, nationalism, environmental degradation, climate-change denial and so on. In this sense, Mouffe's (2009) worry about prefigurative politics leaving the door open to authoritarian Right-wing populists seems justified.

While this is, admittedly, a somewhat polemical proposition, it helps to underscore the odd fact – and, perhaps, strategic blunder – that studies of prefigurative politics have almost exclusively focused on Left-wing movements, the goals of which the authors presumably agree with (see Parker et al, 2014). According to Yates (2015, p 1), prefigurative politics thus generally refer to 'a dynamic distinguishing Left-wing political projects ... from Trotskyism and Leninism, where an organization or vanguard is considered necessary to bring about revolution "from the outside"'. Relatedly, Uri Gordon identifies two different ways of defining prefigurative politics: one is *formal* and 'limited to the very correspondence between ultimate goal and ongoing practice, while remaining silent on their content'; the other is *substantive* and also imbued with particular value content (2018, p 527). While the substantive definition tends to imply that prefiguration is exclusively practised by movements with Leftist values (see Boggs, 1977b; Breines, 1980), the formal definition potentially enables the study of a broader array of practices (see also Yates and de Moor, this volume).

A notable example of scholars adhering to the formal definition (at the expense of the substantive definition) is Robert Futrell and Pete Simi's (2004) investigation of the different organizational practices that allow white power networks to prefigure Aryan dominance. To our knowledge, however, this is the only existing study of prefigurative practices on the Right. But why should scholars of prefiguration not be able to look across the political divide to gain new insights into the phenomenon? Perhaps we might learn something from studying, say, the phenomenon of submissive stay-at-home 'tradwives' of the alt-right (Nagle, 2017), or the Ayn Rand-inspired bankers who recently obtained billions from European treasuries through fraud and speculation with dividend tax, in the so-called 'cum-ex scandal'.

One way to frame the potential benefits of such studies is through the notion of 'reverse co-optation'. Traditionally, prefigurative movements on the Left have been taught to fear co-optation (Breines, 1980, p 427) – and for good reason. But perhaps co-optation could also be conceived of as an important art, one that scholars on the Left might benefit from learning how to employ (Dahlman et al, 2022). For instance, Romand Coles (2016, p 150) details how Leftist movements can play a 'delicate trickster game', co-opting dynamics of neoliberalism or Right-wing populism for the purpose of building resistance to them. Similarly, Christian De Cock and colleagues (2018) argue that the academic Left might advance the struggle against Right-wing populists by borrowing some of their tactics. The study of prefigurative practices on the Right might be able to assist in this process. This sums up the third challenge: what does prefigurative practices on the Right look like, and what can Leftist movements learn from them?

Fourth challenge: circular reasoning

What is the status of prefiguration as a concept? Is it a descriptive term that allows us to understand a particular form of activism or a normative standard for determining the value of activist practices more generally – or both? Whereas the first answer implies that prefiguration is a *conclusion*, which can be reached by studying communities that conflate means and ends, the second answer implies that prefiguration is a *premise*, against which all communities can be evaluated. Combining both answers implies a type of circular reasoning: what is found to be true is true by virtue of itself. In Latin, circular reasoning is known as petitio principii, meaning an assumption from the beginning. This, we argue, is precisely what characterizes some accounts of prefigurative practices.

As Jeffrey H. Reiman (1981) argues, examples of circular reasoning are frequent in defences of liberal capitalism, whose proponents often claim that the right to property is an expression of liberty, only later to claim that liberty can be defined with reference to the right to property. Curiously, the same type of argument can be observed in the literature on prefiguration. One example is Patrick Reedy and colleagues' (2016) ethnographic study of 'individuation' in an alternative organization. The purpose of the study is to explore whether and how prefigurative practices allow the group's members to develop autonomous selves without falling back on neoliberal norms of egocentric individualization. In other words, can prefiguration provide room for both autonomy and solidarity? Here, we quote the authors at length:

> To summarize, our characterization of prefigurative individuation may be seen as relying on the maintenance of social bonds through conviviality, reciprocity and political activism. The ideal of 'do-it-yourself' living … prefigures the non-commodified society to come and seeks to avoid the authoritarianism of the workplace. Shared sub-cultural lifestyles, reflected in dress, festival going, food, music and art, reinforce these bonds and provide opportunities for creative self-expression. The assembly provides a negotiable space in which horizontal democracy is practised and activism organized. In the next part of the chapter we analyse the everyday activities of one group of alternative organizers who use these practices. We begin to answer our initial question as to the extent that such practices facilitated individuation. (Reedy et al, 2016, p 1558)

In this quote, means and ends are conflated in not only the practices of the alternative organization but also the academic argumentation. First, 'prefigurative individuation' is characterized as relying on 'the maintenance of social bonds through conviviality, reciprocity and political activism'. Second, it is argued – prior to the actual analysis – that the group's prefigurative practices (for example, 'do-it-yourself' living, shared subcultural lifestyles, and the assembly) meet precisely these criteria for individuation. Finally, the purpose of the article is stated, which is to investigate whether the aforementioned anticipated conclusion is correct. Ten pages later, we reach the paper's concluding discussion, where it is asserted – once again – that the group 'at least partially' managed to provide space for both autonomy and solidarity 'by forging social bonds supported by interdependence, reciprocity, conviviality and shared values' (Reedy et al, 2016, p 1568). Hence, the premise becomes the conclusion, in the sense that the answer to the research question is assumed from the very beginning of the text.

To be sure, classifying an example of circular reasoning as fallacious depends on the context of the argument (Walton, 1994). In some cases, this can be an entirely acceptable mode of argumentation. For instance, if the initial proposition is phrased as a hypothesis, circular reasoning can resemble logical deduction. Circularity is thus only problematic if it 'blocks the argument from fulfilling or contributing to the goals of the dialogue in which the arguer is supposed to be engaged' (Walton, 1994, p 96). The problem with the example of Reedy et al's study, however, is that it is explorative (or inductive) – like many other studies of prefiguration. This, we believe, makes such arguments poorly framed at best and unreflexive at worst. Our fourth challenge to prefiguration research is therefore to avoid premise–conclusion equivalence by approaching the field in a more open-minded manner. This also involves clarifying whether prefiguration is a theoretical concept, a normative standard or, perhaps, an empirical phenomenon articulated by activists themselves.

Fifth challenge: uber-performativity

Labelling a particular practice prefigurative seems to imply that it somehow forebodes the future. Accordingly, prefiguration carries with it a sense of quasi-reassurance of a certain recursive relationship between the desired future and the daily operations of the social movement. But what is it about prefigurative practices that gives them this almost magical power to anticipate the future? And why do prefigurative practices (such as consensus-based decision-making) carry more weight, in terms of altering the future, than mundane practices (such as emailing or vacuuming)?

It seems that classifying a practice as prefigurative implies an ability to effect change in the world – what we might call 'performativity' (Austin, 1962; Butler, 1990) – that significantly exceeds that of other practices. This might have something to do with the Christian origins of the term. Prefiguration has been used in Christian exegesis (Bible studies) to denote how the Old Testament (for example, the figure of Adam) anticipates the New Testament (for example, the figure of Christ). Accordingly, Gordon shows how prefiguration in the exegetical tradition is a temporal framing 'in which events at one time are interpreted as a figure pointing to its fulfillment in later events' (2018, p 525).

Could it be that a certain exegetical residue still haunts the notion of prefiguration in its current usage, and that this explains the sense of uber-performativity associated with the term? When looking at how the relationship between prefigurative practices and the future has been described in the literature, one can indeed find examples that seem to carry with them a quasi-mystical idea of fulfilment. For instance, prefigurative movements have been described as 'movements that are creating the future in their present social relationships' (Maeckelbergh, 2009, p 68), while the concept of prefiguration itself has been characterized as 'the idea that a transformative social movement must necessarily anticipate the ways and means of the hoped-for new society' (Tokar, 2003, p 78), or as a strategy in which the 'pursuit of utopian goals is recursively built into the movement's daily operation and organizational style' (Buechler, 2000, p 207).

To be sure, the prefiguration literature is quite heterogeneous in its conceptualizations of prefiguration's relationship to the future. Hence, Gordon (2018) distinguishes between a 'recursive' temporal framing (as in the aforementioned examples) and 'presentism', which disassociates from the future altogether and focuses exclusively on utopias in 'the here and now'. In the latter sense, the concept becomes more about individual self-realization, revolutionary lifestyle, an unwillingness to confront a bleak future of ecological devastation and an absent promise of revolutionary accomplishment. As an alternative, rooted in the anarchist tradition, Gordon instead advocates a more 'generative' framing; one that emphasizes how the current practice lays the groundwork for the future by establishing locked-in affordances and path dependencies that act like 'furrows in the road', becoming deeper and more entrenched the more they are used.

While this is certainly a step in the right direction, it still does not account for how and why prefigurative practices would be more effective than non-prefigurative practices in locking in affordances and path dependencies. If prefiguration is an equivalence between means and ends, there is still a certain amount of confusion about which means resemble which ends, and a lack of accounting for the other means and ends that are also always at play (Yates, 2015, p 16). This sums up the fifth challenge, which is to account for why prefigurative practices are, indeed, more performative than practices that are not associated with this particular adjective.

Conclusion

The brevity and deliberately polemical format of this chapter leave little space for nuances and exemplifications of its claims. Let us accordingly reiterate that the chapter should not be interpreted as a denunciation of existing research in the field of prefiguration studies, nor as an attempt to provide a comprehensive overview of the field; rather, the aim has been to provoke and inspire engagement with some of its current challenges. The issues of effectiveness, purity, the Right, circular reasoning and performativity have thus been identified with the ultimate goal of advancing this promising and hopeful field of research, and perhaps even mirroring our objects of study in delineating 'new horizons beyond the given truth' (Dinerstein, 2015, p 2).

References

Austin, J.L. (1962) *How to Do Things with Words*, Oxford: Clarendon Press.

Boggs, C. (1977a) 'Marxism, prefigurative communism and the problem of workers' control', *Radical America*, 11(6): 99–122.

Boggs, C. (1977b) 'Revolutionary process, political strategy and the dilemma of power', *Theory and Society*, 4(3): 359–93.

Bosi, L., Giugni, M. and Uba, K. (eds) (2016) *The Consequences of Social Movements*, Cambridge: Cambridge University Press.

Breines, W. (1980) 'Community and organization: the New Left and Michels' "iron law"', *Social Problems*, 27(4): 419–29.

Brissette, E. (2013) 'Prefiguring the realm of freedom at Occupy Oakland', *Rethinking Marxism*, 25(2): 218–27.

Buechler, S.M. (2000) *Social Movements in Advanced Capitalism*, New York: Oxford University Press.

Butler, J. (1990) *Gender Trouble*, New York: Routledge.

Coles, R. (2016) *Visionary Pragmatism: Radical and Ecological Democracy in Neoliberal Times*, Durham, NC: Duke University Press.

Dahlman, S., du Plessis, E.M., Husted, E. and Just, S.N. (2022) 'Alternativity as freedom: exploring tactics of emergence in alternative forms of organizing', *Human Relations* [online], available from: https://doi.org/10.1177/00187267221080124

Day, R.J.F. (2005) *Gramsci is Dead: Anarchist Currents in the Newest Social Movements*, London: Pluto Press.

De Cock, C., Just, S.N. and Husted, E. (2018) 'What's he building? Activating the utopian imagination with Trump', *Organization*, 25(5): 671–80.

Dean, J. (2016) *Crowds and Party*, London: Verso.

Dinerstein, A.C. (2015) *The Politics of Autonomy in Latin America: The Art of Organising Hope*, London: Palgrave Macmillan.

Epstein, B. (1991) *Political Protest and Cultural Revolution*, Berkeley: University of California Press.

Futrell, R. and Simi, P. (2004) 'Free spaces, collective identity, and the persistence of US white power activism', *Social Problems*, 51(1): 16–42.

Gordon, U. (2018) 'Prefigurative politics between ethical practice and absent promise', *Political Studies*, 66(2): 521–37.

Graeber, D. (2013) *The Democracy Project: A History, a Crisis, a Movement*, London: Allen Lane.

Gramsci, A. (1971) *Selections from the Prison Note Books of Antonio Gramsci*, New York: International Publishers.

Guerlain, M.A. and Campbell, C. (2016) 'From sanctuaries to prefigurative social change: creating health-enabling spaces in East London community gardens', *Journal of Social and Political Psychology*, 4(1): 220–37.

Hammond, J.L. (2015) 'The anarchism of Occupy Wall Street', *Science & Society*, 79(2): 288–313.

Husted, E. (2018) 'Mobilizing "the Alternativist": Exploring the management of subjectivity in a radical political party', *Ephemera: Theory and Politics in Organization*, 18(4): 737–65.

Kokkinidis, G. (2015) 'Spaces of possibilities: workers' self-management in Greece', *Organization*, 22(6): 847–71.

Maeckelbergh, M. (2009) *Will of the Many: How the Alterglobalisation Movement Is Changing the Face of Democracy*, London: Pluto Press.

Maeckelbergh, M. (2011) 'Doing is believing: prefiguration as strategic practice in the alterglobalization movement', *Social Movement Studies*, 10(1): 1–20.

Malone, C. and Fredericks, V. (2013) 'OWS and US electoral politics: an early critical assessment', in E. Welty, M. Bolton, M. Nayak and C. Malone (eds) *Occupying Political Science: The Occupy Wall Street Movement from New York to the World*, New York: Palgrave Macmillan, pp 191–223.

Mimms, S. (2015) 'Is Elizabeth Warren an effective senator?', *The Atlantic* [online], 26 May, available from: https://www.theatlantic.com/politics/archive/2015/05/is-elizabeth-warren-an-effective-senator/449349/

Mouffe, C. (2009) 'The importance of engaging the state', in J. Pugh (ed) *What Is Radical Politics Today?* Basingstoke: Palgrave Macmillan, pp 230–7.

Mouffe, C. (2018) *For a Left Populism*, London: Verso.

Nagle, A. (2017) *Kill All Normies: Online Culture Wars from 4chan and Tumblr to Trump and the Alt-Right*, Winchester: Zero Books.

Parker, M., Cheney, G., Fournier, V. and Land, C. (eds) (2014) *The Routledge Companion to Alternative Organization*, New York: Routledge.

Parker, M. (2021) 'The romance of prefiguration and the task of organization', *Journal of Marketing Management* [online], available from: https://doi.org/10.1080/0267257X.2021.2006755

Pickerill, J. and Krinsky, J. (2012) 'Why does Occupy matter?', *Social Movement Studies*, 11(3–4): 279–87.

Polletta, F. (1999) '"Free spaces" in collective action', *Theory and Society*, 28(1): 1–38.

Polletta, F. (2002) *Freedom is an Endless Meeting: Democracy in American Social Movements*, Chicago, MI: University of Chicago Press.

Reedy, P., King, D. and Coupland, C. (2016) 'Organizing for individuation: alternative organizing, politics and new identities', *Organization Studies*, 37(11): 1553–73.

Reiman, J.H. (1981) 'The fallacy of libertarian capitalism', *Ethics*, 92(1): 85–95.

Reinecke, J. (2018) 'Social movements and prefigurative organizing: confronting entrenched inequalities in Occupy London', *Organization Studies*, 39(9): 1299–321.

Roberts, A. (2012) 'Why the Occupy movement failed', *Public Administration Review*, 17(6): 729–47.

Rohgalf, J. (2013) 'Democracy of the many? Occupy Wall Street and the dead end of prefiguration', *Distinktion*, 14(2): 151–67.

Shotwell, A. (2016) *Against Purity: Living Ethically in Compromised Times*, Minneapolis: University of Minnesota Press.

Smucker, J.M. (2014) 'Can prefigurative politics replace political strategy?', *Berkeley Journal of Sociology* [online], 58, available from: https://berkeleyjournal.org/2014/10/07/can-prefigurative-politics-replace-political-strategy/

Taylor, B. (2013) 'From alterglobalization to Occupy Wall Street: neoanarchism and the new spirit of the Left', *City*, 17(6): 729–47.

Tokar, B. (2003) 'Review of Joel Kovel, *The Enemy of Nature*', *Tikkun*, 18(1): 77–8.

van de Sande, M. (2015) 'Fighting with tools: prefiguration and radical politics in the twenty-first century', *Rethinking Marxism*, 27(2): 177–94.

Walton, D.N. (1994) 'Begging the question as a pragmatic fallacy', *Synthese*, 100(1): 95–131.

White, M. (2016) *The End of Protest: A Playbook for Revolution*, Toronto: Knopf Canada.

Yates, L. (2015) 'Rethinking prefiguration: alternatives, micropolitics and goals in social movements', *Social Movement Studies*, 14(1): 1–21.

Afterword

Davina Cooper

This book offers a rich engagement with prefigurative politics. In this afterword, I address three questions that lie at its heart: What is being prefigured? What does prefiguration do and need? And what academic methods support and advance prefigurative work? Addressing these questions draws lines of thinking offered by this book, together with some additional possibilities. These concern the prefiguration of meaning, radical state practice, building systemic connections, and research-led, do-it-yourself (DIY) simulations of institutional action.

Adopting new meanings

Prefigurative politics is typically associated with two clusters of activity: remaking organizational decision-making structures so that they are more participative, consensus-based and horizontal; and performing everyday social relations in ways that embody cooperation, care, freedom and equality.[1] This reperforming of the quotidian also includes nurturing new forms of subjectivity and consciousness, attending to informal as well as formal hierarchies and, as Laura Centemeri and Viviana Asara (this volume) discuss, forging new relations to the Earth. Prefiguration's alignment with remaking organizational processes, on the one hand, and everyday social relations, on the other, has not been uncontentious, as several chapters describe.[2] Yet, while theorizing has often oscillated between treating prefiguration as a politics of organizational form or one of social living, the two also converge. Paul Raekstad (this volume) argues for the importance of social structural change (such as undoing informal racist and sexist hierarchies) for democratic decision-making to occur. The example of camp-based protest politics – from Greenham Common Women's Peace Camp in the 1980s to the more recent Occupy – also shows how a horizontal participatory ethic for decision-making often combines with new ways of organizing food, care and intimate relations (see Roseneil, 2000).

Decision-making structures and everyday social relations are central to prefiguration. But prefiguration also has a third component: the prefiguration of meaning. New understandings are integral to remaking social practices and organizational processes, but deliberately recontouring concepts is not usually explicitly invoked within prefiguration's terms. In their discussion of the radical imagination, Aris Komporozos-Athanasiou and Chiara Bottici (this volume) draw on Castoriadis' work to explore the importance of the imaginary, how it mediates and shapes society rather than simply reflecting society back, mirror-like, as it appears to be. Importantly, the imaginary is not unstructured or unconditioned, and their chapter considers the limits – identified by Castoriadis – that are imposed on the imaginary by materiality, cognitive coherence and past symbolic constructions. Addressing how the imaginary operates, recognizing it is not a fiction but a shared cultural and symbolic repertoire and mode of social relating, poses questions about how a radical imagination is possible, what it consists of and what it can do. Komporozos-Athanasiou and Bottici's account sits within a growing body of work interested in the prefiguration of ideas – from Margaret Davies' (2017, p 156) work on prefigurative theory, which 'attempts to interpret the intellectual resources of the present and past in a way that opens an alternative way forward', to the notion of conceptual prefiguration, which foregrounds the enactment of new meanings to rehearse and prompt their wider take-up, and which I want to consider a little further here.

Conceptual prefiguration works from the premise that there are multiple ways of understanding concepts, particularly sociopolitical concepts such as gender, property and the state – concepts that combine the tangible, socio-material and imagined in accounts of what they are and in how they are practically enacted.[3] Advancing new conceptual meanings that embody *hoped-for* understandings and definitions has several benefits for Left politics.[4] It can unsettle existing understandings, rehearse new possibilities, legitimate minority practices and make them intelligible, and adjust the contours of the imagined-material thing (what counts as part of it and how its parts go together) to support both its revaluation and repurposing. These possibilities become clearer if we take two contemporary examples: gender and the state – both of which have been subject to progressive, conceptual reimagining. Dominant understandings of gender approach it as the culturally intelligible social life of biologically differentiated dimorphic sex. However, there is a growing tendency across different countries to reimagine gender as plural, mutable and much more complexly and contingently related to sexed embodiment (see, for example, Stachowiak, 2017; Clarke, 2018; Holzer, 2018). In the case of the state, dominant understandings envision it as a hierarchical apparatus governing (or dominating) life, things and land within a defined territory. Yet, state bodies can also be reimagined, including as democratic, horizontal, responsible, caring, permeable and stewardly (see Newman and Clarke, 2014; Cooper, 2019).

These counter-understandings of gender and the state may seem counter-intuitive. They also collide with far more familiar critical analyses offered on the Left, which approach both terms in negative ways. Yet, as the contributors to this book discuss, reality is more open and plural than a depiction of conceptual singularity would suggest. Divergent conceptual understandings shape social life, as individually and collectively imagined conceptual 'cuts' delineate the (evolving) contours of a thing. In relation to gender, these new cuts redefine its parameters (for instance, by reorientating gender to self-perception), add member categories (such as non-binary) and change gender's relationship to other aspects of the imagined-material world. In turn, these adjustments generate a series of new questions: What does gender mean once it is divorced from (or divorcing) sexed embodiment? Can it include an indefinite number of member categories? And does it have an outside – can people live without a gender in any meaningful way within gendered society? Within the confrontational milieu of political activism, these questions are often approached as if a single right answer exists – on the assumption that there is a thing, whether 'gender' or 'sex', that can be properly or improperly accounted for. Yet, the important question is not which definition is right, but what it is that different ways of imagining and actualizing gender *do*. This performative quality is explored in Eleonora Gea Piccardi's chapter, which provides a vivid account of feminist politics in the autonomous Kurdish region of Rojava in North and East Syria. She demonstrates how gender practices and values there became both reimagined and reformed through a 'praxis of de-patriarchization/matriarchization'. Conceptual prefiguration approaches gender through the relationship between enactment and reimagining, recognizing the important and constitutive role played by the tensions between them. Conceptual prefiguration is not simply about new meanings and understandings; it is also about how these relate (or fail to relate) to new kinds of practice.

Prefigurative understandings can have constitutive effects. For instance, a court, statute or organization may declare what gender is in ways that are recognized and which set the terms for the category's usage – at least in particular contexts. But the effects of prefigurative meanings may also emerge in less linear fashion. A declaration by a court or a new law may be resisted or ignored. Even state apparatuses cannot assume that their legally institutionalized assertion of new meanings will become the prevailing common sense. In other cases, where conceptual prefiguration is undertaken by less powerful bodies, the effects may prove even more mediated. Activists redefining the state as, for example, a body that exercises responsible stewardship over its ecological resources do not necessarily lead those bodies currently understood as state bodies to behave in more caring, responsible ways (a point underscored by critics of liberal depictions of the 'good state'). However, this does not mean redescription lacks consequences. Depending on where and by whom it is done, redescription can have all kinds of effects – on wider public expectations, social movement agendas, the terms of political critique and so on. These effects may be desired, but they may also not be. Redescriptions of phenomena, and new cuts to the contours of what something is, are vulnerable to dismissal as loony, mistaken, foolish, ridiculous and so on. Through counter-rationalizations, critics may mobilize and assert a pre-existing common sense – including through legal means. In contemporary Britain, for instance, some public bodies' willingness to take up a more pluralist gender imaginary (see Cooper, 2020a), one that makes room for self-identification and non-binary gender categories, prompted others to use litigation, political pressure and media platforms to press public bodies to approach sex as a formalised, binary, legal status.[5]

Capacity

The power associated with new meanings and practices is an important focus of prefigurative analysis. It is also a reason to incorporate official bodies into discussions of prefiguration. Several contributors to this book explore prefiguration's association with small-scale action. Komporozos-Athanasiou and Bottici (this volume), for instance, describe it as a 'homeopathic strategy'. Prefiguring is also associated with DIY action in contrast to a politics that works through demands on the state. Prefigurative action by state structures receives little attention within the broader field of prefigurative scholarship. Left-wing scepticism about the radical potential and everyday progressive contribution of official bodies has a long history, as Raekstad (this volume) discusses. Even when state bodies claim to be advancing social justice, their decisions, policies, rules and practices are distrusted as watering down or constricting a more radical grassroots agenda. But bracketing state bodies, when it comes to prefiguration, can discount an important terrain of action. It can also be problematic when it inclines to an ethos of purity, intent on remaining uncontaminated by power or compromise. Erik Mygind du Plessis and Emil Husted (this volume) criticize prefigurative projects that seek to remain untouched by the world's maladies and institutional logics. They call instead for a prefigurative politics that starts with 'impure complexity'.

Bracketing state bodies, when it comes to prefiguration, is also anchored in two other assumptions – regarding state capacity and meaning. First, it is often assumed that state action achieves what it sets out to do, and so accomplishes – rather than prefigures – change. State action, from this perspective, cannot be prefigurative, because it has the institutional power to establish a new common sense and new uses. It does not rehearse or anticipate something that, in a more prevalent or expansive form, has not yet come to pass. Second, the exclusion of state bodies from prefigurative action tends to assume a clear-cut division between state and non-state action. Let me start with this second point.

State structures are knitted into many aspects of social, economic and political life in ways that trouble the suggestion of grassroots action at a distance. Jilly Traganou (this volume) observes the complexity – but also the mutating character – of state and regulatory involvement in her discussion of Christiania, a large self-managed community in Copenhagen, established in the early 1970s. The enmeshing of official and unofficial forms also means state bodies can sometimes act prefiguratively, as Lara Monticelli (this volume) – alongside Yates and de Moor (this volume) – considers. Deliberately advancing counter-hegemonic norms, values and valuations has been a long-standing aspect of radical local government activities, from peace and nuclear-free zones to environment, equality and economic justice initiatives (Boddy, 1984; Gyford, 1985; Lansley et al, 1989). Here, state prefiguration foregrounds the uncertain, contested and heterogeneous aspects of state practice, as official discourse and governmental policies and initiatives embody or rehearse ambitions deemed ahead of their time. These are prefigurative to the extent that the state bodies in question lack the force to eliminate or transform existing structures but nevertheless act as if the alternatives they advance are valid (see Cooper, 2020b). Looking for prefiguration within the state also has the effect of orientating analysis and strategy towards an understanding of state bodies as complex terrains across and through which human and other bodies – in interconnected ways – act. This mix of bodies includes frontline staff and service users exercising power against the grain of official state discourse by drawing on the resources, opportunities and contact that state terrain makes available.

Whether prefigurative actors are state, human or organizational bodies, prefiguration works from the premise that actors are neither fully empowered nor fully constrained (or determined) in what they do, or in what their doing does. I want to turn here to three important assumptions that drive how social power is folded into prefigurative politics – assumptions teased out in the course of this book: first, that power can help fashion more socially just worlds – power is not just about relations of domination; second, that the power to act otherwise is possible; and third, that what 'acting otherwise' accomplishes is open, at least to some degree. In part, such openness reflects epistemic uncertainty, since knowledge of what prefiguration's temporal looping can bring forth (as present action enacts future-directed hopes) is necessarily limited. It also reflects, as several chapters discuss, prefiguration's unfixed, undetermined potential – Bloch's 'not yet', which is folded into the real, as Ana Cecilia Dinerstein (this volume) discusses.

Prefiguration operates within an evolving complex world, but its potential also arises because prefigurative practice itself can bring new possibilities into being. The book's discussion of Christiania, Occupy, Rojava and Auroville, alongside other prefigurative experiments, brings this potential to light. A different potential emerges in state-centred initiatives, such as municipal government's involvement in the Palestinian-led movement to boycott, divest and sanction Israel. This example raises questions about state power when local authorities act as players on the international stage. It also raises questions about the authority carried by local state forms of refusal. Withdrawal has an interesting place within prefigurative politics (see Pellizzoni, 2021), as Francesca Forno and Stefan Wahlen (this volume) also consider. Their discussion focuses on refusal in relation to everyday shopping practices. In the boycott, divest and sanctions case, local councils undertook acts of refusal, acting as if they were governmental bodies entitled to engage in symbolic boycotts to show solidarity with struggling communities at a geographical distance. In this municipal case, the right or authority to develop international policies or use procurement powers as a solidarity lever was not preset. While established law and vertical governmental structures shaped council initiatives in this area, and quickly intruded after council committees passed boycott measures,[6] the capacity of councils to act, and the political–legal authority through which they did so, were also things that emerged from local government's acts and policies of solidarity.

Prefiguration's power and reach is not fixed or predetermined, but neither is it unstructured. As du Plessis and Husted (this volume) point out, prefigurative scholarship sometimes assumes an 'almost magical power to anticipate the future' – a potency at odds with critical scholars' more sceptical accounts of other kinds of action. Their chapter also makes the important point that analyses need to consider what success means – what kind of evaluative criteria should be applied to prefigurative action? Certainly, prefigurative practices and politics do not lack critics. As Forno and Wahlen (this volume) explore, DIY actions, when tied to the reinvention of the quotidian self, face criticism for being diversionary, middle class, preservationist and vulnerable to corporate seduction. But critical readings of prefiguration, amid concern with its risks, need to be supplemented with empirically careful accounts of what prefigurative action does accomplish. As Yates and de Moor (this volume) suggest, what is needed are analyses of what prefiguration does and does not achieve – accounts that are sympathetic to prefiguration's ambition while attending to the institutional and historical forces that structure – and, indeed, limit – what prefigurative practices can realize within specific temporal[7] and spatial scales.

One important level of analysis here is the organizational. Mikko Laamanen (this volume), in a discussion of organizing prefiguratively, helpfully explores some of the processes and conditions that support counter-institutional progressive change. Discussion of prefigurative organizing – especially when focused on horizontal, consensus-based decision-making – highlights meeting structures (such as assemblies) and bottom-up federated bodies. Yet what also surfaces is the need for mechanisms that can link together and so help to sustain new practices. Dominant processes are sustained by systemic linkages – resources, chains of authority, qualifications, coherence, enforcement, discipline and recognition, among other factors. These discursive and material linkages support sectoral processes, corset-like, holding their shape and holding them together. Ana Cecilia Dinerstein and Frederick Harry Pitts (this volume) make a related argument in their discussion of capitalism. They suggest prefigurative action needs to go beyond simply withdrawing from or reinventing concrete social practices, such as capitalist employment, to address the mediating forms capitalism entails, including law, state and money.

The importance of systemic linkages and shared social forms can be seen in the case of alternative local currency networks. Research suggests alternative currency networks prove more effective when they are congruent with other parts of people's lives, including the economic and social relations and temporal rhythms that they inhabit (see North, 2007, p 137; Cooper, 2014, p 151).[8] In other words, local currencies work more effectively when they are supported rather than thwarted by other aspects of institutionalized social life. Noel Longhurst's (2013, 2015) work explores the importance of establishing alternative milieus where dense networks and countercultural institutions support social experimentation (see also Fois, 2019). This is about not only the presence of people with shared interests and norms but also the ability to create new routines, processes and habits.

Habits are often treated as antithetical to the experimentation and creativity associated with prefiguration (see Fois, 2019). However, making new social practices sustainable cannot work with complete openness and indeterminacy (see Laamanen, this volume) or where everything becomes a decision – with all the time-consuming and often exhausting, tense and conflictual relations this entails. New practices need to become good sense. Suryamayi Aswini Clarence-Smith (this volume) explores how progressive forms of governance, education and economy became institutionalized over time within the intentional community of Auroville in India – although her chapter also emphasizes the importance of revision and change to the community's identity. Interconnections between sectoral practices, necessary to support new habits and common sense, can develop within comprehensive, communal, self-governing initiatives. But many prefigurative projects are narrower in their focus – a food initiative, a radical school, new gender practices and so on. This focus can make installation less daunting, but fragmentation can leave individual projects or everyday utopias as pockets of radical practice within a hostile (or at least incompatible) wider environment.

Monticelli (this volume) makes a related point, discussing how prefiguration establishes the importance of combining economic, social and environmental issues as interrelated concerns to counter an expansive and multifaceted form of capitalism. Her analysis prompts the question of how to accomplish this joining-up when prefigurative initiatives emerge as discrete and separate initiatives. Can linkages develop – in the form of resources, norms and rationalities, for example – able to support individual projects by creating a more conducive environment, and helping to build broader societal counter-formations? We could imagine, for instance, free universities using alternative local currencies to pay or supplement the pay of staff and suppliers as they stock their canteen with food grown in everyday farming utopias. In turn, such universities might educate students in cooperative practice and have partnership links with intentional communities that welcome students for work experience. Such linkages would not be static; inevitably, they change – and need to change. Linkages might also assume forms that are themselves prefigurative – for instance, initiatives connected through solidarity relations, or a desire to learn, rather than credentials or currency.

The key point, however, is the need for systemic devices that can help to sustain prefigurative practices and amplify their impact. This aspect of countercultural worldmaking parallels the notion of 'path dependency' – which, in Sylvia Walby's (2007, p 465) words, 'lock[s]-in certain paths of development, through their shaping of rewards, power, opportunity and knowledge'. Without systemic devices, the risk is not only of endless decision-making but also that prefigurative decision-making and practice is subject to the powerful systemic countertendencies of the status quo. Take democratic schools which, in Britain and elsewhere, face mainstream imperatives that children obtain educational qualifications. If this is not something that the school offers, they may face recruitment difficulties given the educational, occupational and emotional challenges children can face leaving school without qualifications. Similarly, local currency networks anchored in informal arrangements confront countervailing market pressures, as members get pulled into trades involving more versatile forms of money; face insurance challenges when using their vehicles or expertise for local currency schemes; and experience a limited time envelope for taking part, as local currency trading gets slotted into the temporal availability of non-work leisure time.

Generating new linkages between organized prefigurative practices echoes the anarchist idea of building a new society within the shell of the old. Ambitions for a new society may follow counter-hegemonic lines in proposing a single common alternative. Yet linkages between prefigurative social practices do not have to take such a monolithic, universalizing form. Building on Richard Day's work, Antonia De Vita and Francesco Vittori (this volume) explore a more pluralist, affinity-based approach. They argue for the importance of an intersectional vision that recognizes overlap and interconnection – something that Dinerstein (this volume) also explores, including in relation to 'pluriversal praxis' (see also Escobar, 2020, this volume). A more pluralist approach makes room for many interconnected and overlapping alternative worlds, recognizing also that their co-creation is not a temporally circumscribed and delimited act – a once-and-for-all happening that settles what is – but ongoing as connections between worlds continue to emerge and be forged.

Prefiguration research

Finally, I turn to the question: what can academic scholarship contribute to these processes? This book provides examples of critical pedagogy and praxis (discussed in De Vita and Vittori, this volume); accounts of radical spaces and communities – from Rojava, Christiania and Auroville to Occupy and the World Social Forum; and instances of prefigurative practices in food utopias and municipal activism. Here, in these deliberately experimental ventures (experimental, at least, at their outset), participation in new practices – including by researchers – sparks new ways of thinking. But research itself can also take a more explicitly prefigurative form, including one that is reflexively so, with rehearsals, prototypes and simulations. In his chapter, Raekstad reflects on the importance of practice to building people's capacities and improving the performance of new social relations. Rehearsing other ways of living and acting helps in their acquisition and taking shape (for example, De Smet, 2014; see also Maeckelbergh, 2011). Related benefits emerge when researchers use play and design to explore possible futures, with prototypes to prompt and experiment with new ideas. Prototyping policies, provision and community organizing demands the drawing of connections between critique, design, revision, anticipation and enactment. Yet it is striking how, to date, prefigurative scholarship has not drawn much on the field of design studies, despite rich synergies (for one sociolegal exception, see Perry-Kessaris, 2021).

Prototyping, or the creation of experimental objects, is a promising site for future prefigurative studies. Within feminist and sociolegal scholarship, academics have developed methods that involve producing legal things within a DIY register orientated to other sought-after futures (and pasts). Rather than assuming, for instance, that court judgments, constitutions and laws can only be undertaken by official bodies, researchers take up the task of producing them in ways that draw on feminist, ecological and other progressive values (for example, see Hunter et al, 2010; Rogers and Maloney, 2017). Unrecognized within official legal systems, these experimental legal phenomena do not have the force associated with official versions. They lack the specific traction of the official phenomena that, in revised form, they simulate. However, beyond their capacity to function as critical tools, progressive (even sometimes radical) DIY legal objects show what the law could be like. By inviting people to consider radical policy changes beyond the parameters of current political consideration, experimental legal prototypes stimulate deliberation. But progressive simulations can also do something else. Considering my earlier discussion on the need to forge new systemic linkages, DIY legal objects can contribute to this forging by providing laws or regulatory forms that other bodies engaged in prefiguration can draw on.

This afterword has considered the prefiguration of conceptual meaning, institutional change, development of sectoral linkages and research-based simulations as part of the toolkit of prefigurative analysis and practice. Doing so revisits the different tensions that prefiguration raises, and which this book explores in productive and illuminating ways. These include tensions between experimentation and habits, fiction and reality, present and future, imagination and practice, potential and constraint, and play and work. Traversing different approaches and perspectives, what emerges from this collection is the importance of working with these tensions rather than seeking to undo or transcend them. For it is in the explicit engagement with oppositions of time, being, strategy, practice and thought – in ways that sustain rather than resolve their tension – that a prefigurative attitude arises.

Notes

[1] Embodying social ambitions for the future in the present can also involve Right-wing ambitions, as Luke Yates and Joost de Moor (this volume) explore.

[2] Yates and de Moor's chapter provides a detailed account of the different uses of prefiguration's terms in Left politics and social movement studies between 1968 and 2019.

[3] For instance, property can signal (tangible) things that are owned, but it can also signal relations between people vis-à-vis a thing, entitlements and obligations (the 'straws' of ownership), state recognition, registers of belonging and attachment, and certain kinds of force.

[4] Prefiguring new, preferred meanings – acting as if they are already intelligible and valid – is not restricted to positive terms or usages. Critical meanings can also be prefigurative in the sense of being desired meanings that lack current salience. These may relate to concepts that social justice advocates do not seek to salvage; the project here is one of opposition-building rather than recuperation.

[5] See, for instance, *Fair Play for Women v UK Statistics Authority*, Claim No CO/715/2021.

[6] For example, see *R (Jewish Rights Watch Ltd) v Leicester City Council* [2018] EWCA Civ 1551.

[7] For interesting ethnographic studies that focus on challenges over time, see Reinecke (2018) on Occupy London and the challenge of combining strategic and welfare orientations, and Koensler (2020) on alternative food certification systems. Marianne Maeckelbergh (this volume) very helpfully reflects on the discursive power of different temporal framings through an analysis of prefigurative politics in relation to event-time and process-time.

[8] See also Laamanen (this volume) on time-banking.

References

Boddy, M. (1984) 'Local economic and employment strategies', in M. Boddy and C. Fudge (eds) *Local Socialism? Labour Councils and New Left Alternatives*, Basingstoke: Macmillan, pp 160–91.

Clarke, J.A. (2018) 'They, them and theirs', *Harvard Law Review*, 132(3): 894–991.

Cooper, D. (2014) *Everyday Utopias: The Conceptual Life of Promising Spaces*, Durham, NC: Duke University Press.

Cooper, D. (2019) *Feeling Like a State: Desire, Denial, and the Recasting of Authority*, Durham, NC: Duke University Press.

Cooper, D. (2020a) 'Taking public responsibility for gender: when personal identity and institutional feminist politics meet', *feminists@law* [online], 10(2), available from: https://doi.org/10.22024/UniKent/03/fal.968

Cooper, D. (2020b) 'Towards an adventurous institutional politics: the prefigurative "as if" and the reposing of what's real', *Sociological Review*, 68(5): 893–916.

Davies, M. (2017) *Law Unlimited*, London: Routledge.

De Smet, B. (2014) *A Dialectical Pedagogy of Revolt: Gramsci, Vygotsky, and the Egyptian Revolution*, Leiden: Brill.

Escobar, A. (2020) *Pluriversal Politics*, Durham, NC: Duke University Press.

Fois, F. (2019) 'Enacting experimental alternative spaces', *Antipode*, 51(1): 107–28.

Gyford, J. (1985) *The Politics of Local Socialism*, London: Allen & Unwin.

Holzer, L. (2018) *Non-Binary Gender Registration Models in Europe: Report on Third Gender Marker or No Gender Marker Options* [online], ILGA-Europe, available from: https://www.ilga-europe.org/resources/ilga-europe-repo rts-and-other-materials/non-binary-gender-registration-models-europe

Hunter, R., McGlynn, C. and Rackley, E. (eds) (2010) *Feminist Judgments: From Theory to Practice*, London: Bloomsbury Publishing.

Koensler, A. (2020) 'Prefigurative politics in practice: concrete utopias in Italy's food sovereignty activism', *Mobilization: An International Quarterly*, 25(1): 133–50.

Lansley, S., Goss, S. and Wolmar, C. (1989) *Councils in Conflict: The Rise and Fall of the Municipal Left*, Basingstoke: Macmillan.

Longhurst, N. (2013) 'The emergence of an alternative milieu: conceptualising the nature of alternative places', *Environment and Planning A*, 45(9): 2100–19.

Longhurst, N. (2015) 'Towards an "alternative" geography of innovation: alternative milieu, socio-cognitive protection and sustainability experimentation', *Environmental Innovation and Societal Transitions*, 17: 183–98.

Maeckelbergh, M. (2011) 'Doing is believing: prefiguration as strategic practice in the alterglobalization movement', *Social Movement Studies*, 10(1): 1–20.

Newman, J. and Clarke, J. (2014) 'States of imagination', *Soundings*, 57(1): 153–69.

North, P. (2007) *Money and Liberation: The Micropolitics of Alternative Currency Movements*, Minneapolis: University of Minnesota Press.

Pellizzoni, L. (2021) 'Prefiguration, subtraction and emancipation', *Social Movement Studies*, 20(3): 364–79.

Perry-Kessaris, A. (2021) *Doing Sociolegal Research in Design Mode*, London: Routledge.

Reinecke, J. (2018) 'Social movements and prefigurative organizing: confronting entrenched inequalities in Occupy London', *Organization Studies*, 39(9): 1299–321.

Rogers, N. and Maloney, M. (eds) (2017) *Law as if Earth really Mattered: The Wild Law Judgment Project*, London: Taylor & Francis.

Roseneil, S. (2000) *Common Women, Uncommon Practices: The Queer Feminisms of Greenham*, London: Cassell & Co.

Stachowiak, D.M. (2017) 'Queering it up, strutting our threads, and baring our souls: genderqueer individuals negotiating social and felt sense of gender', *Journal of Gender Studies*, 26(5): 532–43.

Walby, S. (2007) 'Complexity theory, systems theory, and multiple intersecting social inequalities', *Philosophy of the Social Sciences*, 37(4): 449–70.

Index

References to figures appear in *italic* type.
Reference to endnotes show both the
page number and the note number (87n1).